SOLITARY IN JOHANNESBURG

QUENTIN JACOBSEN

SOLITARY
IN
JOHANNESBURG

LONDON
MICHAEL JOSEPH

First published in Great Britain by Michael Joseph Ltd
52 Bedford Square, London, W.C.1
1973

ISBN 0 7181 1109 5

Set and printed in Great Britain by
Northumberland Press Ltd, Gateshead
in Baskerville type, eleven on twelve and a half point,
and bound by James Burn at Esher, Surrey

PREFACE

On October 24th 1971 the South African Security Police raided the homes of at least 115 people of all races in a nation-wide swoop at four in the morning. Thirty-seven of these were detained. Ahmed Timol, an Indian schoolmaster, fell to his death from the tenth floor of the John Vorster Square police station on October 28th and another Indian, a medical student called Mohamed Essop, who had also been arrested, was found seriously ill from injuries he had received while in custody, in the Verwoerd Hospital, Pretoria a few days later.

I was arrested on 2nd November. *The Times* of 5th November reported: 'The object of the present police activity in South Africa is to find the source of political pamphlets discovered in the possession of Mr Timol. Police spent most of to-day in the Jacobsen's studio and there is speculation to-night that they suspect it to be connected with the production of the pamphlets.'

This book is a factual, chronological account of what followed. Nothing has been invented and much of the dialogue has been taken from police interrogation notes and court transcripts of the trial. Obviously these have had to be condensed since, in all, they come to over a thousand pages.

I have not set out to write a specifically political book, that is, one about the South African situation in general. If anyone wants the facts about Apartheid, they can be got from the United Nations or from Father Cosmos Desmond's book, *The Discarded People* as well as many other publications.

TO MY
MOTHER

CHAPTER ONE

I opened the door, still a little sleepy, and the man standing there said, 'I am Commander'—I didn't catch the name—'Chief of the Ideological Crime Squad.'

It was the dagga I thought of. The books they might not find but the dagga was in the bottom of the drying cabinet.

George was down by the darkroom but as half a dozen police pushed their way in, I knew it was no good trying to tell him to dump it, there was far too much of it. The man who had spoken was about my height. He had fair hair and would have made a good extra in a mountaineering film. The others, a small crowd behind him, all in plain clothes, I would have put in the drawer marked 'doubtful' but they could be used in a football crowd sequence.

'I'm looking for a coloured man called Quentin Jacobsen.'

'I'm Quentin,' I replied, 'but as you can see, I'm not coloured.'

To begin with we all got on very well. I explained to them that if they could be fast, I'd appreciate it because I had a lot of work to do that day.

'Well, Mr Jacobsen, we've had certain complaints.'

I thought for a moment that some bastard had spotted us with black girls in the car. People do that, they report you if they think there's the smallest chance of breaking your scene.

One tall guy prodded me in the stomach and said, 'It's all over. Just sit down and shut up.'

I saw very little opportunity to do anything else. For one moment I did think of dashing down to the darkroom and tipping out a ten-gallon drum of petrol in the hope that it would burn either the dagga or the film, but the screw top would have taken far too long to get off.

The same man asked, 'Where do you live?'

'Here.'

'I have a son about your age. I'm glad he doesn't live in

such a slum.' I was just going to answer back when Ugly Face turned round and said, 'Didn't I tell you to shut up?'

Number One asked how many people lived there and I explained myself, my brother and two other people, Dave and Martin. Another of them turned round and said, 'Who's he?' indicating George Wagner. I told him and added that he had started working for me the night before. Ugly turned round from looking at him. We both had very long hair; mine hadn't been cut for six months.

'This is some kind of commune, isn't it, you bloody buggers?'

I started wishing I'd had my shave. Number One said they were going to search the whole place and, wondering if Ugly was going to interrupt again, I started to explain that each of the cupboards belonged to a different person. From then on it was a little like going through Customs. Dirty socks became as controversial as books. God, I wished I'd never bought a book in my life. The dictionary was put into a big cardboard box. *Aggression* by Conrad Lorenz raised even more eyebrows.

'But it's about fish!'

And when they found *Existentialism from Dostoievski to Sartre* they knew they had it in the bag. I'd only read the chapter on Nietzsche, who had seemed about as right wing as you could get

'Every time we get this book,' said Ugly.

'Which book?'

He held out a book without a cover. I thought it was *The Human Zoo*.

'Marcuse, *One Dimensional Man*.'

'Martin's,' I said. 'He borrowed it from a friend. I haven't read it.'

It was put in the box. Then a big colourful book on skindiving.

'Whose is this?'

'Mine. It's mine.'

'Well, I hope you read it. Mr Venter is one of our finest men.'

A small good mark.

'Yes, it's a very good book.'

Into the box too, went the telephone book. I only hoped they wouldn't spend too much time reading it. Our filing cabinet came next. It was a little odd. It started with a top drawer marked 'Environment' which contained maps, aspirins, bandages, and pile-cream. The next two drawers were marked 'Studio'. The first thing to come up there was a bombshell, Ebrahim's I.O.U. to me. One of them shouted excitedly, 'Got it!', and with a stern, angry face passed the slip of paper over to Number One. This confused me at first. I didn't know if they were acting or not. I couldn't see that it was so important.

'How long have you known Timol?' said Number One.

'Who's Timol?'

'Come on! Don't be stupid. Ahmed Timol, the schoolteacher.'

'Oh, Ahmed! I've only met him once to try and collect the debt on the paper you've got.'

He put the paper carefully into his file after everyone had fingered it. Another policeman said, 'Better take the typewriter, too.'

They asked who did the typing and I said Martin did. I never type anything.

I then realised that Ahmed was their lead-in and for the next ten minutes or so they asked me everything I knew about him. It was quite a relief to me because I didn't know anything about him. I didn't even know he was dead. The police said it had been headlines for two days. 'Of course you knew.' I said I'd heard but it hadn't occurred to me that it was the same Ahmed and I hadn't really registered his last name. More blank expression from the police. Number One said, 'How come? Before he died he described the whole of this studio, even down to the orange skirting-board.'

'Ebrahim must have told him,' I said.

'No, he's been here. He knows you, he knew the studio.'

I couldn't understand it at all, but it suited me fine. I said, 'Look, I've got a client coming in on a job at ten o'clock. I would prefer if you'd leave before he comes. Or shall I cancel it?'

'No, don't cancel it. We might be through by then.'

So I still had hope. It was nine-thirty. They might not find the carrier-bag or the *Cookbook* by then. I just had to keep calm and hope.

One of the main policemen at this point decided to make a search of our pockets. I dislike carrying as much as a bunch of keys, but on this occasion I did, so that had to be explained to them. That was the combi, that was the front door, that the studio, and there was one other I couldn't remember; it might be the old flat at College Mansions. The words 'College Mansions' had the same effect as that old children's game where you all stand still when the music stops.

After a pause, one policeman said, 'College Mansions! You really pick some peculiar places.'

'I didn't pick it, someone gave it to us.'

'What's his name?'

'I don't know. I never met him.'

There were roars of laughter. 'Don't be a funny bugger.'

After me they went over to George. The policeman patted his jeans, stopped, and put a hand in George's pocket. Had I been in his position I would have giggled, but George merely looked more hurt than ever, and I was a little surprised when, amid a round of applause, he exhibited a finger of dagga. But as the pace hotted up this incident was forgotten. More dagga was found in Dave's jacket and in a film canister. So Number One deduced that this whole studio was a front for some international smuggling ring. It was hard not to laugh.

'This place stinks,' Number One said. 'I've been a policeman for fifteen years and this place stinks.'

By this time I was going through my bank statement to prove how much turnover the studio had had, but it was of little interest to them. Then the telephone rang. Musical Chairs was what they played this time. Number One dashed over to the phone and carefully lifted it up.

'Hallo! Yes, this is the studio. Who is it speaking please? I'm afraid he's out. Who is it speaking, please? Hallo? Hallo?'

God, I thought. What third-rate acting.

He turned to me and said, 'Who do you think that was?'

'If you'd let me answer the phone, I might be able to tell you.'

'No, Mr Jacobsen, I'm afraid not.'

Then halfway through the negative file a different policeman found a photograph of a water-tank. More congratulations. I explained it was a photograph of a water-tank.

Number One said, 'We can see that.'

'Martin took it,' I said. 'He thought it was beautiful.'

'What, that bloody old thing?'

It added up; books on aggression, maps, drugs, and now photographs of strategic points.

'Mr Jacobsen, where do you sleep?'

'I sleep here.'

'Where?'

'Well, sometimes by the wall there, but generally over there by the fire.'

'And where does Martin sleep?'

'Martin sleeps by the telephone but he's not staying here very much. He and Dave sometimes stay over at Trafalgar Street, I think, or Regent Street.'

'And anyone else?'

'Yes, I have a twin brother called Henry. He left on the 25th. We all sleep in sleeping bags on the floor.'

'Mr Jacobsen, who is the brains behind all this?'

'Well, I suppose I shot most of the work.'

'But this is just a front.'

More negs turned up, this time of a girl with a hair-shampoo bottle. I hadn't wanted to do the shots but an art director asked me to do them as a favour.

'She looks black.'

'Well, it's a negative. I didn't want to shoot it.'

The time was 9.45. If I could get through the next ten minutes without trouble, I might still win. But what was going to come up next? The telephone rang again and there was more excitement.

'Hallo, yes, who is it? No he's not available. Hallo?'

He put the receiver down. 'It was the same person as last time.'

Answering in that voice and without saying 'Jacobsen, Cohen and Smith' wasn't going to get him anywhere. He asked where the others were and I said I thought they were at Trafalgar Street. I knew they were either at Pretoria or at Stan Field's place but the longer they stayed out the better.

After doing the studio, the men went on to the darkroom, and the first things they dragged out were George's stuff that he had brought the night before. There was a tea-chest and a large suitcase and it was this that amazed even me. Apart from the hundreds of black and white shots of black women, there were pieces of feminine underwear, and night-dresses. I felt a little like a mother who finds nude magazines in her son's room. Why on earth had he brought that stuff here? It added to what already seemed a sufficiently complicated situation.

I kept on saying, 'I have nothing to hide. Do try and hurry up so that I can get on with my work.'

I was trying very hard to appear as normal as possible. I asked if I could use the phone to book a model for a job. I let them ring the number for me and booked the girl for twelve o'clock. It was very short notice but I had a provisional out on her from the day before. Then I asked if I could go into the darkroom to get things ready. I didn't think they would fall for that but it was worth a try.

At about five-to-ten I said, 'I would like you to go now.'

Number One said, 'Just let us finish the darkroom first.'

My heart was pounding away. If only I could distract their attention from the darkroom somehow. Then Ugly opened the drying-cupboard door, looked inside and, in spite of the dark, saw the bag right at the bottom. Slowly he took out the carrier-bag and inside it found another. He opened the second and looked at me with a very big grin. I asked him what it was and he said, 'Come on, you know what it is.' I didn't think my lying was all that bad but my first reaction was, 'It's Henry's. I knew he smoked but I didn't know he'd left that amount in the studio. I don't smoke at all. Henry smokes a lot.' Both of us then trotted out to Number One.

'This place is just a cover for an international smuggling ring.'

Again I insisted that we earned twelve thousand rand

doing photography, and that I had a client coming at any moment.

'It's a very serious matter, drugs.'

I tried to agree with him. Then he decided to go into the darkroom, too. I could have opened the window to let in some light but at that moment I thought the less light the better. But the police decided to drag everything into the studio, mainly empty suitcases and boxes. One small, black suitcase from under the enlarger was opened and at that moment I felt as if I had come a little too suddenly to the ground floor in a lift; he had found the ten-by-eight box with all the prints and negatives of the *Anarchist Cookbook* and the *US Army Manual on Sabotage and Demolition.* It took him some time to realise what he was holding. It was basically five years of my life. When he had read half a page or so he got up from a crouching position, smiled like mad, then grabbed me by the arm. I didn't know whether to ask what it was or deny it but I never think it's good to deny things till you know what they are. I knew my fingerprints were on every page, so I felt it would be a little silly to deny all knowledge of the book.

'Henry brought it in with him and he asked me to do a few prints. I haven't read them. I don't know what they are.'

'This is Communist propaganda for terrorism. Where is your brother now?'

'He left a week ago, on the 25th.'

There was silence. Then a knock on the door. I said it would probably be my Schweppes client. It was, and it was very funny seeing this young art director walk into something he didn't have a clue about. He said, 'Hey, what are you doing? Stop that.'

'What do you do, son?' asked one of the policemen.

'I'm an art director for an advertising firm.'

'Turn out your pockets.'

'What's this?'

'Never you mind, just do what you're told.'

'They're security police,' I managed to say. Ugly told me to shut up again. Another policeman started to frisk his body and legs.

'How long have you known the studio?'

'Three days. I came here for the first time three days ago about this job.'

'Did you talk politics with Mr Jacobsen?'

'No, of course not.'

'Can you prove where you work?'

'Yes, look up the company in the telephone book and ask anyone there who I am.' While they did this I managed to say, 'Sorry, about this. I don't think I'm going to be able to shoot that job.'

He said, 'Well, I hope it's nothing serious.'

'No. No. Just a misunderstanding.

And after a brief description over the phone and him giving his name and address, he was released.

Once the police had the prints of the books, they were satisfied and the search was called off.

'We are detaining you on suspicion of a drug offence,' said Number One.

'The drugs belong to Henry,' I said once again.

'We'll see about that,' said he.

One of the more passive ones said, 'Get all your things together, shirts, socks and so on. You'll need them.'

'But I'll be coming back here.'

'No. Not for some time.'

'Well, I'd better cancel my work then. I'll show you the numbers in the book and you can dial them. I just want to tell my clients to find another photographer.'

They agreed, so I went ahead. I rang VZ and cancelled the butter job, and JWT the soap job, and the model. Naturally they all wanted to know why, but the police wouldn't let me give any explanation. All I could say was that I was afraid I couldn't do the work. I put all my things into a big suitcase. I took my folio with all its shots and my precious life insurance policy as well as my badge collection. What I didn't know then was that the policy isn't good for suicide for the first two years.

George and I were taken separately. I went down first in the lift, then at the bottom the policeman asked me whether I preferred to be handcuffed or would I prefer to be shot. This wasn't a joke. I said I preferred to be shot. We walked

14

round the block to their car. I was lugging my big case and trying to look innocent. When we reached the spot where the police car should have been they started swearing in Afrikaans. I asked what was the matter and they said somebody had either towed the car away or pinched it. Their embarrassment was painful. I said helpfully that it wasn't far to the car pound; it was down on Bree Street next to the Phoenix pub. The three policemen argued about whether to ring for another car or pick up the old one and then decided to get their own, which meant I had to carry my very heavy case over to the Phoenix. Once there, we all peered through the fence looking for a black Dodge. There were cries of joy from the police when they recognised it. We all walked round to the entrance and they told the African policeman there that he had a car of theirs. The African, very courageously, said they couldn't have it unless they paid the fine. There was more laughter. Out came identification papers and more insults but the African obviously didn't want to lose his job.

'Please, Baas! Just walk round to Simmons Street and see Baas. Bring back your paper and I can release car. Please, Baas, I can't let the car out without the paper.'

Absolutely exhausted from carrying the suitcase, I accompanied the policemen to the office. There I was left downstairs with two of them while the third went upstairs to see a friend who knew the department. While we were waiting, I remember a girl in an out-of-date mini-dress went up the stair and the two young policemen whistled. The girl turned round and smiled—at me.

The police then said, 'What do you think of our girls? Not a bad lot, are they?' I was tempted to say, 'They are all fat and stupid,' but instead I said they were very much like the Australians.

'Take a good look,' said one of them. 'It may be the last for some time.'

'I don't see why. I haven't done anything.'

'What about those books?'

'The books belong to my brother.'

'We'll see about that.'

The third policeman came down, talking to an official who

was saying something about 'We'll see it doesn't happen again. See you at tennis next week.'

As long as you're sports conscious you can get away with anything.

I said, 'Do you play squash?'

'No,' said the young policeman.

'Fives?' I asked.

'What's that?' I explained it was like squash but without a racket.

'No, I don't play fives.'

'Well, come on, let's get the car.'

Back across the road, past the Phoenix. I could have done with a beer by now. On to the car lot. The policeman waved his bit of paper. The African bowed. 'Thank you, Baas.'

I got into the back with a policeman on either side of me and the one in front drove. The big black car was stifling. The plastic seat smelt. After reversing the clumsy thing we managed to get it into position to leave. When the driver insulted the African at the gate he said 'Thank you, Baas.'

The wind coming through as we drove relaxed me a little, then, as the car engine warmed up, I heard the driver curse.

'Blisken God! Blisken Jesus!' The car started behaving oddly and the driver got more and more angry but we managed to get halfway across town before it completely stalled. Apparently the automatic choke was sticking and the engine was flooding. We all sat in the back of the car while the driver swore at the engine. I thought he was going to flatten the battery, but instead the other two got out, leaving me in the back alone. They started to push and after a few yards the driver let out the clutch, the car tyres screamed and an African on a scooter smashed into the back side of the car. The driver, furious, got out and walked over to the Black who had fallen off his scooter. He did not recognise the police and started to say it was their fault. They took his pass number and the number of the scooter and climbed back into the car. Finally, to my relief, we spluttered into the car park at the police headquarters in John Vorster Square.

CHAPTER TWO

The car park is on the ground floor. There are two lifts that go directly to the tenth floor, where an old man presses a button which makes a steel door open. The whole police station was designed only a few years ago at enormous cost and it was proudly boasted that it was quite impossible to break out of it, or even into it. On the tenth floor my police escort nodded to the old man; he pressed the button and sure enough the door slid open. Once we were in, the door closed. The corridor was a good fifty yards long and had grey walls with glass panels and rooms leading off on both sides. We went into the second or third room on the left, where I put my suitcase down. Then we went down to, I think, the second floor—it may even have been in an adjoining building—to the department for drug offences.

The police interrogator there had all his diplomas and promotions framed on the wall. He was softly spoken and deeply concerned. After a quick five-minute philosophical speech directed at me while we both looked out of the window, he told me and anybody who might be looking in that dagga was grown by communists to corrupt our youth into laziness and debauchery. 'We will not tolerate it; it will be stamped out; new laws are coming in which will change the whole situation. It will not be long before our country is clean again.' He then stood up and took a cigarette packet from his pocket and offered me one.

I stood up too and said, 'Thank you very much, I don't smoke.'

'Sit down,' he said. 'I haven't finished with you yet.'

'The dagga in the studio isn't mine. It probably belongs to Henry. It's got nothing to do with me.'

'But it's your studio, isn't it?'

'I admit I do most of the work but I can't dictate what the others should do. I don't know half the people who come in. They are friends of the others. I can't check everybody who comes in and out, can I?'

'Where are the others?'

'I think at Trafalgar Street, I don't know the number; it's a house at the end on the right.'

'What about the dagga in David's jacket?'

'I don't know. I didn't think he smoked.'

'Well, it looks to me that he's an addict. How many others are there?'

'I really didn't think he smoked. I know my brother Henry smoked a lot but he's in London at the moment.'

'Well, Mr Jacobsen, you're not much help, are you?'

'I'm sorry if I can't help you, but Henry is in London and Dave's at Trafalgar Street, I suppose.'

'Have you anything else to say?'

'No.'

So he got up and took me to the office next door. George Wagner was there. He took my place in the interrogation room and I stayed behind with another plain-clothes man in his mid-thirties, who seemed quite cheerful. It's obvious that they love their job. He showed me other big cases that he'd worked on and, inside a glass case in a corner, some 'Durban Poison' and some 'Malawi Grass' which comes stuffed into bamboo cane. I knew this already but I didn't want to spoil his fun. There were more pills than anything else, mainly amphetamines, slimming and the anti-depressant types, not as striking as the grass. The objects I found most exciting were parcels which had been sent through the post and been intercepted. There they were in their half-open state, looking very lost.

After Wagner had his interrogation, we were both taken down and round into the front entrance of the ordinary police station, where we were given over to the prison authorities. Behind this small unimposing front we were taken through a complete vehicle-loading bay. As far as I could see, at least five trucks could load up at once through separate bays and channels. It was clearly designed for a very quick turn-about. One guard took us to the first gate which was opened from the outside by another. We went in and I innocently commented. 'There's always a first time for everything.' The guard replied, 'It's your first time then? Well, congratulations. It's my first day too.' He was very nice and on the way up told me what his wages were and showed me his uniform. It's odd. They don't get much.

Upstairs on the second floor George and I were told to sit down and wait. After a while I felt it was all right to talk to George and asked him what he'd told the police. He told me and I said, 'Stick to that and we'll go far. Remember you know nothing about the books, so don't make any guesses.' While we were talking, a long line of Africans marched quietly past us and stopped by a door. While they were waiting, a few of them started what I can best describe as blowing kisses at us. I wondered if I was being accosted.

They kept saying, 'Please, Baas,' and then they'd make a hiss-hiss sort of noise. Then it suddenly occurred to me—it was cigarettes they wanted. For some unknown reason I started to speak French, 'Je ne fume pas.' George added, 'We've just been busted.' A guard put his head round a door and shouted something and all the blacks ran forward and turned left into a small room. There was two minutes' silence and then the most frightening noise of metal falling on metal, and screams and shouts. This went on for several minutes and both George and I were terrified.

'This is outrageous. What next?' I thought.

Then the noise died down and very quietly the Africans started to come out. I was practically a nervous wreck by then. I hardly dared look, but when I did, to my absolute relief I saw they were carrying a vast number of dripping aluminium plates, a bit like dog bowls. In fact that describes them very accurately from more points of view than one, because later we had to eat from them and they smelt of grease, like my last dog's breath.

After the Africans went out a white prison officer shouted, 'Stand up!'

George and I looked round. Nobody else was in the hall, so slowly we stood up.

'Come in, come on, get in!'

We walked into the office.

'Name?'

Simultaneously, 'Quentin'. 'George'.

'You over there, shut up. Name?'

'Quentin Charles Bulow Jacobsen. Sorry it's a bit long.'

'Don't worry. I've got all the time I need. Age?'

'Twenty-five.'

'Any watches, pens, knives or cash?'

'Yes, I've got twenty-five rand and some silver.'

'Put it on the table, then. Anything else?' He wrote out a white slip of paper in duplicate, made me sign it and gave me the top half. 'All right, get out!'

I sat down outside while George got his slip and then we both waited on the seat. I was just thinking how exciting the whole thing was when a white prostitute and a coloured drunk were brought in. The drunk couldn't stand, so he was dragged everywhere. The prostitute, on the other hand, knew exactly what to do. She demanded the use of the telephone and even got a phone book; she rang up a friend and told her to get hold of her lawyer who was called such-and-such, and somebody else to get money from. I was very impressed and it occurred to me it wouldn't be at all a bad idea if we did the same. So after she finished I asked politely if I might telephone.

'No, you'll be getting a visit from the consul to-morrow.'

'Oh, great. Consular visit, eh? Well, thank you.' I went back and told George. He was a little upset at this, because he'd just been to his own consulate about giving up his German citizenship for South African.

'You bastard, George! What on earth do you want to become like one of them for?'

'I like it here.'

'You want your head examined.'

Wagner in his strong German accent said,

'No, it's good here. Maybe not right here and now but in Botswana it's very nice.'

Every time the big main door was opened, we both got up. Eventually it was our turn to leave the hall and go upstairs. If I remember rightly, we were on the second floor and went up to the third. The fourth floor is, I think, for women. A guard opened the door from the outside and another guard opened his door from the inside. We were directed to the store and told to get four blankets and a mattress each. After dragging these over to a cell, we were locked in.

It was a large cell, twenty-two feet by eighteen, with a

20

cream ceiling, grey walls and black floor, just like our studio but upside down. There was a light in the middle, a lavatory in one corner and a metal-barred door which opened inwards on to a small hall which had a solid door which also opened inwards. The solid door was left open so that you could speak to other prisoners across the corridor. I peered across to have a look. The first one I saw was only wearing his underpants and looked very young. 'Here, what are you in for?' he shouted.

'Dagga, I think.'

'What do you mean "think"?'

'Well, I don't know, I haven't been charged yet.'

There were about six in his cell. The others were sleeping. I asked him how long he had been there, and he said, 'Forty-five days.' He asked me what time it was and I said I thought about six. I asked him what time supper was, and he said at sundown, which would be in about an hour.

'Here, have you got anything to read?'

'No.'

'Do you want something?'

I thought I might as well, so he threw across a photographic comic. I walked back to George who was sitting on his mattress and told him he could have it when I'd finished with it. I read a few pages and decided to walk. Now that I was locked up it was necessary to do a little thinking.

Henry was out, so that was to the good. Dave and Martin weren't caught yet but that wouldn't take long. Seadom and Buki were not in either the studio diary or Henry's Unicef 'Wild-Life' diary which I knew he had left behind, so there was no need to bring them in at all. Ian Hill was in Henry's diary and he had left a record that might have his name on it. I'd try and leave him to the last. If I was lucky the others wouldn't talk. There were still some beer shots waiting at the lab. I must try to ring the client about that, and do some invoicing. It was nice, in a way, to be relaxed for a bit. I had been working very long hours and I could do with a holiday. George was still worrying about his naturalisation papers.

Supper took hours to arrive. We heard the noise of it being taken out of the lift and put on a table outside. Someone came round to check how many prisoners there were, doled the food out and, eventually, served it. I got a dog bowl with a small piece of meat, some boiled potatoes and some very dead vegetables, much like school food really, and coffee in an old Coca Cola can. The plate was forced under the grille door by an African and the coffee was left standing on a cross-bar. There were no spoons. One ate with one's fingers. The food was all right and the coffee was excellent —good, hot, milky, sweet coffee. Then they closed the solid door and said good-night.

That first night I really felt at home. It was exciting and at the same time there was no rush. Anyone who has been in advertising will know what I mean; no-one could possibly ring up and ask for something immediately. But it was a little noisy, which made it difficult to sleep and in the middle of the night it got very cold, too, and more and more it was changing from a camping holiday to a prison camp. By morning I was shivering and waiting for my breakfast. The noise of breakfast arrived hours before it actually came. The solid door was opened and coffee, two boiled eggs and slices of bread were shoved through. Having someone to talk to did make moaning worth while, and the sentimental comic was a change from Spinoza. I decided to sleep in a bit. I thought of Malcolm X when he was in jail, doing isometrics and reading the dictionary.

Presently the police came in, this time to take us down for fingerprints. I made a small and pathetic gesture of protest. From what little I knew of liberty, I seemed to remember that my fingers belonged to me. They said I was quite right.

'If you want to make trouble, we can go to court to-morrow and get permission. It just means waiting twenty-four hours.'

'Well, I think you should tell me these things. I shouldn't have to ask.'

The policeman who took my prints was young, very tanned, and had hair longer than mine. I almost asked him why he was doing the job. I felt very let-down by all these young policemen who were so adamant in their conservatism and their belief in some sort of divine right, and yet so convincing in their nonconformist image.

After signing the prints and washing the ink off my hands,

I went back to my cell. George came in later. He said he'd seen his consul and he'd been very angry but he thought he might get off with a small fine and possibly deportation. Then a policeman came to collect me for my consular visit. I went down to a room on the second floor where I met Mr Biggie, the consul. He was unmistakably British: tall, broad, with a moustache, a pipe, pipe-cleaner, hanky in breast pocket. His usual comment was a non-committal 'I see.' He was accompanied by a girl I can best describe as like a slightly overweight sparrow. It was her first day on the job. She was very talkative and full of enthusiasm. I told them I'd been detained because they had found dagga in the studio and some books that might possibly have been banned. I didn't know.

'I see,' said Mr Biggie. 'Books?'

'Well, just a couple of books, you know.'

'Yes, I see, but what books?'

'I can't remember exactly, but I think one's called the *Anarchist Cookbook* and the other the *US Army Manual on Sabotage and Demolition* or something like that.'

'Mmm, I see. Yes, it does put a slightly different light on things, doesn't it?'

'Well, that's a good way of putting it.'

'You're well, are you? Good! Yes, I see. Well, we'll see what we can do. That seems to be about all, doesn't it? What messages would you like sent to your parents?'

I asked him to telephone my father in Bishop's Stortford and tell him I'd been detained on a drugs charge and get him to contact my brother Henry. I didn't want to give him my home address because it might have led to embarrassment for Henry. As it happened, a friend of Dave's rang up my mother and said that on no account must Henry return to South Africa and a telegram arrived later to the same effect.

After they left, I was taken to my first spell of interrogation. This was on the tenth floor of the other building. I was given a seat and asked to start at the beginning.

'Beginning of what?'

'Well, what about your full name?'

'Quentin Charles Bulow Jacobsen. You can put two dots over the "u" in Bulow if you like.'

'Age?'

'Twenty-five. Born 23rd of the first, 1946. My twin brother Henry was born half an hour later.'

'Where was that?'

'In Leicester, England.'

'Parents?'

'My father is Bent Bulow Jacobsen; he's Danish. He's a scientist, and my mother is Susan Jacobsen. They're divorced.'

'Does she do anything?'

'She was a teacher, but she's retired.'

'Brothers and sisters?'

'My oldest brother Gilbert is in America. He's married, and my second brother Nicholas is also married. He lives in London.

'What do they do?'

'Gilbert is in computers and Nick works in art school. Then there's Henry, my twin. He worked with me in the studio.'

'Where were you educated?'

'I went to three schools: Barrow Hill Road School for a year, then the George Eliot School in St John's Wood for five years, and the King Alfred School, Hampstead for five years. They're all in London.'

'And after you left school?'

'I emigrated to Australia when I was sixteen, on my own.'

'What did you do there?'

'Worked. I did practically everything from road-laying to bus-conducting. I ended up doing photography, came back to England, and did a year at Guildford School of Art doing photography.'

'What qualifications have you got?'

'No paper qualifications. My qualifications are all personal experience in advertising and journalism.'

He went on to question me about all my relations, including aunts and uncles and Danish and Scottish cousins, some of whose names I was very uncertain of. Then all of them started in on what countries I had been to. It amounts to forty and must have sounded a little odd. I don't think they'd been anywhere at all.

'I haven't been to East Germany, Russia, or any other communist country, but I passed through Bulgaria to get to Yugoslavia. I've also been to Mozambique, Swaziland and Lesotho. I've been down the Suez Canal to Aden but that's all. I've also been to Gibraltar and Malta.'

'How come you've travelled so much?'

'It's in my blood to travel. My father took us on holiday round Europe when we were children. But, in fact, most of it's been on work.'

'When did you arrive in South Africa?'

'April 21st, 1971.'

'Who did you come with?'

'Henry, my twin brother, Martin Cohen and David Smith.'

'Who are the others?'

'Martin's an Australian I met in London and David I met through Martin. They were at school together in Australia.'

'All right. Let's start with Martin. Tell us about him.'

'Martin comes from Sydney in Australia. He has been in business, something to do with stocks and shares, and he's been a computer programmer. He has a degree in mathematics.'

'Where is he now?'

'So far as I know he's still in South Africa.'

'And the other guy, David Smith?'

'He comes from Sydney, too. I know he went to the Architectural Association school in London. He has a degree in architecture.'

'And now Henry?'

'He's my twin brother. He went to the same schools as I did and then went on to the London School of Economics for a year and then to Leicester University.'

'And why did you decide to come to South Africa?'

'I came here to get work, because work was slacking off in England.'

'And when did you arrive?'

'On April 21st, at Jan Smuts Airport.'

'Well, we've checked your passport and it says the 22nd.'

'I know it says the 22nd, but it's wrong.'

'How come it's wrong? What flight did you come in on?'

'It was a Trek Airways flight about ten in the morning.'

'And there were other flights before that one?'

'I suppose so; I don't know.'

'And you want me to believe that all the passport stamps that morning had the wrong date on?'

'Yes.'

'Well, I don't. It's impossible.'

'It isn't impossible. I pointed it out at the time and he said it didn't matter.'

'It's impossible. And another thing I don't believe is that you have a twin brother.'

'Why?'

'Why, because it's a well-known fact that people fly in twice on different passports to make it look as though they have a double.'

'Well, I do have a double, and as it happens, he's out of the country.'

'We still don't believe he exists.'

'I don't care what you think.'

He left it at that and went on.

'What South African people did you know before you came here?'

'I had no South African friends and I've only met a few people since I came, mainly through business.'

Then he asked me in detail about everything to do with my business, especially about my bank accounts, who had recommended that particular bank and why. He asked me what political discussions I'd had with people.

I said, 'I'm not interested in politics. I'm interested in economics, not politics.'

Next it was the I.O.U. from Ebrahim to Timol, not once but over and over again. When they'd been at it for at least three hours, they decided to take me out to Roodepore Indian High School where I told them that I'd met Ahmed Timol in connection with the I.O.U. It was a great relief to know they were still on the wrong track. We drove to the school with the police radio going full blast in Afrikaans. I was with the man I got to know well as Mr Bouwer, and a younger policeman who had a bulge in his pocket. There was the usual 'Do you prefer to be shot or do you want hand-cuffs?' I preferred to be shot every time. I did often think of running for it, but if I did it would be in the city, not out in the suburbs. Mr Bouwer sat in front and I sat in the back with the other one. We talked about photography, films, books. Like me they hadn't read much. I tried to keep subjects competitive, knowing their fondest hate of communism. If I had known any rugger songs it would have been an excellent time to hum them. I told them we had got lost the time we went out there. Did they want me to direct them the way we had actually gone or would they prefer to go straight to the school? They didn't see much point in getting lost first, so we went straight to the heart of the matter.

In my interrogation I had told them exactly what we had done, going out—meeting the wrong Ahmed and being redirected on to Ahmed Timol. We retraced our steps exactly and even got the wrong Ahmed, who remembered everything. The disappointment of the police was heartbreaking. I even offered to go and see Timol's mother and see if she remembered me, but they didn't feel there was any point in it. So we drove back to the station. I tried to feel depressed. It had been such a disappointment for the police. Back at John Vorster Square they rang Ebrahim's brother at his textile store, and he came up to the station and corroborated my story down to the 'bent sou' he said he wouldn't even give me for the I.O.U. It was really all going very well. Then they asked me if I would like to go back to the studio and settle up my work and get some clothes and things, which seemed to me to have both good and bad aspects. It could be that they meant to deport me and wanted me to straighten my work out first. Or, on the other hand, it might mean we were settling in for a long, cold winter. But just then it was still a matter of interrogation. Bouwer and his mate went off duty and their place was taken by two more men. Question and answer continued. It went on all night until I think the police felt that things were falling a little flat. Eventually I asked if I could go to the lavatory. Both the policemen accompanied me, through the steel doors, turn to the right opposite the lift. As I walked in, an orange light was coming through the frosted glass of the window and I realised it was sunrise. I thought of *Citizen Kane*. I could have been a reporter working all night on a story, unshaven and a little unhappy at the editor's opinion. Mine, too, was only a story and not a very interesting one. The police waited outside but I had to leave the door ajar and as I washed my hands by the window in the cloakroom they practically held on to me: The window clearly worried them. I glanced in the mirror and made a face at myself: 'Mouldy again.' I would have liked a shave. And so back to the interrogation.

An African knocked and came in with a trolley.

'Coffee?'

'Yes, two sugars and milk.' I wondered what he felt like. It was oddly comforting. Seadom used to make me coffee.

After seven, I think, breakfast came up, coffee again and scrambled eggs. The police ate theirs with me. Presently the interrogators of the day before came on again and the night ones left. There had been two different sets, one lot in the evening and another at night. Now it was Bouwer and his young friend again. I was quite glad to see him. He asked how I was and I said I was a bit bored but not tired.

'When are you going to tell us something interesting?'

'You mean my sex life?'

He looked up. 'Have you had black girls?' Not a bad shot in the dark.

'I genuinely prefer blondes.' A slight psychological slip, I realised. You can't prefer unless you know, but he didn't seem to notice.

'What do you think of South African girls?'

'Oh, great. Just like Australians.'

It was a strange conversation so early in the morning.

Then he went on to read through the previous day's interrogation. I thought of the cliché, 'That's my story and I'm sticking to it.' He seemed to think the same too.

'Why did you get mixed up in all this?'

'All what?' I asked. These do-you-still-beat-your-wife sort of questions are quite catchy when one is tired. I looked at the two men. One had torn the top pages out and the other was reading the carbon copies left in the book. They had both been home to beds with sheets and wives. Bouwer wore a blue-grey suit and the young one light blue shorts, a matching shirt and white knee-length socks, and he had a bulge about where his appendix would be. When Bouwer had finished reading the top copy he went out of the room and gave it to somebody to deliver somewhere.

Later that morning we went back to the studio. We used the same black Dodge, and needless to say, halfway up Market Street there came the same shout of 'Blisken Jesus!' They hadn't fixed the choke yet. Broken down and double-parked against the vegetable trucks, we stamped our feet like children. Everything the police did I did too. If they laughed at Blacks, I laughed. If they stamped their feet, I did too. Anything to agree with them. After a wait of five minutes to let the plugs dry out, we tore off again. This time we parked right outside the studio. I wonder how many people thought, 'Quentin's done well, got a chauffeur-driven car.'

On the fourth floor I saw that the police had only locked the wooden door and not the metal shutters. As soon as I saw this, I was angry.

'Anybody could have smashed the window and gone off with the lot. Don't invite crime by being lazy. You should know enough about that. I've got all my life savings in there.'

They tried to look a little guilty.

'Who's got the keys?'

'Not me.'

'Nor me.'

'Well, do you think I still have them?'

'No.'

'But the way you've locked up we don't bloody well need them.'

I got hold of the padlock and twisted it off, screws and all. The police tried to object but it was in my hands already.

It was good to see the studio again.

'Anyone for coffee?' I asked. Apparently not.

Then Mr Bouwer said, 'Anything you want to chuck out put in a box.'

There was a box outside that I used for rubbish so I put it in the middle of the studio. Bouwer was standing there with his hands in his pockets saying, 'I can't understand it. You had everything good, an interesting business, a car, money, models walking in and out. How much do you pay for steak in England? Two rand a pound. And as for pine-apples and mangoes, you can't even get them. You had one of the biggest studios in Jo'burg, and look at you now! I feel really sorry for you.'

It was hard to know what to say. I could complain that I was innocent, but without being charged I didn't know what I was innocent of. On the other hand, I'd had about enough of business just then. I wouldn't have minded all that much being deported.

'Anything you want to return to clients,' Bouwer said, 'put in piles for them to collect.'

'You mean negs and things?'

'Yes, and all the equipment. Can you leave it somewhere with one of your friends?'

This must, I thought, mean deportment. Things could be worse. I went through negatives and separated them into five groups. When I came to the prop cupboard it really seemed a shame. I had fifty pounds' worth of glasses that I'd bought on beer, wine and brandy jobs. I had pints of vodka and brandy that I could do nothing with except re-turn to the client. What a waste! Cigarettes too, pounds of loose tobacco and dozens of new packs, all going back to the client. As I got it all set out, the police rang the agencies and explained that they must come down to the studio and pick up their things. I went on tidying up. It was quite re-laxing and I found it a relief. It was hard to think what other end there might have been to the studio. But the end this was: of that there was no doubt. I rang up a friend that I knew had a studio and asked him if I could leave my equipment there. He came round with his assistant and a Black. We all had a jolly good laugh. The assistant had hair down to his shoulders, and someone asked 'Who's your girl-friend?' I offered my friend the darkroom sink and our gas camping-cooker on which Henry had made curry. There were yellow drips still left on the chrome. Henry used to squat on the floor beside it and spit bits of ginger into the coffee as they do in India. When, I wondered, would I see him again, or, for that matter, the cooker? All the equipment went with my friend, together with the surfboards, the ether, the pressure cooker, the flashpacks. I had hoped to be able to tell him to dump the lot and I think now that this 'happening' was a put-up job anyway, because many of the things I threw away came up later as exhibits. The police were hoping that I might give them a lead by trying to throw something away. No doubt they went through every little scrap of paper in the waste. It was suggested later that the enlarger might have been used for blowing up microdots. Again, I said I didn't know. It was obvious that it couldn't have been, but it looked better not to know too much. Like the glycerine in the bottle, the ad for the Chemical Exhibition and the newspaper cutting about Bantu education, with a story about African Explosives accidentally included. All Dave's and Martin's things I left, although I admit to stealing two of Martin's shirts and a pair of underpants. At the time I joked to myself, 'I'll need them in court.' As it turned out I did. I hadn't particularly liked doing all that work. Much of it was boring and badly paid by English standards, and I don't particularly like sleeping on the floor. I'd miss the telephone but even that wasn't totally unpredictable. Quite often one got the right number. When I walked out of the door I knew that I would never see the place again. I was just having a last look round when I noticed Dave's shaving brush and the studio razor. Mr Bouwer smiled and said, 'Go on, you bugger, have a quick shave.' Anybody would have thought he was a nice man. I hadn't any hot water and the kettle had gone, so it had to be a cold shave, close, and in a hurry. I let the water out and we left.

On our way back to the interrogation room at John Vorster Square we passed an open door and I caught a glimpse of Dave's red jacket. So Dave, and, I guessed, Martin had given themselves up. The police chose a room some distance from the one where Dave was. My interrogation book was brought in and the new interrogators signed on where the old ones signed off.

After forty-eight hours of going over everything again I was feeling pretty gaga. I really didn't know what I was saying. If I fell asleep, they would ask me if I wanted to stretch my legs. It was my opinion then that the sooner I told them everything the sooner I would be deported, so I didn't mind staying up to help them. But with all the excitement earlier I just couldn't keep my eyes open any longer. When I was fifteen we used to do the London to Brighton walk so I knew what it was to be completely exhausted. So they took me back to my cell. Only this time George had gone and there was a note on the door, not from George but from the prison authorities, saying in Afrikaans something about no talking, no letters, no papers, no books. This was it. Even the comic had gone. I was left with only my jacket, my spare shirts (I had another two with me), spare socks, my Johnson's baby powder and a toothbrush. And a mat on the floor. The light was left on all the time, but it didn't matter. I was asleep already.

CHAPTER THREE

I don't know when I woke up. The eggs were cold and I had no method of telling the time. The noise outside sounded like a cross between a railway station and a swimming pool, with school meals thrown in. I ate my two eggs but saved the bread; it was good to have something to nibble on.

I hadn't really explored the cell the night before, so the first thing to do was to operate the flush a few times to see how that worked. I wondered whether, if everyone did it together, we could flood the place. It might be good fun but it would be difficult to organise. Next to the lavatory there was a small wall and, on the far side of that, what looked like a belly-button turned inside out. It could have been a point for a shower. Why didn't they use it? I badly wanted a shower. That was probably the reason; people with nothing to do would have used all the water trying vainly to come clean. On the other side there was a concrete block against the wall. It could be used for sitting on but I preferred my three-quarter-inch felt mat with three blankets on it and a fourth folded up for a pillow. In fact I found the felt mat very itchy, so when I slept I put one blanket under me.

Apart from the bulb in the middle, which was left on all the time, except for total blackouts which happened quite often, there were reinforced glass windows six feet from the floor behind quarter-inch wire mesh and steel bars. In the morning the sun would struggle through to reach a few square inches of white Englishman and as the sun moved round I too would move my mat to meet it. I'm sure it made no difference, but it was a good excuse for doing nothing and at the same time it didn't look defeatist. After two hours of no more than a narrow beam of light I had to wait a further two hours before I could do anything with it again. If I jumped up and caught hold of the bars I could peer out of the window, but all I could see was other windows, and I never saw anyone look out of them.

Two days passed quite quickly. I slept a lot during the

daytime and walked up and down, but made no system for time-wasting yet. It didn't really seem necessary; I still imagined I would be deported quite soon. Then the police came for me again and I was almost glad to see them.

'How are you?'

'All right.'

'Fine.'

'I wouldn't mind something to read.'

'Well, you won't need it. We've come to ask you some more questions. Put your trousers on and a jacket.' (I found it far more comfortable to walk round in a shirt and underpants.) I hadn't had a shave yet or any exercise outside my cell, so a trip up to the interrogation room would break the boredom. I thought to myself, 'If you tell them nothing you can only make them suspicious.' The best thing was to explain everything in innocent terms.

Halfway through his spell of interrogation the older police officer suddenly burst out, 'What I don't understand is why you buggers always pick on our country and try to tell us how to run it. Why don't you go to Northern Ireland or Tanzania? There's a cabinet minister there who burns his floorboards when he runs out of coal. He's the sort of stupid bugger who needs teaching, a damn sight more than our Blacks do. You come over here and you think you know it all. Well, I'll tell you something. South Africa has the highest gross national product of the whole of Africa, and our Blacks have more fridges than they do in any other African country. Did you know that? That's it, you see. You don't bloody think. South Africa's got more telephones and cars than all the other African countries put together, and what we can't take out of the air we dig out of the ground.'

In some ways it was a relief to hear this hard and bitter elderly man lose his temper, lies and all, but I hoped it could be taken as the little pep-talk they give you before they put you on the plane.

'Our country is built on a gold mine and you British have always wanted it. But I tell you you'll never get it. While we were fighting your bloody war, your soldiers were over here fucking our wives. It was the same in the Boer War. Although we were outnumbered seven to one we beat you

34

because our strength lay in our trust in God.'

I didn't dare say anything. He was shouting like a madman and I was half asleep out of sheer fatigue.

'You bloody English burnt our farms, took our men without warrants and then accepted the evidence of the Blacks against us. Do you know who invented the term "concentration camp"?'

'Sorry, are you asking me?'

'It was the British, do you hear? Thousands of our wives and children died of typhoid and malaria in YOUR bloody concentration camps. You complain the African is being treated badly but what do you think our fathers have been through? A hundred years ago the Transvaal was nothing, nothing. They built this place and when they were dying of hunger we had to beg for food from you British. And do it in English, too.'

At the end of this I really felt quite guilty. It was late evening by then and at one stage there had been as many as eight policemen in the room, who had dropped in just to see how it was going. They were clearly waiting for the breaking-point, and it is true that this kind of lecture is very exhausting.

Eventually the man calmed down a little. It was interesting that the other policemen in the room weren't in any way embarrassed at his losing his temper; they just sat still and nodded agreement at his argument, whereas I sat rigid, afraid to answer him in any way at all.

'We're wasting our time with this statement,' he said, 'you've told us absolutely nothing. We know all about the telephone exchange. Why don't you tell us about that? Or about Modderfontein?'

I was in a very tricky position. This was all new material coming up from some source. Martin, Dave or Seadom—I didn't know who at this stage. But not to answer would only have made them more suspicious, so all I could do was to say things like, 'Well, we had thought of it, but we haven't done anything.' But they seemed to think that even thinking of doing something was enough to convict you.

New interrogators came on.

'Jacobsen, that's a Jewish name, isn't it?'

'It may have been hundreds of years ago, but it doesn't really matter, does it?'

'What religion are you?'

'Church of England.'

'Which one?'

'Not Presbyterian, the other one, the main one.'

'When was the last time you went?'

'I go every Christmas.'

'That's not much use, is it? How were you raised at school?'

'Well, it was quite a big school and all mixed up so they didn't have any religious instruction. We had a community meeting in the morning, called Council.' As soon as I had said this I knew I had put my foot in it.

'What sort of school do you call that?'

'Progressive.'

'Oh, we've heard that one before. Old Helen Suzman's lot. I can just imagine it, full of wogs.'

'I left anyway when I was sixteen. School didn't interest me much. By the way—I've remembered. I think I'm Anglican.'

'You mean one of the Dean's lot. You'd be better off being an atheist. Did you ever see him, old Putty Face?'

'Who?'

'The communist Dean, ffrench-Beytagh.'

'No. I read about his case in the paper. What did he do?'

'He was planning to take over our country; he even incited some old women to acts of violence and had ANC leaflets as well as money from communists in London. He was in it up to here.' He pointed to his neck. 'Once the communists get hold of someone, it's like a bad apple, he goes rotten and nothing can stop it. By the way, have you ever been to the Race Relations Board?'

'No. Why?'

'Oh, they're a bunch of bloody so-and-so's too. Trouble-makers the lot of them. "Evolution not revolution," that's our answer. Why can't people let things take their natural course and leave us alone?'

After continuous interrogation for two days and nights, I was virtually incapable of thinking. Half the time I didn't know

36

whether they were giving me question or answer. When things got very bad I was made to stand up and stretch my legs. 'Have a little walk' they'd say. 'Try and keep yourself awake.' I would get up and ask to go to the lavatory, or maybe I'd have a cup of coffee and then sit down again to more interrogation. I realise now I should have objected. I remember one morning when Bouwer came in after they had just confronted me with new information from someone else, I just completely broke down. I couldn't see any way out; someone was telling them the lot and that was it. Tired, dirty and unshaven, I went out to the lavatory, and as I was washing my hands, Mr Bouwer came up to me, put his hand on my shoulder like a father, and gave me some toothpaste. I was very touched but it was the last straw. It was probably the smallest tube of toothpaste one could buy but I knew it had come out of his own pocket and nobody else's.

'Come, do your teeth as well.'

'Can you lend me a hanky?' I sobbed.

He talked slowly. 'Yes, go on. You really are a very silly boy. Why didn't you just stick to your photography?'

'I don't know. I ... Oh, God I'm in a mess.' I was sniffing with exhaustion and fear.

'Come, clear the whole thing up,' Bouwer said. 'We know it all already. It's stupid to hold out on us. The sooner you tell us the sooner we can deport you, but we can't do that till we check everything, can we?'

I tried to pull myself together. I did my teeth and put the toothpaste back in my pocket and went back to interrogation.

Night came for the third time and by now I just felt like a tortoise without its shell; I had to prop myself up with my hands.

'What's wrong with you? Anybody would think you haven't had any sleep.'

I talked very slowly. When it's tired a child gets angry, but I was sad and exhausted. 'You know how long I've been here. I haven't slept for two days and three nights.'

'That's nothing. We're just beginning. Have some coffee. Stand up! Shake your legs a little!'

37

'I really think this is a little pointless. I'm very tired. I would be able to remember things much better in the morning.'

'What about my overtime? I could have been out with my wife at the Bioscope and I've cancelled the lot to see you.'

'I didn't know you cared.'

'Don't be smart. I'll make the jokes.' He paused and then began again. 'Why did you come to South Africa? Who sent you?'

'Not again! I've answered that hundreds of times. Nobody sent us. Work was getting slack so we decided to come here. I've been practically everywhere else. Why shouldn't I come here?'

'Because you want to ruin our country, that's why. Why did you bring in ANC leaflets?'

'That's a new one, isn't it? I've never seen any leaflets.'

'But you've been there haven't you?'

'How do you know?'

'Don't ask questions. I do the questions. You stick to the answers.'

'All right. I've been there. So what? A friend of mine, Ebrahim, asked me to go with him.'

'You mean the one you lent money to?'

'Yes. Why?'

'You mean you just sit there and don't think it's important?'

'Well, it might be. I don't know. I don't want to be rude, but doesn't your coffee taste funny?'

'No. It's the same coffee I'm drinking.'

'Well, mine's a bit bitter. This is one hell of a coffee. I ... well, I think there's something in it.' He offered to change cups but whatever effect it was having on me it was doing the same to him. We were both very wide awake. He went back to his questioning.

'Why did you go to the ANC?'

'Look, I went there with a friend out of interest. I'm a member of the press. I really don't see what's wrong in seeing the friend of a friend who happens to work at ANC.'

'Well, what about the books?'

'What books?'

'You know damn bloody well. You brought them into this country didn't you?'

There was a pause.

'Henry did.'

'Henry did, Henry did! If I bloody get my hands on him! You know he's back, don't you?'

'No.'

'We sent him a telegram saying you were very ill and he must come back.'

'Do you really expect me to believe that?'

'He's your twin brother, isn't he?'

'At least I'm glad you accept the fact that I have one, now. If I was ill he would phone to find out. Anyway he sent a telegram from London saying "Arrived safely. Letter following".'

It had occurred to me that this wasn't very original. Anyone could have sent it, and I wondered if they could have picked Henry up at the airport without me knowing it. It made things very difficult. I had no real proof that Henry had got to England; there had been no letter and the telegram wasn't at all convincing. 'I still don't believe you've got him.'

'What difference does it make? We know you are the leader.'

'Leader of what?'

'The whole thing. It was your idea to come out, wasn't it?'

'Yes.'

'And your idea to go back, too.'

'Well, yes, I had some money to collect in Paris. I had to go back.'

'And it was you brought the books in, wasn't it?'

'All right, I admit I brought the books in, but only Henry helped me to print them.'

'Great, but we know that already. Now tell us something new. About the bus sheds or Modderfontein.'

'I have. We've been through all that.'

'No, you haven't.' He paused. 'Jesus, you have a lot of nerve coming here.'

'I don't think so.'

'You don't think so. Well, you tell me what would happen if you blew up Modderfontein Dynamite Factory?'

'I don't know.'

'Well, for a start, you wouldn't bloody live to see it.'

Slowly I began, 'Before you can get democracy in this country...'

'This is a bloody democracy. It's a white democracy.'

'I don't call that democracy.'

'Bloody Africans don't deserve a vote; they're too stupid.'

'I know they're stupid but it's because you don't feed them and you don't educate them.'

'Yeh, but you must understand, they don't want education.'

'How can they know what they want unless they try it?'

'Quentin, listen, you don't know. I've been in this country more than forty years. You've been here for five months and you think you know it all.'

'No, I don't. I'll even admit you won't get democracy until there's an industrial revolution which will let the African learn enough to be an important part of the community. I don't think the Whites can advance any further unless they teach the other half something.'

'We are teaching them.'

'That's not what I read.'

I realised I shouldn't say these things. It was providing them with a motive, but I was so tired, and in view of what they knew already it scarcely seemed to matter.

They dropped that subject and went on to ask me about my girl-friends and what hobbies I had, where I went in my spare time, where I bought my car, my typewriter, cameras and so on, who had applied for the telephone and if I was a member of any club or political group. I said that the only thing I belonged to was the National Union of Journalists as a free-lance photographer.

That evening, after Bouwer left, two fairly young interrogators came on the job; one could see they were totally inexperienced but I suppose even policemen have to learn on somebody. I felt like a patient in hospital who is being used to illustrate some disease or other to young medical students who appear interested out of politeness. The bearded one told me he had done philosophy at Wits. I said I was a

Nietzsche fan and agreed with him that man's greatest weakness was fear and laziness. I don't really, but I thought he'd like it. He brought up Spinoza and I promptly denied ever having heard of him, then stupidly asked if he'd seen the film of *The Fixer*, which had been on the week before at Witz. I remembered taking Seadom and Buki and Martin and Dave, and saying, 'No, it's not about junkies, but something much more relevant.' As indeed it was. Here we were a few days later, all, like Alan Bates, detainees and we must all in our detention have muttered, 'I am Yakov Bok, and your brother.' It's funny, both Dave and Martin used to come out with pet phrases like 'Now is the winter of our discontent,' and a line from the Woodstock record, 'Alan Faye, Alan Faye, can you come to the information booth? Your friend's on a trip and it's a bummer.'

Another thing I remember talking to the young interrogators about was the statement 'There's no success like failure'—a sort of trial and error philosophy that appeals to me. I have been subject to so many accidents. I owe my existence to a genetic accident: I am an identical twin. My arm was broken doing the high jump; I lost the tip of my middle finger in the woodwork room at school, making an eggcup for my grandmother; my nose was hit by a hockey stick and my knee by a hockey ball; my index finger was broken by a man who opened his car door when I was passing on a motor-bike, and my teeth by a madman at a party I went to dressed as a cop. These are all me, they contribute to the way I run, write, walk and eat—and I love them all. One must be vulnerable and unpredictable. The Timol affair, however, though fatal for him, was beginning to be my greatest accident, the longest and the most expensive.

Those two interrogators struck me as being simply 'packers', there to keep the ball rolling till the heavies came on again after they'd had eight hours' sleep. I didn't think they wrote a single word in the interrogation book, but we did a lot of talking, mainly about films and books and ideas. It was an odd compulsory relationship but unforgettable. However, by the time Bouwer and his mate came on again, the effects of my drugged coffee had worn off and I doubt if I was very much use to them.

CHAPTER FOUR

How many days I slept after the seventy-two hours' interrogation I have no idea. Now there was no-one to talk to, no books, no pens, no letters, nothing. And no clock. So I found the first way of passing the time was to re-invent it. The only thing I could do was to jump up and hold on to the bars of the window and look out at the shadow the sun cast on the paving below. I could only hang on for twenty seconds or so at a time, but I managed to count the number of one-foot-square paving tiles and from that roughly work out the height of the building opposite. There are 360 degrees in a day, and twenty-four by sixty minutes means 1440 minutes a day. Dividing 360 into 1440 means one degree equals four minutes. I might have been completely wrong but it was good fun, and I now had a very large and inaccurate clock. And there was a bonus. At twelve o'clock a siren screamed and sure enough the sun was exactly parallel with the wall, so much so that it showed up the texture of the brick and proved for good measure that the wall was vertical.

But, actually, to tell the time was more complicated. I assessed the height of the building opposite at thirty feet, and since the base looked like one-square-foot paving, three squares equalled a tenth of the height, so nine degrees should be nine times four minutes or roughly half an hour. Then I checked that with my walking clock. My cell was twenty-two feet long, approximately seven metres, so I had to do 144 times back and forth to cover a kilometre, walking at about ten kilometres an hour, say a thousand times in half an hour. 'All right, Quentin, this is not a race, but see if five hundred times there and back does equal three squares.' After doing it a hundred times I couldn't resist peeping out through the window to see what sort of progress the sun was making. He was doing all right. It looked roughly a third of a square. This was quite exciting. By nine hundred I found my walking was a little behindhand. If I was going

42

to reach a thousand by the twelve o'clock siren I would have to hot up a bit. By the end I was looking out of the window every ten runs, and as the siren went I was doing a very slow 999-and three-quarters for the second time. By working the thing out backwards it was possible to know when they were late with lunch—not that one could do anything about it. Sometimes they missed out altogether but at this stage it, didn't matter too much. When I mentioned it to the jailer he was very apologetic; he thought I was still in interrogation.

Nothing would happen all day. No bath, no exercise, just three plain meals. Quite early on I began to change my walks; sometimes I walked round the room and over my bed; sometimes I tried a more complicated pattern: I would walk across and back again till I reached a certain number, or a multiple of that number, or a higher number that ended in the original number, and then I would turn right. This may sound quite inconsequential but it isn't so. Take nine, for instance. You start off at wall one, walk across to wall two, back to the original wall three, and do this up to nine. Then turn right: Keep doing this till you get to eighteen, and turn right again. Turn right again on nineteen and go on to twenty-seven. Turn right and again on twenty-nine, then thirty-six and thirty-nine and so on. Believe it or not, ten, thirty, fifty, seventy and a hundred and ten will always be on the same wall, and on the opposite wall you will have nought, twenty, forty, sixty, eighty and a hundred. But ninety will be all on its own on the side wall. This system of nine holds good into the thousands, by which time I lost count. But the initial discovery was again an accident of real excitement. I immediately envisaged computers having to change, and whole new life-patterns emerging, on the famous new Jacobsen Turn Right Cycle. Bang would go decimals; everyone would be turning right into a new era. I tried doing it with seven, three and eleven but nothing else has the recurring element of nine. From now on, nine was my number.

One morning during my 'nine' period the police came in, very anxious to get me cleaned up for a visitor. They took me quickly down to the Police Sports section of the station and on the way down I mentioned that I hadn't had breakfast. They were very apologetic and took me straight to the kitchen where I got two fried eggs on toast and coffee; then I went up to the showers for a quick shave and what they call in Australia a 'shit, shower and shampoo'. During my shower I had a good scratch and to their horror the police saw great red marks round my body.

Bouwer was terrified.

'What the hell's happened?'

'It's all right. I've got a delicate skin. It runs in the family, I can't help it. There's nothing to worry about.'

It was obvious that, though I was going to rot in prison, at least I was going to do it with kid-glove treatment. After the shower I was made to put on my best shirt and my suit, too. Who was going to visit me I had no idea, but it was clearly somebody pretty important. We went down and along to the other building and there was Mr Biggie, the consul. I had only seen him a week before and there really wasn't much to say. I was in good spirits. I'd just had breakfast and a hot shower and I couldn't complain. He didn't look too happy so I told him not to worry and in my usual way gave him what my mother calls my 'With-one-bound-I'll-be-free' line. But he didn't seem to agree. I didn't attach all that much importance to the visit, but in fact it was my last human contact with the outside world for the next fifty days. The only other thing was a note that came from my mother. It was given to me to read once. I was told before it was given to me that I couldn't keep it, so I read it very slowly. It was all on one side of quite a small sheet of paper and written with a black felt pen in Mum's unmistakable handwriting. It said that she was deeply concerned for me and so was everyone else. The telephone rang constantly. Henry had got a job assisting a photographer friend of mine called Tony, and I must keep a stout heart. I broke down and cried for joy that Henry was safe, that Mum knew where I was, and that other people seemed to have heard, presumably through the media. So things were moving. My next reaction, though, after this relief, was a feeling of absolute loneliness. I felt sick for home and my mother and Henry. I thought of that letter for days after. I tried to read some second meaning into every word that I could recall. I decided it wasn't all that final, nor particularly pessimistic, and it was very reassuring that Henry was safe.

That apart, it is true I had a two-minute conversation with a visiting magistrate who asked me if I had any complaints. I said I didn't know what my rights were, so how could I complain? I had no exercise and nothing to read but was I entitled to any? He didn't even answer—just ticked my name off a list and went.

As time went on I became, oddly perhaps, more self-conscious and eventually plain selfish. The warder used to peep through the spy-hole in the door and I used to try to appear as normal as possible, though normal I never was and hope never to be. The temptation to stand on one's head and sing, or practise walking on one's hands was very real. I resisted that temptation but felt I really should keep physically fit. So, quite apart from my mathematical experiments, I walked for exercise. After meals I would walk round my cell and over my bed a hundred times and do ten press-ups, then touch my toes a few times and finish with a bit of shadow-boxing. Later I substituted running on the spot for the shadow-boxing in case they thought I was being aggressive. There are so many problems of self-expression in jail. If you're passive and depressed they may think you are guilty, or if you are aggressive they may think you are militant and so a terrorist, and if you are in the middle and show nothing much they may forget you. So I made up my mind to be polite and good-humoured and as interesting as possible without sounding mad. But with no-one to talk to and nothing to read it is difficult not to become introvert.

Budgies, if they're lucky, have a mirror with a bell on it; all I had was a police spoon. They don't trust you with a knife and fork. It was a beautiful spoon, very heavy chrome plate, built to outlast several lives, and when I was using it, it became a third eye. As it left my mouth, I could see myself, the window on the right and the door on the left all reflected in the spoon: the Son, the Father and the Holy Ghost. When I reversed the spoon I got a very distorted view of myself. I've always thought I had a big nose and the spoon didn't help it. I became very preoccupied with myself. With the aid of my towel I measured my legs in relation to my thighs, and my body in relation to my total leg length. I found scars on my legs that I had forgotten about and lumps in my jaw line that I'd never known I had. Over the next four or five months I was going to find out a lot of useless information. Every time I sneezed or farted it was a major event and worthy of recognition. Every fart was, as it were, hand-chosen and especially smelt, if for nothing else than to prove that I was still human and my body was still functioning. There was always a shortage of soap and when I did get my hands on some I used it for modelling. I still had to use it to wash with, but at least I acquired the admiration of my jailer. In a very patronising way he inquired 'Who is it?' The soap was red but the shape I made was black, not black and beautiful but black and angry. I had some other soap which I had brought with me from the studio. This was a small white bar and it became my blonde Arian girl-friend, very beautiful, very clean and a bit stupid but worth a smell. My Johnson's baby powder became an American ex-girl-friend, tall, dark, and an embarrassment whenever she opened her mouth. The red soap was my Swazi girl, very good value but short on water. I had to find a substitute for everything and there was practically nothing available. There was even very little writing on the wall, though I do remember 'Work is for sheep'. Again, it could be dangerous to comment on that one. Better leave it alone.

After all my marathon walks I felt limbered up. I could put the palms of my hands on the floor, not merely touch my toes, and I could bite my toes—something I hadn't done since I was a baby. I could walk anything up to ten thousand times back and forth, which worked out at something like eighteen miles a day. I was determined not to go to sleep during the daytime and not to go to sleep until it was dark. I didn't want to confuse my timetable. I must work during the day and sleep during the night.

I stayed in this big cell for about three weeks. I pretended not to be tense or worried, only a little bored. Then one evening supper was rushed in to me rather early. A police-man (they were always in plain clothes) came in and said, 'Get everything quickly together. You're off.' He slammed the door and left me thunderstruck. Off! that could only mean one thing, deportation. I'd told them all I could. It took me three minutes to get ready and then I waited for my ride out to the airport. I waited and waited, all dressed up and nowhere to go.

I thought, 'Why have they done this to me?' They said, 'Get your things together quickly. You're off.' Well, I had got everything together quickly and I was still sitting there. I wondered if Dave and Martin were going too. I hoped so, then we could all get drunk together on the plane.

'Come on, I'm ready.'

My head was splitting with the action inside it and the lack of action outside it. Where was the outlet? Then it came. Three heavies; I could hear them approaching, loud and happy. The door opened.

'Come on, you're off. There's a car downstairs for you.'

I explained I had a suitcase to get and twenty-five rand. We collected these and went on down. It was late sunset. My case was put into the boot and I was bundled into the back between two of the heavies.

'You're going to like this trip. Oh God, you are!'

I didn't dare say anything. Once the car had started I couldn't have cared less where we went, just so long as we went. The two men in the back were fat, overgrown schoolboys, smelling of beer.

'Do you know where you're going?'

'No, I haven't a clue.'

'Oh, didn't they tell you?'

'Well, they always said I was to be deported. I suppose I'm being deported.'

'What a surprise we've got for you!' There were big laughs from his brothers. 'Do you know the Pretoria Road? You should, you were planning to blow up half of it, weren't you?'

I made no comment.

'You rotten commie homo bastard! You thought you could get away with it. Well, what about that, eh?'

Big laughs from his friends, and the stink of beer made me cringe at the driving. The big, black Dodge, shock-absorbers gone, thundered down the road to Pretoria, bouncing all over the place. What was happening next I didn't dare

47

to think. It didn't look like deportation and yet I had my case with me. As the car sped further and further from Johannesburg and the airport, my head seemed to spin round and round; a real migraine was setting in hard. After being in a closed cell for nearly a month it was quite frightening to be driven at high speed. I realised I wasn't standing up to solitary as well as I had thought.

'Well, boy, what do you feel like now, you stinking black-woman lover?'

No comment. There wasn't much they didn't know. I wonder who told them that.

'Why don't you get a hair cut?'

'I'd like one, actually.'

'Actually...' he murmured, 'why don't you talk properly, you British bastard? We learnt your language. Why haven't you learnt ours?'

'I've been very busy working.'

'Still giving us that one, are you? You'll work here all right and for a long, long time.'

I made no comment. My head was aching too much and the speed of the car worried me. I wasn't holding up too well. My talk-back wasn't coming and I realised that, for the first time since I was stuck on a glacier in Norway when I was fourteen, I felt genuinely frightened. Eventually we arrived at Pretoria Central Prison and I got out of the car. And I thought I heard angels singing. It must have come from some other part of the jail, a black part, because they were going like hell, beautiful, perfect singing. The front door opened and before me appeared a massive, steel-barred wall. That was unlocked. We went down a corridor. It was like my first day at school, only without Henry. The big men talked very fast in Afrikaans. I was looking up at them, afraid. Then they had their last laugh, and I was left standing with my case, dumped in the hands of someone else.

He turned to me.

'All right, no talking, no whistling, no singing, no books, and no bickering. I can't stand moaners.'

I nodded my head and followed him through more doors, all immaculately shining. The floor was positively clinical, far too clean for my liking. We turned left at the third corridor, through another steel-barred door. My cell was number eight. Opposite me I could see a small room with a bench in it, like a chapel. The door to my cell was thick steel, supported on three enormous hinges. It closed after some argument. In the old jail the jailer always closed the door but here I found I was expected to do it myself. I also found that here one had to call everyone 'sir', and when there was a routine check the officer would shout 'Stand Up!' and I would have to rush over and stand as near to the grille as possible. The atmosphere of the place was quite different from that of the other prison. The cell was tiny, six feet across by seven feet long. There was a hard wooden shelf about a foot off the ground, which had a three-quarter inch felt mat on it and four blankets, plus sheets. There was no doubt about it, this place was very clean. My case was locked up next door, which was a communal cell for three but not in use.

I asked through the grille if I might have some aspirin for a very bad headache and the warder said he'd ask the doctor next day. I said nothing but hoped my head would be better by then.

What a day it had been! In three hours my hopes had gone to the moon—and back. What frightened me most was that I was beginning to be frightened. In the cell there was a small sink where I could get drinking water. In my last cell I had got water by pulling the lavatory lever and catching the incoming water in my hands. I could see out of a small window that angled down so that the warder could see I wasn't doing anything I shouldn't in bed. I tried to have a little walk, but with the cell only seven feet long and the bed on one side and the bog on the other there really wasn't more than six feet to walk in. I felt very strange while I walked, as though everybody was staring at me. The glass window gave me no privacy at all. I made my bed up, thought for the first time about praying, decided things weren't quite that bad yet, and went to bed.

CHAPTER FIVE

I was wakened by a kick at the door.

'Up!' I stood up and leapt to the door and stood with my nose to the grille. Quite an old man looked at me.

'That shirt is filthy.'

'Yes. I couldn't do any washing at the last place.'

'Name?'

'Quentin Jacobsen.' There was a pause.

' "Sir", that's what you say. "Sir".'

'Yes, sir.'

He walked away and I was left wondering whether he had finished with me. He didn't come back, so after five minutes or so I stood at ease and went back to make my bed. I took it completely apart and made it absolutely straight and without creases. I had slept with my head under the window, but when the guard saw this he told me to make the bed the other way. This meant they could see me more easily and my pillow—and it was nice to have one—would fall off on the floor. So I re-made my bed. In this cell there was no writing on the wall, only a calendar scratched on the door: someone else had done three months' solitary cramped up in this small space. Poor bastard! But I hoped I wouldn't get the blame for his writing.

'Breakfast!'

I leapt to the door, which opened: a plate of porridge and a cup were handed to me and I was told to dip the cup in a churn of black coffee, and then slam the door. I ate my porridge very slowly. Then I heard a jailer shout 'Finished?' further down the corridor, answered by shouts of 'Yes, sir.' My door was opened and I was told to put my plate out at once. The spoon had to be jammed in between the bar and the mesh on the outside of my door. I had hardly touched my porridge but I was allowed to keep my coffee cup. Now there were problems. The coffee cup was very heavy metal; that took all the heat out of the coffee, but on the other hand the porridge was too hot and there was neither sugar nor salt on it. At the next meal, which came at twelve, there was a plate of vegetables and mealies and a piece of meat. I quickly took the plate and slammed the door only to realise that my spoon was outside and because of the need for haste I didn't dare wait. I finished along with the others. The door was opened and I put my plate out. The warder asked where the spoon was. I said I had left it outside by mistake, and he told me I was a stupid bugger, which didn't surprise me. Then he slammed the door, and said, through the grille, 'You can sleep for an hour now.' This confused me for I never sleep during the day and I didn't want to change my habits. Sure enough, an hour later they came round and woke me. When they did, the older jailer told me I must wash my shirt. I was more than grateful to be able to do so because it was the first time in three weeks that I'd been allowed to wash anything.

'Where's your other luggage?'

'Next door.'

'Get it.'

I opened my case and he overturned on the floor.

'It's all filthy. Wash the lot.'

'But only my shirts are dirty.'

'Wash the lot.'

'All right. Where do I go?'

'Down there.'

I was led further down the corridor opposite some of the other cells, numbers six and seven in fact. My cell was number eight, and I saw about five others. They were all about the same size as mine but these had a card stuck outside along with the spoon.

We went into the bathroom and he said, 'Fill the bath up and start washing.' I started on my shirts and, thinking that, like the meals, everything must be done in a hurry, started scrubbing like mad. After I'd finished I had to take them over and show them to him. Without looking, he said, 'Again.' I didn't argue. I went straight back into the bath and did them again. After I'd really scrubbed the shirts to pieces, he looked at them and said, 'Again.'

'Where?'

'Those white spots, get rid of them.'

51

'But that's the bone of the collar.'

'Don't argue. Do it again.'

I went back and did it again. Then I started on my other clothes. All this time the prisoner across from me was watching. I didn't feel entirely lost. The warder sat on the edge of another bath and smoked. An African would come in every half hour and ask if he wanted coffee and he would take about a minute to decide. When 'Stand up!' was announced he stood up, and hid his cigarette under his hand and I stood up in the bath with my brush in my hand. An official walked in and asked me what I was doing. I answered him and he smiled and went out. I went back to my washing. I washed my towel, my cavalry twill trousers, two pairs of white jeans, everything, twice—everything in fact except me. Then I was given prison clothes and made to hang my washing in the chapel opposite. I was given a grey-green day shirt and trousers and a blue shirt and trousers which I was told to wear at night. I didn't mind this at first. Then it occurred to me that they were all symbols of a long stay. I did want to wear my own clothes but on the other hand I didn't want to wear them out before I got to court.

Quite soon supper came. I think it was about three-thirty. The sunlight came in at an angle of 45 degrees. I grabbed my spoon and got my ration, which was soup, bread and, surprisingly, a small piece of butter and some brown sugar. I remembered my porridge in the morning. I must try to save some of the sugar. The soup was thick pea soup and very good. There was an occasional bit of stalk in it but it was good and thick and hot. I lapped it up in record style. 'Finished!' was shouted, the door was opened, the plate went out. Then the door opened a second time and the spoon went out. I would have to get used to this new routine. In the other jail we didn't get spoons to begin with but when we did we were allowed to keep them. Here everything had to be kept outside. All my soaps, my toothbrush and so on went next door. All my old identity had been removed and I was left alone.

The other prisoners down the corridor would start to talk in Afrikaans, and even a foreign voice was a comfort in a way. Occasionally the warder would shout 'Hulop!' which,

I suppose, meant 'Shut up!' and they would stop for a while and then drift back again. Over in the African section the nine-to-nevers were praising the Lord in hymns of great strength, while over in our section someone started up on 'Once I was lost and now I am found' and finished with

Jesus loves me. This I know
For the bible tells me so.
He doth count me with his sheep
In the fold when I'm asleep.
Yes, Jesus loves, Jesus loves me,
The bible tells me so.

I wished I had a bible. At that moment I had nothing at all. Wearing prison clothes depressed me. Now, I thought, this is hard. I can no longer pretend to be innocent. I don't really care what happens to me. I've tried my hardest but I'm not as strong as I thought. I'm like a drunk drowning. I must keep walking and not let them know I'm slipping. This is the beginning, the beginning of nothing. Where will I go from here? What good can I do, stuck here? All I can do is prove I'm weak, mind over matter, breakfast, lunch, supper. I wasn't born alone and I'm not really alone now. I wonder if people think I'm still stuck in Jo'burg.

God, this place is sick. I must look like some mentally defective animal walking back and forth, ninety-nine a hundred. I miss you, Dave. 'Assonance', that's what he called it. It was one of his favourite words—'beat the meat', 'stone the crows'. A hundred and five, a hundred and six, I think better when I'm walking. I would like to do my press-ups but the cell isn't long enough and the lavatory is in the way. Well, Quentin, remember you used to knock the RSPCA, but, buddy, no animal would do this to you. I should smuggle out a letter: 'I am a human being shut in a box six foot by seven and I'm not going to make it. I need help badly. I'm not as strong as I thought I was. The walls look nearer every time I walk up to them.'

A hundred and twenty-six, a hundred and twenty-seven. At two hundred I'll have a piss. Better have a drink first to store up for the next one. Sometimes it doesn't come out straight. I wonder whether it's worth correcting because when it goes on the floor it gives me something to do. A hundred and fifty, a hundred and fifty-one. Got to save that sugar for breakfast and I must remember to get my spoon tomorrow. Come on, a hundred and sixty-nine, a hundred and seventy. A hundred and eighty, a hundred and eighty-one. If I warm the metal cup in my hands, it won't cool the coffee down so much. I'm almost at two hundred and time for a pee but there isn't much to pee. Try and hit the other side of the water. I stopped. I saw myself in the water. My hair was long. I hadn't seen myself for almost a month and I'd had only three shaves and those were without a mirror. I looked at myself. 'Well, you're all there.' The water rippled and I disappeared.

I took some bog paper and wiped the floor and as I did so something made a noise, like a piece of metal falling. I put my hand down and felt around. I touched a thin sliver of steel. I turned round to see if anyone was looking. This was it. I felt it might almost have been planted: half a razor blade. Should I leave it there or hide it somewhere else?

I'm going to need this, I thought; it's an answer, a gift, and I need something. I don't really want to die. I just want the excitement of pain to prove I'm still alive and willing, or is it kicking? I mustn't do anything till I know it's the absolute end. They haven't actually charged me yet. I have to wait until I know it's hopeless. It only feels hopeless but it's not the end yet. Pain, yes, pain would be a pleasure, to cut myself and see red blood, to get sympathy and to relieve guilt. It's all in the future, something I can think about now, but when it comes, it will be final. I'd got to hide this silver blade, half-broken and very blunt. I put it in my pocket. I have hope, I thought. This won't last, but now I can at least call my end without them knowing it. I was happier. I walked round the cell with my hand in my pocket, feeling the blade. It was very blunt; I didn't think it could be much use; I must try and see if it would do anything. I looked out through the grille. No-one was in sight, so I took out the blade, pulled up the leg of my trousers and started to cut the skin. Is it the skin that's tough or the blade that's weak? After quite a bit of hacking I managed to make a cut about half an inch long and a quarter of an inch deep. It was on the inside of my calf, in the muscle. 'Well, that's not bad;

I feel better already. It's beginning. I've got to stop now and hide you: you are for harder times, not now but when all hope has gone.'

I felt I had asked for pain and must suffer, if for nothing else, because I had failed to live in solitary. What depressed me most was that I couldn't hold on to what I'd got. I did think I was a stronger person, but maybe my strength lay in knowing when I was beaten. The light was failing and the rain started to beat on the glass roof; it was like the monsoon. The heat vanished and I felt quite cold. The rain poured down. I wiped my eyes. Rain, you bastard, flood the place! The voice of African hymns drifted in again through the sound of the rain. There was a sudden flash through the glass roof and the late thunder echoed. It poured and poured. It released a lot of tension in me and I think I smiled. It was exciting; the noise of the rain was telling me I must go on. I was not alone, the storm was with me. I looked up at the lightning. You tell them there's still a bit of spark left in me too. But still the pain was on. Why should I suffer for something I hadn't done? And after such a good life too. Why should I have to end it so pathetically? The thing I missed most was not being able to love someone.

It's hard to have so much to give and no-one to give it to. I tried to hang on to what little faith I had, most of that in children. I owed so much and wanted to return it. I thought of Tinker, our old short-haired terrier, and of Lindsay Grant and the Amorys, who had been so kind to me in Australia. At five o'clock a siren whined and it reminded me of an old radio programme, 'A Year to Remember, 1944'. The whining 'All Clear' interrupted the peace. I wished I had a radio like the one we had as children, which looked like a miniature Odeon, warm with talk, Dick Barton, the Goon Show, and the nine o'clock news. It was odd to remember that one of our hamsters died in that radio. Once Henry and I, when we were little, listened to *The Lord of the Flies* in bed together, terrified. We listened on shared headphones from a crystal set, just loud enough to hear and late enough to keep us awake all night. It was good sleeping in jail. I never dreamt of being in jail, though I once dreamt that the Americans were building a stone bridge to the moon, using cheap black labour. I woke up as the bridge fell down.

I thought, 'I'll just do another thousand turns and go to bed.' The storm died down and I finished the thousand, almost embarrassed because I seemed to be the only one still up. It was still daylight. It might have been six or seven. As I finished walking, I sat down on my bed and thought, 'I've been here three days; I was at John Vorster Square three weeks, so I've got seven more days before I finish the first month. I've got to last out a month. It would be weak not to last out one lousy month. Well, I've never prayed before and I don't think it can help much, but God, help me not to hurt myself. I don't mind the pain but I do want to finish this.'

I opened my eyes, took off my grey prison clothes and put my blue prison pyjamas on. I don't normally wear pyjamas but if they gave them to me I must wear them. They were brand new and a piece of loose thread was dangling from one leg. I pulled it off, chewed it for a bit. Although time was dragging terribly, I mustn't lose count of the days. I got my comb and started to count off twenty-three teeth, a tooth for each day, and when I got to the twenty-third I wound the thread round the tooth. It was getting dark now so I lay on my bed. I could hear my heart; it was like sleeping with another person. My mind was no longer part of my body but my spirit didn't care; the night had come. Although I don't remember my dreams, I know they were not about jail. I was drifting into my old world of people. It was like arriving at a party a little late, but finding it good that the others had started without one.

I awoke with a kick at the door and a shout of 'Stand up!' I hauled my body upright with my eyes still sticky with sleep. I bounded to the grille, hands to side, back straight, chin up. His ugly face was inches from mine. I didn't think, just stood there, not quite awake.

'Jacobsen!'

'Yes, sir.'

'You stink.'

'Yes, sir. I haven't had a bath or a shave for eight days.'

'Is your cell clean?'

'No, sir. I would like to clean the floor ... sir.'

'I want it scrubbed, walls, floor, door.'

'Yes sir.'

Then he walked on down the corridor and I relaxed a bit, but as he came past again, I stiffened to attention. I never knew what else to do. I couldn't turn my back and make my bed, so I always waited till they were out of the corridor. When he had gone I quickly changed into my grey clothes and made my bed, reminding myself that I mustn't forget to get my spoon. Eventually a warder and another prisoner came round with breakfast. I grabbed my metal cup and breathed into it so that I could have my coffee as hot as possible. When the door opened I picked up the plate of porridge and then the coffee. On the way back I bumped against the door and spilt some of the coffee on the floor. I put it down, seized some lavatory paper to wipe it up with, picked up the cup again and closed the door. As soon as I had done so I realised that once again I had left my spoon outside. I signalled to the prisoner who was serving and he called the guard who gave it to me.

'You mustn't forget your spoon.'

'I'm sorry.'

'You're always sorry.'

'Yes, I know. I'm not used to this place yet.'

'Don't worry, you will be.'

The guard went on to the next cell and the prisoner whispered, 'What are you in for?'

'Terrorism,' I said.

'Shit,' said he and went on.

I put the last of my sugar on my porridge, finished it and licked my spoon clean, ready to go outside again. Door open, plate out, spoon out.

'Please, sir, I want to clean my cell, sir.' I didn't really, but I did want something to happen.

'Later.'

I closed the door, wound another day on to my comb and waited. Might as well do a little walking.

I had notched up a thousand or two before the bucket of water came. There was soap, a scrubbing brush and a promise of polish for the floor later. I started to scrub the walls. They were perfectly clean already; in fact the whole jail looked as though it had just been built, but I didn't mind, it gave me something to do. I enjoyed it. No, that's an exaggeration; I endured it with confidence, even enthusiasm. When they came for inspection, I was a little scared because the blade was in my pocket and my trousers were soaked. It would have been awkward if they had told me to change them. They examined the walls and okayed them. Where there had been spots that wouldn't come out I'd covered them with Bouwer's toothpaste, like make-up. I was told to scrub the floor and polish it. After doing this, I put the bucket outside.

All over the prison people were cleaning—not just Blacks doing the usual polishing but Whites actually doing a bit of dusting. I hadn't had a bath or a shave yet but I didn't dare ask. Then a head warder came up and said I was to have exercise. I didn't believe it. It was the first time exercise had ever been mentioned. My door was opened, then a door into a yard. It was sunny outside and as I went in I was told to walk round to the left. I immediately counted the distance; it was about thirty metres square and had a very tall wall. I was told to take my shirt off. The sun felt good. As I walked I counted the number of times I went round. The warder started picking up stones and threw them like cricket balls at the walls as I went round. I knew he wasn't trying to frighten me; he was just bored. I would have loved to join him but instead his friend did. Later, he got up on a platform near the roof and started loading a gun. I started walking faster. It sounds silly but, being exercised for the first time, I thought, 'Maybe this is it.' I might be 'Shot while trying to escape'. When I'd walked round about seventeen times, the original warder said, 'Get out!' I grabbed my shirt and shot back to my cell.

Some time later he called me out to have a shave. I was given an old plastic razor and he stood near me while I shaved in the room where I had washed my clothes. There was a steel mirror on the wall, but it was very scratched and I couldn't really see my condition. I felt much better when I'd finished. He checked I'd left the razor and escorted me back to my cell. Then I realised that something was definitely on. Top prison officers with faded tattoos on their arms and without the usual cigarette, kept walking round looking worried.

Then finally it arrived; a group of government visitors was being shown round, my cell first. The door opened and I stood to attention.

'Any complaints?'

'Yes, I have no reading-matter. And I'm depressed.'

'What I mean is, have you any physical complaints, food, clothing, blankets?'

'No.'

There were smiles all round. Everyone congratulated everyone else and went on to the next cell. My door was closed and only then I realised I should have complained about having no exercise except for that morning. The other prisoners complained in Afrikaans so I couldn't tell what my rights were. The visitors all eventually left and we were told to stand at ease—at least that's what I assumed the order meant. I'd had my chance. I should have complained about many things, but how could I when I didn't know what the rules were? Later, when lunch came round, the prisoner serving it whispered, 'Have you got anything to read?' and when I said I hadn't he said, 'Bloody ask for it. You've got to have something.'

My spirits rose considerably. I must ask for something to read. What did I want? Something really big, like the complete works of Shakespeare or a dictionary, anything long and difficult. I thought of all the long books I haven't read, like *War and Peace*. But that was Russian. *Lord of the Rings* —that was long, but who wrote it? I could always get the Bible or even just pen and paper.

When the medicine man came round I asked if I could have some anti-depressants but he just smiled and said he couldn't do anything; the doctor would have to see me. I knew this was just a brush-off, but if I asked for the doctor he would probably say something like, 'Why, are you cracking up?' I've got to be strong. I mustn't show I'm breaking.'

Days went by. It was the end of my month and I couldn't take any more nothing: nothing to read, nothing to do; no exercise, no work, no-one to talk to. I'd had a month's complete isolation. I can't. I won't. Why should I take any more?

I'm not going to rot here. I would prefer just to forget the whole thing. If I told them this they must charge me or deport me; they must do something. 'I can't take this. The mesh, the glass, I want to smash through them. I want to kick the walls. I can't breathe any more. The cell is getting smaller. Everytime I breathe I feel I'm flooding the place. I want to get out. I can't take it. I can't do walking without them staring at me. They know I'm going mad; they want me to go mad. My breathing is heavy, my arms feel as though they are in a strait-jacket, my teeth are sore from grinding them. I feel my head pounding. There is a plain-clothes man outside and he's watching me, a man about thirty-five, in blue shorts and shirt. Trying to look innocent, you bastard. What does he want? He goes away. I should have told him I want to talk. Come back!' I suddenly make up my mind. I can't face any more nothing. Something's got to happen. I called the guard. 'I want to speak to the police.'

I thought he was going to laugh but he didn't. He took it very seriously. He said he would ring them up, and came back and said they were coming. I felt relieved in a way, though I didn't see what good it was going to do. I just kept on walking. Then I asked when they were coming and he said they were on their way. Time was dragging. I'd done my bit; I'd given up. Why couldn't they do their bit and come and get me? Something had got to happen; I couldn't do nothing any longer.

Eventually two very young, plain-clothes policemen arrived. I broke down and cried. 'I can't take any more. I must have something to do. I must talk to somebody.'

They walked with me into a little store full of prison files and asked me what it was I wanted to say. I said it was nothing much, just that the dagga in the studio might be Dave's.

'Well, we know that,' they said. 'Isn't there anything else?'

'I don't think so, but I must have something to do. I feel completely suicidal. If I don't get something to read, a bible or even a dictionary, I'll go mad. I don't want to live any more. Please try and get me some books.'

'I don't know about books, but we'll see what we can do.'

And they went away almost as sadly as I went back to my cell.

CHAPTER SIX

There I waited and walked, desperate. I had to get out. I
was waiting for it. I had to get out. I couldn't be let down.
I had to get out. I walked and walked. I didn't want to ask
the warder again what time he thought they might come,
I just had to wait and hope. Much later, after miles of wandering, I heard Mr Bouwer's voice and, like a child whose
parents had forgotten to collect him from school, I broke
down again.

'Sorry, we've been very busy,' Bouwer said.

'This is not interrogation, it's punishment,' I managed to
splutter out.

He looked at me and said, quite kindly, 'Well, how are
you?'

'You know very well how I am,' I said slowly. 'I've got
nothing. I've no hope. I haven't even anything to read.'

'Well, you see, Quentin, if we give you something to read,
you'll only forget what happened.'

'But you haven't asked me anything for three weeks!'

'Anyway, change your clothes and get your suitcase.'

I didn't look at him. 'Where are we going?'

He paused. 'We've got a bit more interrogation for you.'

I cheered up slightly and changed quickly. It gave me some
hope. That 'Get your case' bit means I'm not coming back
here, I thought, and if I'm not coming back here, I must take
my blade with me. The whole situation was very childish,
with Bouwer standing there like a father, telling me to get
changed and me, like a child, crying because I had missed
him and he'd been late. And on top of that my secret toy,
the blade, had to be hidden. As I took my trousers off I
managed to swap it into my jacket pocket. It meant everything.

Bouwer told me to put everything into my suitcase, soap,
folio, socks, the lot. I smiled wryly as I put in my life insurance policy. I'd taken it out originally to get an over-
draft; now it became an incentive, a bonus card. 'That'll teach

the buggers.' I put my suit on because I needed to; I wanted to look smart. When I was ready I picked up my suitcase and walked out with Bouwer, and felt almost as if I should hold his hand. When we came to the gates, I was signed out and I asked if I could have my money, my twenty-five rand, but Bouwer said it wasn't necessary, I'd be coming back to a different section of the same place. My heart sank. I tried to ask him how much longer—did he think—I would still be there, but got the usual answer, 'It all depends on you; the quicker you tell us everything the better for you.' So we were back to square one. The quicker I tell anything the more confusing it gets.

Past the last gates and out into the open. I felt as though I had been saved from drowning. We got into a small, old, blue VW car which belonged to a man I hadn't seen before. It had two doors, so the seat had to be pushed forward to let me into the back. The new man was, I found out, Colonel Ferrara, who was later in charge of my case. He didn't say much but I have remembered his fat, pig-like face uncomfortably ever since. He was the next worst thing to Swannepoel.

'Well, you're in trouble aren't you? I hope you really have something new to tell us—or did you just want to get out for a while?'

'I certainly have to admit it's tight in there.'

Then slowly, as he drove through the town, he said, 'Look, I know how you feel, but we want to clear the whole thing up.'

I stared at the back of his seventeen-inch collar and replied, 'I don't call being left in alone for three weeks much fun. It doesn't seem to me that you've really been trying to clear things up.'

'No, no, you're wrong,' he said in his loud, broad Afrikaaner accent. 'We've been very busy. Your friend Seadom told us a lot.'

I stared out of the window at the people flying past.

'What did he say?'

Fat Neck nodded his head solemnly up and down. 'That's our business. What we want to know is, who sent you? And why?'

I frowned and fumbled with my fingers. 'Nobody sent us. Dave and Martin will tell you that,' I said, still looking out of the window.

We were now in the old centre of Pretoria. The car turned right past a museum and stopped outside what was really a very beautiful old building. Bouwer knocked and asked if it was all clear. All clear it was, so in we went. Some of my old interrogators were lounging around reading picture comics. One turned round and said, 'You're looking smart! How are you?'

Realising that I was wearing my suit instead of the jeans they were used to, I said, 'Fine, a little shaky, but...'

Bouwer told me to walk down the right passage to the end room, which I did. It was an old building; the walls were three feet thick and the windows had bars, and shutters strong enough and airtight enough to withstand tear gas or molotovs or hand grenades. The place was a regular little fort. The shutters were open slightly and one could hear the noise of scooters whizzing past. The room was painted grey and on the walls there was a series of air-photograph maps, and big charts showing the different makes of foreign guns. There were files and more files, and in one corner some weights for weight-lifting, and in the other a small hot-water boiler. Tea was brought in and the black tea-boy sneaked a glance at me. I smiled at him, not especially because he was black but because he was the tea-boy. Bouwer and Ferrara were to take the first interrogation shift.

Bouwer bent down into his brief-case and pulled out my notes. He plonked them on to the table.

'Not much use, is it? Seadom's a bit more interesting,' he said.

I didn't reply. It was like a school-teacher complaining about my homework. I didn't know what to say. I just stared at it.

'Let's start at the beginning again,' Bower said. I wondered what beginning they meant. We all sat down and my book was opened. This time Bouwer did the writing and Colonel Ferrara asked the questions, and I, so to speak, played the gramophone, not out of strategy but because I had told them practically everything already. All I could enlarge on was the detail, the colour of people's shirts and what we ate. The interrogation was becoming more and more like a fashion-food magazine and less and less like political crime. 'Dr Dadoo of the banned South African Communist party was reported to be seen wearing a conservative three-piece suit. And then we went for coffee.'

'No, I can't remember if he takes sugar.'

'Did the other man use an inhaler for asthma?'

'I don't know. I didn't ask him.'

'No, but did you see him?'

'I can't remember much about him. He was sitting next to me. I wasn't looking at him.'

'Did Dr Dadoo...'

I interrupted, 'Yes, he had his pipe.'

It was all so predictable. I realised I shouldn't try to be clever but we had been over all this before. But I did remember one small detail. When I had taken my press-card out he had looked at it very carefully. I had thought it a bit odd. The Colonel and Bouwer looked at each other in excitement. Bouwer spoke. 'Well, he might have been a member of the press or something.'

'I don't know. He didn't say much.'

They were both very excited by this. I didn't understand why. I tried to explain what he looked like and when I had done my best Bouwer copied it out a second time separately and rang someone about having a telex sent off to Ziggie and Carl in London immediately.

'Now we'll know the truth,' he said. 'That second man is one of ours.'

I was a bit shaken. It was true that I had never been introduced to the man but I scarcely thought Dr Dadoo wouldn't have known who he was with. On the other hand, in interrogation one grew to depend on the police and I couldn't see the advantage of their lying to me.

'Did you ever hear of a man who went to Russia and later on to China? He was a policeman. We managed to get him in.'

I hadn't, and clearly I had no means of checking up, but the police obviously thought he'd done well and I was left to infer that this was the man with Dadoo. Another policeman came into the room and took away the separate note that Bouwer had made, to send, I suppose, to London.

Then Bouwer got me to draw a kind of flower and write my name in the middle of it. He explained that that was Swiss Cottage where I lived in London and all the petals were the surrounding suburbs and he wanted me to tell him the names of all the South Africans I knew, petal by petal. I said I didn't know any who lived near me at all. But he insisted.

'Who are the people who live in the flat above yours?'

I said there were some Australians there; I couldn't remember their names, but the name on the letterbox was Haynes. A policeman said quite casually, 'Tell us about him?'

'Well, as far as I know he's an accountant from up north somewhere who bought the flat and then decided to let it out. What his first name is, I don't know. I've hardly seen him.'

It was clear that they knew this already, so they must have been watching the house. Then he pointed to a petal of the flower above where I had written my name.

'And do you know any South Africans in this northern suburb?'

It was a pointless game. I knew hardly any South Africans and the ones I did know were totally non-political, but Bouwer had all night so they took down addresses as, with some difficulty, I found three in all when we'd gone through all the petals. Then I found that they meant Indians as well and that produced two more. Next I remembered a few South Africans I'd known in advertising in Australia, and these were added to the list. And back we were again to my going to the ANC and my meetings with Aziz and Dr Dadoo. They loved listening to that but again it was pointless because they couldn't prove anything and it was not illegal in English law and it had happened in England, so I thought there was no harm in talking about it. Again they started asking who sent me and again all I could say was, 'No-one sent me.'

They tried another angle. 'You tell us who sent you, then maybe you could be a state witness against him.'

It was a good way of passing the buck, but no-one had sent me.

'When you went up to the Anti-Apartheid Movement with Ebrahim, who did you see?'

'I saw a young girl who was trying to sort out newspaper clippings. The place was a bit of a mess, actually.'

The two policemen laughed.

'We know it's a bit of a mess, but who did you see there? Just this young girl? Do you think she was a voluntary worker?'

'I don't know.'

'Do you know who runs it?'

'No, do you want me to guess?'

'No harm, have a go.'

'That man who started up the CND, Collins, Canon Collins.'

'What, that bloody communist? What do you know about him? Did you ever see him?' They had a pained expression on their faces.

'No, it's only a guess. I've never seen him.'

'But you know about him?'

'I've read about him in the South African press, that's all. I've never met him or anything like that.'

'God, man, you bloody booger, you know him all right or you wouldn't have said his name.'

'I really don't know him. It was just a guess. Is he head of the AA?'

'No, a woman is, but Canon Collins is just as bad, in fact, worse.'

'I can't help that, I've never met him, or this woman.'

'What about the girl at the AA?'

'She was young, a voluntary worker possibly. I don't know.'

'What did she look like?'

'I can't remember. Ebrahim wanted to find a cutting about acid being thrown over him outside Wits during a demonstration.'

'It wasn't acid, it was paint.'

'I don't know what it was. Anyway, the girl couldn't find it so we left.'

There was a pause.

66

'What do you know about Defence and Aid?'

'Nothing.'

'"Nothing, nothing." What about Canon Collins?'

'I tell you, I don't know Canon Collins.'

'But you know he's head of it.'

'Head of what?'

'Defence and Aid.'

'I didn't. I just guessed he was head of the AA, that's all.'

'God, man, you know lots, you're just telling half of it. Where did you get your military training?'

'You're joking. I could never get into the army even if I wanted to.'

'Why's that?'

'I get collapsed lungs very easily.'

'You look healthy enough to me.'

'That's half the problem. You don't see it. It just happens suddenly. I might be walking or running...'

Ferrara, who was doing the questioning, interrupted, 'Or on the job?'

We all laughed.

'Or on the job. Suddenly you can't breathe.'

'Breaks my heart, it does.'

'Oh, it's not painful or anything.' There was a slight pause, then I added, 'I suppose I got military training in advertising. I remember reading the Che Guevara book on guerrilla warfare and thinking how like advertising it was.'

He thought about that.

'You know, Quentin, you always evade our questions. You're smart and clever with words.'

'Have you ever worked in advertising?'

'I'm a policeman.'

'I know, "Me doctor, you nurse."'

'What was that?'

'Nothing. But anyway, if you worked in advertising, you would know it's a cut-throat business. It is, I suppose, modern warfare. The similarities are very funny—campaign planning, product identity, finding your competitors' weak points, it's all there.'

'Quentin's rambling on again,' said Bouwer. 'You know, I quite like you but, by God, you're a bull-shitter.' I tried to interrupt. 'Just shut up when I'm talking. This whole bloody thing is a complete waste of your time. We can keep you here for months, years if necessary. You're not helping us at all. You bloody leave out half of everything. Why did you go back to England?'

'Well, to pick up money in France from my agent and read books on South Africa, like *The Discarded People*.'

'You could have read it here. You didn't need to go to England for that.'

'I thought it was banned.'

'You could have asked Miss Horrell of the Race Relations Board for it. She knows the whole bloody thing off by heart.'

'That's very nice, but I've never been to the Race Relations Board.'

'What about the Christian Institute?'

'I've never been there either.'

Normally, in jail, I drank a lot of water and consequently I had to get rid of it, but even when I wasn't drinking I found the need remained, so I asked if I could go to the lavatory.

'Yes, anything, but we'll come with you. Do you want something to eat? Hamburgers or something, and milk?'

'Great. Any chance of a bar of chocolate?'

'Maybe, but you know this comes out of my own pocket?'

'Why don't you get it back out of expenses? Or I'll even pay for it myself. I've got money in the bank.'

'No, Quentin, don't worry. They pay all right.'

'How much? Go on, how much?'

'Ah no, but we manage, don't worry. I'm going on holiday soon though.'

'Where will you go?' I said politely.

'Me I'm going to stay at home and do absolutely nothing, like you.'

'Like me? God, that's no holiday, I can assure you. Outside with a glass of beer, maybe.'

Colonel Ferrara called out to an African to bring three hamburgers and then asked Bouwer if he wanted one.

'Yes, but no onions, they make me fart.' The African wanted to smile, but managed not to. 'And three pints of milk.' Bouwer gave him a note and he went away. I stretched my legs and asked again if I could go to the bog. We crossed the room past the weights—I was dying to have a go at them —and on into the main room. Bouwer called out 'All clear!' and got 'All clear!' back, and we went on down a beautiful tiled corridor to the lavatory. Bouwer looked in to make sure there was no-one there and let me in. When I came out they looked, as they always did, so worried that I was sure that someone had committed suicide in the bog not so very long before. I could read it in their faces. I washed my hands and looked at myself in the mirror. There was a spot coming up on my right cheek. Better have a quick go at that while I had the chance.

'Come on, Quentin. What are you doing?'

'I've got a spot on my face.'

'Leave it alone and come on.'

I washed my hands quickly, thinking of *Midnight Cowboy*. Says Jon Voigt, 'You've got a sick boy on your hands and what are you going to do about it?' I'd seen the film eight times and I still couldn't get it right. I'll have to see it again.

'Coming, coming.' We walked back—'All Clear!' 'All Clear!'—past the weights—into my room, our room. As we sat down Bouwer harped on about how lucky I was to have this holiday, free board and lodging, nothing to do. 'Any other country would have shot you months ago!'

'That's a nice thing to say!'

'You've told us nothing.'

'I haven't done anything.'

'But you were going to.'

'How on earth can you prove that?'

'We will. Now you've had your shit. Here's your hamburger and milk. After this let's really get something written down.'

I opened my plastic bag and tucked straight into my hamburger. Bouwer opened his and saw onion. He turned and cried out, 'Where's that bloody coon?' An African rushed in smiling. Bouwer shouted, 'I said, "No onions".'

'Yes, sir.'

'Well, what's that?'

'Onions, sir.'

'Get me another and bloody well pay for it yourself.'

'Yes, sir. Thank you, sir.'

I asked if I could have it and Bouwer handed it over.

'The milk's a bit off,' I said. Bouwer opened his carton and had a sip. 'It's just been in the fridge too long. When it's been in too long, it goes a little bitter. There's nothing wrong with it.'

'I can't find my fruit-and-nut bar.'

'God, man, you're in jail. You're bloody lucky to have interrogation.'

'I've got money. I can pay for it.'

'You've told us nothing we don't know already and here you sit eating hamburgers.'

'Look, I've worked very hard in this country. I'm owed at least 1500 rand. I don't need free holidays. I can pay for things. A couple of books would help.'

'If we give you books, you won't think of anything new.'

'I haven't done anything.'

'It's not what you've done, it's what you might have done.'

Bouwer's hamburger came. He inspected it and there was a quick argument in Afrikaans over the change. Ferrara had finished his already and went to call the African for coffee. We had that and went back to interrogation. This time it was on the Modderfontein Dynamite Factory. After a few minutes a small fat man bounced in. The other two stood up looking very pleased and they all shook hands and talked in Afrikaans. Then the new one turned to me and spoke in a very broad accent.

'So, you've blown your cover and the birds have flown.'

'Sorry, I don't quite understand.'

'Your cover's blown.'

'You mean we've been busted? Actually, now that you say it, I do remember reading something about the language of spies in the last *Time* magazine I saw. I do remember "blown your cover".'

'Always the right answer. Lie as much as possible to confuse the enemy—and then commit suicide!'

He was shouting so loud and bending over me so close I didn't dare make any comment. He turned to the others and said in a lower voice, 'He knows.' Then back to me again.

'You're not as stupid as you look.'

He got behind me and bending over so that his arm came over my shoulder, he picked up a biro and started writing on a piece of paper.

'You know what this is?'

'Charcoal.'

'And this?'

'Sulphur.'

'And that?'

'Saltpetre.'

'You know what they all make?'

'Yes, gunpowder.'

'You see, you're a bloody terrorist, aren't you?'

Then he laughed very loud and marched from the room, his great, fat neck overflowing out of his white collar. He really looked as though he might explode at any moment. God, I thought to myself, what a ham actor. The others looked very sad.

'Who on earth was that?' I asked Bouwer.

He said almost regretfully, 'That's Swannepoel, one of our greatest men. He's not very well at the moment. He had a heart attack a few months ago and lost a lot of weight.'

'Doesn't look like it to me,' I said.

Then Ferrara asked, 'How do you make a bomb?'

'Well, I suppose you get a battery and a clock of some kind and some explosive.'

'Draw a picture.'

'No, I really don't know how.'

At this point two other men came in to take over and Bouwer and Ferrara got up, stretched and explained to them what to do. The new couple were quite nice. One I had seen before. He was very tall, quite young with darkish blond hair brushed straight back, going bald already. He was from Rhodesia and had taken my fingerprints the second time in Johannesburg and I remembered talking to him about job reservation. He'd even admitted it was unfair. The other one was new, up from Capetown, small, quick-talking, with thin, black curly hair. He wore a pink shirt and looked slightly camp; I could imagine him watching queers in a public lavatory.

He tore out pages, gave them to the tall one and started to read the counterfoils. I suppose they must have read for more than half an hour. The small one explained that he was new on the job. What was it all about? I explained briefly for the hundredth time. Then he took out a list of questions from a file. They were about communes, mainly the one in Melville. He told me to start right at the beginning, about going there in the first place. I rolled it off, how we had gone in and there was no-one there and no-one came in so we left.

He said, 'If I write that everyone will think I'm going mad.'

'Well, it's what happened. This girl opened the door. I couldn't see her, she didn't turn the lights on. Then she went back to bed. We went into the kitchen and made ourselves coffee. Sorry, I missed out a bit. She said—that's the person who opened the door, I don't know who she was—she said we should make coffee. She said the others had gone out for a while but they would be back in fifteen minutes. So we made coffee. No-one came in from the outside so we left.'

'I can't write that down. It's not proper English. I will write it down and add a bit in the margin that you're mad.'

I was already yawning.

'I don't know how else to put it, because the people—I mean the woman who opened the door—she never appeared again and no-one else came in, so we stayed fifteen minutes, had coffee, no-one came in from the outside, so we left. I know it sounds odd but it's what happened. I didn't meet anyone else there at all. It was an odd place. There were newspaper cuttings on the wall.'

'Hold it. Slow down.'

I finished. Then he tilted the book sideways and wrote in the margin 'This person is mad.'

'No-one came in from the outside. It's mad.'

I laughed and said, 'It sounds odd but I can't think how else to put it.'

'Go on. What was on the wall?'

'Oh, various proverbs and sayings, quite a few political ones. I can't remember them.'

'Not one? What a pity, it would make it sound more interesting.'

'Well, the last lot only got me into trouble. I'm not doing any more guessing.'

'Anything else about the house?'

'It was pretty dirty.'

'Hold it. I'll just write that down. "It was pretty dirty." You know we've arrested three people there, two students and a teacher from Wits?'

'No, I didn't. What under? Communism?'

This interested me. Actually arrested three people. Well, things were moving. Why was all this interrogation going on in Pretoria anyway? Maybe Jo'burg jail was full up. The tall one opened a book of photographs of people, mainly young students, and asked me to point out anyone I recognised. I turned over the page. He asked me if I was absolutely sure I didn't know anyone on that page.

'No, I don't think so. I might have seen them up at Wits but I don't know any of them.'

'Not even Ian Hill?'

'He's not on that page.'

'Yes, he is.'

'Where?'

'There.'

'That's not him. Ian's got blond hair down to his shoulders. That guy's hair is quite short and as black as boot polish. That's not him.'

'It is.'

'Well, he must have dyed his hair or something. Anyway, these shots all look the same. Everyone looks guilty.'

The tall one said, 'I took that shot. What's wrong with it?'

'Well, he just looks like all the others. They all look guilty and depressed or desperate. They're useless from the point of view of recognition. The best shots of people are spontaneous or taken without them knowing.'

They both smiled. 'Like this?' He put the book down and took out a packet of large pictures.

'Who's that?'

I stared at it.

'That's me. It's very good. I look really great. I'd like a copy of that. Who took it?'

'One of our men.'

'When was that?'

'A few days before you were busted.'

Now I remembered a yellow VW combi was parked outside the studio for almost a whole day, right on a bus stop. I should have realised they were the police. In fact, I remembered wanting to go up to the guy. I remembered now. The young blond one who took my fingerprints the first time: that was where I had seen him before. He had been in the van, shooting people as they left the building. They put forward another photograph of me—or was it Henry? It was very hard to tell. It had the same shirt in each shot but from that angle I couldn't see the parting in the hair. They took out another and were contemplating whether to show it to me or not, but the light was coming through it and I knew who it was without being shown it.

'Don't worry. I know who it is.'

'How?'

'The shape. He's unmistakable. It's the guy who works next door.'

'Tell us about him.'

'That's all I know. He's got a funny shoulder. One higher than another. That's all I know. I've seen him in the lift.'

'What else?'

'He works next door, in the store. Each morning they come up to get more supplies, I think for the camping shop in Rissick Street. That's all I know.'

They showed me another shot, this time of a guy who worked above us, at French's. That was all I knew about him. I had his number in my book in case something went wrong, like the roof leaking. I didn't know him. Quite a few more shots came up, of Africans who work in the building, some of whom I had lent money to and others I just knew from meeting them in the lift. I always say good morning to people in the lift and sometimes the Africans would come up to look at what we were doing. I think some of them used to borrow money, not because they needed it, but because they liked an excuse to come up. They always paid it back.

74

There were so many photographs. All the girls from the Regent Street commune were there. One, I knew, was pregnant. The photos were miserable and I began to feel depressed too. Everyone seemed to be inside. It was so unfair. These people had done nothing, yet they looked guilty. I didn't mind being in jail because of the books but these people had absolutely nothing to do with that. But what could I do? To say they had known nothing would only do more harm than good. They showed me one more, of a girl I knew.

'She's opened up, not on this case but the other one. Told the lot. She'll get off as state witness. There's no problem. You could do the same. You tell us who sent you and then we can say you were incited by them. That's all we want.'

'It's a nice idea, but unfortunately no-one sent us. You could say conscience sent us.'

'Who's Constance?'

'No, not Constance.' Oddly enough we did know a girl called Constance. 'Conscience. Maybe you don't have one. It was entirely my own idea to come to South Africa, no-one else's.'

The one from Capetown changed the subject altogether.

'How many times have you been to Capetown?'

'Only the once. It's very nice but too far to go by car.'

'Who did you see when you were down there?'

'A photographer, Leslie Dexter.'

'You mean Captain Leslie Dexter.'

'Yes, that's the one.'

'Why is he called Captain?'

'I haven't a clue. I thought he was called Doctor Dexter in the trade because he fixed people's problems for them, but when I looked his name up in the book, it said Captain. I don't know why. He's quite young. A good bloke. Does a lot of work.'

'Yes, I know him. My brother's a photographer. There are good models in Capetown. It's the best place in South Africa really, but the wind is bad in winter, blows down telegraph poles regularly. For someone like me who's light, it can be quite difficult, just walking down the street. Quite a few people have been killed by the wind.'

75

We rambled on about Capetown and various models we knew and I asked him if he would like to see my folio. He would, so we went into the main room. Both policemen were quite impressed with my work. My folio isn't aggressive in any way at all and it made talking about sabotage seem very remote. The small policeman looked wiry but when he put down the photographs he had in his hand and picked up one of the weights I'd seen lying in a corner, I was quite shocked. The poor man couldn't lift eighty-five pounds with two hands. I had been doing my press-ups for some weeks, so lifting this amount with one hand was no problem at all.

The tall one had a go on the weights and then I asked again to go to the lavatory. By then most of the lights in the building were out and we had to tip-toe down the corridor. Apparently the other interrogators were sleeping in the map-and-file room so we had a full house. Again the routine of 'All clear!', 'All clear!'. Back at the interrogation room, we spent the rest of their eight hours talking about Capetown.

The next two interrogators to come on were an old hand from Schleswig-Holstein and his blond mate who looked ideal for the part, but far too young to have any punch at all; but old Schleswig was full of beans. He read the previous shift's notes and then rapped out, 'Stand up! You don't need a seat, you lazy bastard.'

He had a habit of clenching his fists slowly and turning away. Then suddenly he would look at me.

'God,' I thought, 'another ham actor.'

'Who sent you?'

'No-one.'

'I don't want that answer. I've read that already. I want something new.'

'I've told them everything.'

'It's not enough.'

He signalled to his off-sider to go outside for a bit. Then he got up and said, 'We know everything about you. Why do you hold us up?'

'Look, I'm really quite tired. Do I have to stand up?'

'Yes.'

'This is pointless. You're treating me like a child.'

'I'm not a child,' he shouted. 'I'm not a child.'

'I didn't say you were a child. I said you were treating me like a child.'

He obviously didn't understand me, because the more we argued the more he spluttered, his German accent getting worse and worse. Finally he came over and punched me in the throat. I was astounded. This was the one thing that all the other police were terrified should happen, but here was this old man who should have retired years ago, losing his temper over nothing. I stood dead still, as if nothing had happened. I think this only made him more angry. He came up to me again; this time I was a little frightened. But all he did was to pull my hair! What a let-down! Hair-pulling's the sort of thing one did to girls in kindergarten. Then he went outside and called his mate in. And on they went.

They wanted to cover the meeting with Aziz. It was a futile situation. They couldn't prove anything. I could more or less say what I liked, or indeed what they liked, because nothing I did then was illegal in England. But Schleswig became so aggressive that in the end I just made it up. By this time, after standing in the corner for some hours, I was very tired. It was also acutely embarrassing. The shutters were open a bit and I'm sure people outside could hear everything this idiot was shooting off. Then, through the crack in the door, I saw someone signalling, with a finger to his lips, that he should be quieter and making a kind of patting gesture with his hands which I think was meant to indicate that I should sit down. I pretended not to see. But the old man quietened down slowly and then left the room. It was a little like hack opera with the other man conducting him from behind the door.

When he left, his assistant took over, an Aryan wonderboy who had been in the police for seven years, he told me, and had just recently been promoted to the Security Branch.

'What's it like?' I asked.

He answered very slowly and in the most uninspiring manner possible. 'Very interesting.' Then silence.

'You shouldn't let the old man ask all the questions,' I said.

'I'm very new, I wouldn't know what to ask.'

'Anything. Don't be afraid.'

He sat up. 'Well, what do you think of South Africa?'

'I'm glad you asked me that. No-one else has so far. It's surprisingly different from England, but, in fact I've learnt to love your country.'

'What do you think of the Springboks?'

'Well, my brother's a vegetarian and I prefer steak. Venison, I find, is a little sweet. Henry thinks it must take a lot of courage to eat your national emblem.'

'I didn't mean that. I mean the Rugby team.'

'Oh, not that mob!' I said, quickly adding, 'I mean I think it's a great shame they can't play any more.'

'Hell, man, they're good.'

'Yes, I'm sure they are.'

I'd had some pretty odd questions put to me in interrogation, but this boy beat them all. He was still a child. He hadn't even got spots yet and I thought his chance of getting his stripes was just as unlikely.

'What do you think of your partner?' I asked him, and he replied apologetically, 'I think ... I think ... I don't know. I don't like him.'

'I have to admit I, too, think he's a bit past it.'

'He's always like that, you know, very noisy and shouts a lot.'

We talked on for some time after this mainly about photography and then Old Schleswig came back and apologised stiffly, but apparently quite genuinely, for hitting me. I accepted his apology and said something about its all having been a misunderstanding. Then he joined in the conversation about photography.

In the course of the conversation he mentioned, to my intense interest, that America had devalued the dollar again and South Africa had followed. I was fascinated. When Britain had last devalued I'd been stuck in Afghanistan with a Nigerian and when we heard it over the radio we were off down to the bank so quickly with our travellers' cheques that we got there before they heard. Stuck in jail, it was sad to think of all this news flying by. In passing, too, he mentioned the Indo-Pakistan war with about as much interest as if it had been a cricket score. This was the first and only news I ever got in three months. I'm sure they only told me

that much to get a political reaction. By then it was afternoon again. I hadn't slept for thirty-six hours but I was all
right.

Bouwer and Co, returned from their sleep behind the
files but I think that in their break they had been up to
something. Their attitude had changed.

Bouwer said, 'Well, Quentin, there's not much more we
can do for you. From here on, you're on your own.'

I didn't quite understand what they meant but Ferrara
explained. 'You know you can't cry wolf every time you feel
the walls closing in on you. Unless you tell us something
new, you are just wasting our time.'

'I've told you everything.'

'No, you haven't. We know you're the brains behind the
studio.'

'Brains behind what? I haven't got any qualifications. All
the others went to university; I didn't. I just know about
photography.'

'Do you know anyone in the British Secret Service?'
Ferrara asked.

'No. Do you mean M16?'

'Yes, British Intelligence.'

'I know the photographer son of one of them. His telephone number's on the back of my press-card.'

'How long have you been with them?'

'What, me in British Intelligence? You must be joking.
Look, my mother's Scottish and my Dad's still a Danish citizen and since I left school at sixteen I've spent more time
out of England than in it. Apart from that, I failed my "Eleven
Plus".'

'There you go,' Bouwer broke in: 'You always turn questions aside. We know you're the brains behind this and it's
you who are going to suffer. Unless you tell us who sent
you it's you who are going to take the rap.'

'Rap for what? We haven't done anything yet.'

Both Bouwer and Ferrara were hotting up again. 'But
you bloody well thought about it and you can get a minimum
of five years for that.'

'If I did think of sabotage, how is that breaking the law
if we didn't actually do anything?'

79

'Because it's conspiracy. You weren't alone. There was your brother and the others.'

'Conspiracy my foot.'

'And then there were the books. On that alone you can get anything from one to ten years under the Suppression of Communism Act.'

'What, for a couple of pages from an American book? Are you sure it's banned?'

'That's not the point. I'm telling you, Quentin, I like you and I've got boys of my own about your age but, thank God, they have more sense than you do. But believe me, you're in trouble.'

'Deep trouble,' Ferrara added.

I could only repeat, 'But I haven't done anything.'

'But you were bloody well thinking of it.'

'I don't know any law, but if someone can get five years for just thinking ... well, how can you prove it?'

'Don't worry, that's our problem. What we want to know is who sent you.'

'I've told you. Why don't you check with Martin and Dave?'

'Because we're asking you. You're lucky we don't make you stand on bricks like the English press says we do.'

'Did you know Old Schleswig made me stand all the time and then punched me in the throat?'

There was consternation.

'What, he hit you?'

'Yes. It's all right, he apologised later.'

'The bloody fool!'

'No, it's really all right. It was a misunderstanding.'

They were both very disappointed with Schleswig but I stood up for him as best I could. I told them I had said he was treating me like a child and he had thought I had said he was like a child. He had just misheard. It was all right. He had apologised.

The two of them talked for a bit in Afrikaans and then decided to break for hamburgers. Someone was sent for them and I went to the lavatory, accompanied as usual. Once inside and sitting there on my own, I realised that I had to protect myself somehow. Judging by that last lot of interrogation, things weren't going too well. I'd got to get that razor blade hidden or they would find it. On the inside pocket of my jacket there was a label. I hacked the sewing on one side and slid the blade in, pulled the chain, looked at my spot and went back to the interrogation room.

While we were talking about nothing in particular, I asked Bouwer, 'Why do people die when they're hung?'

'Well, it's a small bone in the neck.' He put his hand back to find it. 'The rope knot is on the side and when the weight of the body pulls against the knot, the bone breaks sideways.'

'I never knew that. I thought you died through lack of air.'

'No, no. Haven't you seen them in photographs? The neck is actually broken. It's quite painless.'

I don't think they imagined I'd try this, but it was for that reason I asked. My mind was made up. I'd had enough.

After Bouwer and Ferrara left, I had eight hours with a pair from South West Africa. By morning I had gone forty-eight hours without sleep and I could hardly understand what they were saying. I don't think they wrote any interrogation notes at all.

They were replaced by two more men. I was so tired by then that I remember nothing of their shift though it lasted another eight hours. My interrogation book was on its last pages, page ninety-eight to be exact. The policeman read through what I had said to Bouwer and Ferrara, clearly felt jealous of what they had got, and asked if I had anything to add. I said, 'No,' half asleep. Then he started on Timol again. After a page and a bit we were literally on the last page of the book.

'Look,' said the Capetown one, 'only a few lines to go. Tell us something really good so that I can get promotion and you can go to Robben Island.' I asked him what Robben Island was and he explained it was a long-term political prison. 'Not a bad place. You can do medicine there and get a degree. Other people have.'

All I could say was that I couldn't keep awake any longer.

'Nothing for our last page?'

'No, sorry, no promotion. And no pay rise for Bouwer either.'

'Well, Quentin, I think you've had it. Better get you back to jail.'

I'd been sixty hours without sleep by then, the last forty-eight of them non-stop interrogation.

We drove to an older jail at the back of the new one which I had been in earlier. I signed for what I had left and reminded the police I still didn't have anything to read and asked when they would be back. They said, 'Tomorrow.'

I was taken up to my new cell. This part of the jail was very old. There was no plumbing, just buckets, but the cell was larger than the last, with bed-sheets and a table and chair. They took my case and searched me thoroughly. I just managed to keep awake until they left me.

CHAPTER SEVEN

Every jail seems to have a different system. There are some where you say 'Sir' and some where you don't have to. When I awoke, some time around lunchtime, they seemed pretty pleasant. The food was left outside and when they opened up you collected it and put it on the table. Then they locked up again and, hours later, came round to fetch the bowl. No hurry here. It was quite a big cell, some twelve feet by six, slops-bucket in one corner, water-tank in the other. There was still nothing to read. I didn't really expect them to give me anything. When the guard opened up to get my plate I asked him what day it was and he said it was Saturday December 4th. Well, I thought, it seems as good a day as any other to choose. Why wait for Sunday? It's a poor heart that never rejoices and it's going to be a short life but a merry one.

I started to walk back and forth. If to-night's the night, then I'd better not look too different. Just a little walking, nothing out of the ordinary. It's been a good life. I've had my share of luck and I'm not complaining. I've had incredible freedom, leaving school at sixteen to go to Australia, and then after that to India. That was by motor-bike. Then back to Australia, by air that time, and afterwards practically everywhere else. I have reached twenty-five but I had hoped to live to be fifty. I know I'd never get a pension because I haven't paid any stamps. I had hoped to have children. I always thought I'd call my first child Atalanta if it was a girl. I think out of all my girl-friends I really loved Friday best, or at least I missed her most, but it was a relationship based on ignorance. We never really knew each other. But then most love is a matter of imagination, anyway. I had hoped my relationship with Julia might—I don't know—progress. Still, I've had my share. I can't complain. No, if there's any-one to blame for this mess, it's me. Pity about my debts. I would very much like to have paid them and there was enough in the bank. But my other debts, debts to society? Not the lost library books but the trust I was given to begin with: for that I feel bad. But five months more solitary and five years of whatever it is on Robben Island is something that my mind simply cannot envisage. And it's not as though apartheid has anything to do with me personally. I could sympathise, but I can't fight any longer.

I've had a hell of a lot—and thrown most of it away. It's a waste of something—not time because I have done quite a bit, but nothing is saved. It has all gone. If I love children, it is because I was loved when I was a child and this I have failed to pass on. No, when I go, it will not be because I don't feel loved but because, here and now, I can't return it and, in a purely selfish way, I can't endure any more. I'm not as depressed as I was. In a way, the thought of going makes me feel better, more relieved. And I don't feel guilty, not for what I've done. I do feel hopeless, and bad about the others who are stuck here on my account, and for that there is a great relief in going. They can't very well hold them after I'm dead.

Now this game will be my very last, so plan it to win. No pyjamas and they might not leave me with my shoes and clothes. The best thing was to hide the blade in my toothpaste. I could also use a bit of that to try to sharpen it. But with the table up against the wall, if they looked through the spy-hole they'd see what I was up to. Now, if I sat on the table and looked towards the window, I could block the view, I got my tube of toothpaste, the one Bouwer had given me, unrolled it and put the half-blade in at the end and closed it up again. That was the beginning. If they came in and took my clothes, I was still all right. But if the blade failed, I was going to need a second approach. I could try hanging myself. The window looked high enough and a sheet would go round through the bars all right, but that seemed a bit ordinary for me. I thought and I thought. I needed something more mechanical. The liquid in the slops-can might be poisonous but it seemed unlikely in jail. The bed now: that was solid and heavy, that must have a use. We arrive in the world by way of bed so why not go by bed? It even looked like a hospital bed. Only when I came into the world, I didn't do it

alone; I came with a friend. I paused. I hadn't thought of
Henry till then. If he were here I wouldn't be like this, but
I was glad he wasn't. I felt he'd got to continue my life for
me.

If I pulled the bed out a foot or two and lifted it till it
balanced, and then pulled it down by the bedcover, the
weight of the bed falling on my neck should break it. The
bed was heavy and I could tie the water-container to the base
to weigh it down. I'd use the blade first and, if that failed,
the bed. But the blade should be mounted on something
to make it easier to hold. My comb would be good. I hadn't
marked up the last few days and I wouldn't need it now. I
could use the cotton thread to help bind the blade to the
comb. So I unravelled the cotton and tied the three pieces
together. I had slept so soundly the night before that I
couldn't remember if the light had been on or off. I looked
up at the window. Most of the panes had gone but in one
there was a jagged piece left in. This, I thought, could be
used. I pulled the chair over to the window, looked quickly
at the spyhole, jumped up and felt the glass. It was quite
loose. There was no problem there. I got down and put the
chair back. But no. I would use the blade and if that failed,
the bed. So I sat down on the bed and pretended to look as
normal as ever. The blade was safe but I must get my comb
ready. It was black and had a thick end and a thin one. I
chose the thin end. The blade would have to bend round
the teeth, so the thin teeth would be better. If I broke out
two of every three teeth and bent the blade down in a zig-
zag like a saw, it should work. I chewed the remaining teeth
down to about a quarter of an inch and it was ready. Supper
hadn't come yet and I didn't know when it was due but I
felt it must be fairly soon, so I thought it would be best to
start walking and keep it up till supper arrived. I had two
shirts with me, a rather nasty yellow one and a rather beautiful lilac-pink one which I had had to scrub till the white
bones of the collar were showing. I'd wear that one. If
they looked through the spy-hole the contrast with the blood
would be slightly less obvious. The bed, I felt, I could do.
I would wrap the bedcover over the end so that if I was in
a hurry, all I needed to do was lift the bed, balance it at

about seventy-five degrees, place my head sideways on the chair and pull.

Then I thought I ought to make a list. I thought of my toothbrush and tried scratching with it on the table to see if it would mark the wood. It left, not a scratch, but a shiny mark that you could only see from a certain angle. I didn't really want to leave a message but a list of names, just to let them see I wasn't utterly alone. First Mum. Or should it be Mother? Mother, it was; then Henry, Julia, Dad, Gil, Nick, Mary, Charlotte, that was the family. And now friends. How does one start a list for what is basically one's funeral? By the ones one has known longest or by the ones who come into one's head first, like Alan, who always used to say, 'Now I'm going home for a good cry.'? And the other Q., and Johnny and Bob Comber and Chris, Tony Horth and Tony Huston and Friday, whose name wasn't really Friday. It wasn't many. But Joan should be added and Henry's Brenda. And for that matter, Tinker, my old dog, though in fact he was the only one of my friends who was dead already. Just a list of names, no message, no motive—or should I write the 'Studio's Democracy, Liberty and Equality'? It seemed a bit corny and old hat but still it was what had got me here, so I left it. And so, with these words marked next to my list of names, I waited for my last meal and sunset. I was much happier knowing that I was going to leave this mess, much freer, and for the first time in weeks I had a feeling of release.

When I least expected it there was a sound at the door and a small fat man came in and said, 'No singing, no whistling, no standing on the chair looking out of the window.'

I asked him for a bible. He replied, 'No reading matter.'

'Thank you,' I said and he left. I reassured myself that I wasn't missing much. If I had been given a bible or even a dictionary I don't think I would have tried. Possibly later, but not then.

A few minutes later supper came. I really can't remember what it was. I know it wasn't soup. I ate it slowly, thinking, 'I'll need the energy.' And then on reflection, 'Maybe not'. All I had to do now was to finish slowly and look as normal as possible. No tears, no praying, no last-minute questions once I'd made up my mind. It's as good as done. I made this decision basically a week ago. This cell is better, this bed is better, so to-night's the night. I walked on and on. I don't remember anyone looking in through the spy-hole. The electric light in my room gradually filled-in the shadow cast by the window. Soon it would cast a beam outside. The red of the sky turned to a deep blue. I'm a bit worried about my shoes. I could use them to get the weight of the mattress right up to the top end of the bed where it would be most use. I was just about to take the blade out of the toothpaste when I saw a slight movement of the spy-hole cover. I pretended not to notice and went on to turn back the sheets on my bed. The shoes I'd better leave by the door in case they want me to put them out later, I'll use the pillow to wedge the mattress up. It looks less odd.

Just then the light in the room suddenly went out. I was astounded. For a whole month I'd slept with the light on and they had to go and turn it off! It's not the end. I can find things and in some ways it helps. I decided I'd better ... I'd better get into bed. I undressed but kept my shirt on. I felt around for the toothpaste, got the comb and took everything to bed with me. I got the blade out first and started to try to sharpen it by grinding it with toothpaste on the base of my cup. I don't know, but the noise frightened me. I was afraid the guard would hear it and come in. I stopped, licked the paste off and put down the cup. I started to unwind the thread on my comb and, when I'd done that, wedged the blade amongst the remaining teeth. In the dark, it was a little odd. I had to do it all under the covers so that if he turned the light on I wouldn't be caught red-handed. The blade in, I wound the cotton round it. Now I was basically ready. I had a sock somewhere to tie round my arm to make the arteries stand out. My god, in the dark this is stupid. I'll have to go entirely by touch. I can't see anything. I put the blade down and found the sock and then, holding one end in my teeth and the other in my right hand, I tied it round my left arm, pulled it tight and waited. I was terrified they'd put the light on and come screaming into my room. I don't need to rush things; this is something I've got all night for. I counted my pulse. It was good and strong. I could feel it well, both at the wrist and the inside of the elbow. All right. It was absolutely dark so I started. I got the comb, felt the blade with my thumb, then slid it across my arm where Bouwer had told me. I couldn't see anything but it felt good, not annoying like a headache or a migraine but clean, exact. I worked it back and forth almost like masturbating. It was my body. No-one was looking. It was a substitute for I don't know what. This was living, feeling, not waiting but doing. I was going at myself like a dog at a bone, hungry for meat, almost chewing. My arm felt warm, slippery. In some awful way there was something sexual about it. Slightly guilty and yet not caring, I hacked on. I didn't want to end it; I was almost enjoying it. I clenched my teeth in determination, sweated and pounded, up and down. By now I was sure I was swimming in blood. The comb was loose and the blade and the thread wet with blood, my blood. When I've slept with a girl, each part of her has had a different kind of warmth, a breast, a buttock, the womb. My blood was warm and slippery. It was sick but I enjoyed it. And yet it wasn't really working. I wanted to float. I wanted slowly to forget everything and float away. I put the comb down, felt to see if the blade was still there—yes, it was—and felt my arm. Not much of a hole. I've got to do better than that. My feet were sweating and that felt like blood too. I felt my wrist. A pulse was coming through strong as ever, bugger it. I started to hack at my left wrist. After bouts when I clenched my teeth and hacked at it I felt round to see how much blood was coming out. Very little, really. I couldn't understand it: I'd been going at it as hard as I could. Then I swapped hands, wiped them on the sheets and had a go at my right arm, but my arm was just as strong. I was quite amazed. Only five weeks earlier, when I'd been making a prop for an Amstel beer ad with a stanley knife it had slipped and gone right through my jeans, leaving me with a good two-inch cut. This blade was useless but anyway I'd keep going. I tried to open up the old cut on my thigh but I couldn't find it. Then in pure madness, I just cut all round the old wound, then back at my arm and wrist, anywhere. If I couldn't get an artery, then anything would do. I waited to feel if I was weakening but it was no use pretending. I thought of sleeping for a bit to see if, when I woke, I'd be weaker but my breathing was fast and the idea seemed hopeless. The only thing left was to try the bed. The comb was quite useless, not really painful but pointless, and when I went to feel if the blade was still on, it had gone. There were only the teeth and the cotton. In desperation I went back to my left arm. The hole was quite big by now; my index finger could move inside it. There was something there. If I could only break it! My finger felt it but my arm didn't, so it couldn't be a nerve. It must be a vein or an artery or something. I got my comb again and got the last tooth, the end one a little bigger than the others, round it, ground my teeth, tugged and pulled, and in the end felt nothing give but the comb. I thought I'd won because when I felt my arm it was sopping. Then I found something hard imbedded in it and realised to my horror that it was the tooth of the comb. I had to do something. The comb was broken and I was only bleeding. I waited, feeling my arm again. I was not dizzy at all. I felt my other arm. It was almost dry. The bloody thing was drying up on me. Christ, what the hell are you made of? Leather or something? Give it time; wait and see how it goes. Start again, find the blade, get the cotton. Yes, get the blade. I patted around in the dark, found the blade, got it back into the comb and started in on my wrists again, first the left and then the right. They would bleed for a while, then, literally, dry up on me. You bastard, I thought, it means the bed and as soon as they hear that bed fall, that's it. It's got to be once for all. I stopped for a while and listened carefully. There was no sound other than my bastard heart, going stronger than ever. But there was no guard, that was the main thing. I waited a bit longer, then went into action.

I got out of bed, jammed the pillow along the mattress to get the maximum weight at the other end. I went over to the water-tank and lifted it. It weighed a ton. But if I put that on, when I lifted the bed all the water would push the lid off and they'd be bound to hear it. So I forgot the tank. I pulled the bed out from the wall slowly so as to make as little noise as possible, lifted it up till it was balancing almost at right angles, then brought it down gently to mark the spot on the floor where it would fall. Then I put the chair in the right place next to where the bed would come down. Quickly I lifted the bed up again, got the cover in one hand and, holding tight with the other to the chair I was kneeling on, put my head sideways, and pulled the cover. Come on, what's holding it up? It felt as though I would go on counting for ever...

I woke up and couldn't understand what was happening. I was sleeping on the floor. My arms hurt, my head was splitting, and my left ear was bleeding badly. I was still holding the cover in my left hand. I couldn't think what had happened. It felt like a motor-bike crash, only there was no bike. I couldn't see anything and my ear was beginning to throb. I staggered up, very unsteady on my feet. What on earth was happening? I tripped over the chair and realised I was in jail. 'God, let me die! I don't want this, just let me die!' I must try again. No-one has come yet. My neck hurt and my ear throbbed. Come on. This may need more of an angle on my head. I picked up the chair. I couldn't understand why the guard hadn't heard. I lifted the bed right back to its top height, then yanked the cover again. Come on, get me this time! I felt the bed come down. It didn't knock me out this time. It just smacked me like a brick on the head. I reeled in pain, but the bed held me there. I had to lift it off my head which was exploding with pain. This was not the death I had planned. This was a vicious, brutal, bloody mess and totally unsuccessful. I was more alive than I'll probably ever be again. The pain was like childbirth, self-inflicted; this was a miscarriage, a totally useless pain. I began to shout, 'Guard, guard!' There was no answer. For God's sake, I've failed. 'Guard!' Still no answer. Time stuck to my hands, to my head, each second marked by a throb of pain, not just agony but failure, and not just failure but guilt. This whole thing was ending in nothing. It would only lead to more complications. I had failed in every way possible, except one. I wasn't bored any more, only guilty and disgusted.

I went on shouting and eventually my light went on and someone looked through the spy-hole.

'Guard, I'm sorry. I tried very unsuccessfully to kill myself. My head hurts and my arms, as you can see, need stitches.'

'What have you done?'

'Oh, for Christ's sake! I tried to kill myself.'

'Have you got a knife in there?'

'No. Look, can you get me a doctor or something?'

'I'm afraid I can't open up because I'm on my own here. I'll have to go and get the boss.'

'Why can't you open up?'

'Because you might attack me.'

'Look, I've just tried to kill myself. I'm hardly likely to start on someone else. Oh, piss off and get a doctor, but hurry.'

The frightened eye left the spy-hole and the cover swung back. I was left with myself, stupid bastard me, and the stupid comb. And where was the bastard razor blade? I pushed over the chair and walked over to the bed. The white sheets looked like an American flag, only red stars on white instead of the other way round. It looked as though there had been a fight. I tried to hide the blood. It had been a shocking thing to do. I didn't feel sick, I never do, but I did feel guilty. I'd never hurt anyone before, but I had now. In a way it didn't matter that it was myself, it was still inexcusable. Violence is violence.

After a long wait, quite a number of people arrived. First one looked through the peep-hole and asked what the matter was. I said again that I had tried to commit suicide, 'But, as you can see, very unsuccessfully.'

'What did you use?'

'A razor.'

'A what?'

'A razor,' I shouted, 'a very blunt razor.'

'Put it on the table.'

I put it on the table.

'Don't touch it when we're coming in.'

'Oh, for Christ's sake, open the bloody door and stop playing games.'

The door opened and three small men, in their sixties at least, stood there. The original guard was quite thin and had a small moustache. He looked very worried. The other two were fat, one in a nightshirt, the other in full uniform, scrambled egg on his cap, and rainbows on his chest.

'My boy, while there is life, you must live.'

'Oh, god, if you call being locked up in solitary with no exercise and nothing to read and no foreseeable future—if you call that life, you can fucking well keep it! I've had enough.'

'Look, there's no reason to swear. We can bloody well leave you till morning and put you in a strait-jacket.'

'No, no, I'm sorry. I've just had it. I didn't mean to be rude. But I don't want to live like this any longer.'

'I'm afraid I can't help that. I'm just in charge of the jail. I don't make the rules. You'll have to see the police to-morrow.'

'I don't want to see the police.'

'You're their prisoner. You'll have to, now. Where did you get the blade from?'

'I found it in the other jail and smuggled it in in my jacket pocket.' I reached for my jacket to show them the torn hole.

'I see. And what's this bedcover doing tied to the bed?'

'Well, I tried to break my neck by letting it fall on my head.'

'Sorry, I don't understand. How?'

'Well, I lifted the bed up and then pulled it down on my head.'

'Not a bad idea. Original.' He looked round. 'It means we've got to take all the furniture out.'

'I don't mind. I can walk more easily with the furniture out.'

'But if you try any more, it's the strait-jacket. Understand?'

'No, don't worry. I've had enough.'

The man in uniform told the fat one to go down and get some bandages. 'And some stitches,' I added. He asked why and I showed him my left arm and he said, 'And some stitches.'

He went and we just stood there.

'Well, it was a pretty stupid thing to do, wasn't it?'

'Yes, I know. I'm sorry.'

'I really can't understand why you did it.'

'Because I haven't a chance. I can be stuck here for another five months and then get at least five years without anyone batting an eyelid.'

'Five years is not a lifetime. I've known men to do five years and come out better men for doing it.'

'Well, I'm not like that. I wasn't born alone. I'm a twin and I've always had a life full of friends. I'm not good at solitary. If they would just give me something to read. Surely it must be possible to get me a bible.'

'I don't know. I'll try. But you must behave yourself.'

The other old man arrived with bandages and needles and so on. The two of them, like overgrown boy scouts, prepared me for stitches. The thin one looked on. He wasn't happy at all. It was obvious that he'd been sleeping on the job, or someone had, and he looked more guilty than I did. I didn't want a local, so they just stuck straight in but then on closer inspection they found that all the same a small artery had been cut so, very reluctantly, they said we'd have to go down to the prison hospital.

'Oh, great,' I thought, 'anything to get out of that prison cell.' I put on trousers and helped to carry the plaster and stuff back down to the hospital.

The thin warder was told to stay behind and tidy up. I think he was quite anxious to do something; he looked really sick. Anyway, I and my two overgrown scouts, who were wearing long shorts, trotted off down to the hospital. It was pitch dark and completely quiet. I don't think there can have been many in the jail or, if there were, they were all asleep. The two old men knew their way without having to put lights on. Then they opened up a wooden door and turned on a light. The room was, as everything is in South Africa, clean beyond all reason. With my blood-stained shirt and my long wet hair, I must have looked obscenely out of place. On the wall were pre-war photographs of people giving artificial respiration. That system went out years ago. The kiss of life is the thing now. There was a steel bed in the corner with a white sheet on it. I was told to go and sit on it.

'But I'll make it dirty.'

'Don't worry. Sit on it. Put your head down. How did this happen?'

'When the bed hit me.'

'Oh, yes. That was pretty pointless, wasn't it? It's impossible to die in jail. Didn't you know that?'

'No.'

'Well, the cells are designed to make it impossible.'

He started to cut great wads of hair off the left side of my head just above the ear. I was sitting down listening to the noise of the scissors and watching the hair fall on the polished floor. It was quite good fun. Who knows, I might even get a cup of tea out of it. A dab to the head stung a little. What a relief! It was all over.

'Does it hurt?'

'No, I don't mind the pain.'

'Does it hurt, man?'

'No, not really, just throbs a little.'

'God, you're stupid to even try this.'

I wondered how many others had tried. I think he liked doing it. I think he got a kick out of it. 'Middle of the night. Somebody somewhere needs me. Mercy dash.' That's why he put his uniform on. I certainly liked it. I thought, 'If I go to Robben Island, maybe I can do medicine and become a hack surgeon. It would be good fun.' It was exciting, much better now. I wasn't just me any more, I had cuts on my arm and a big pink bit of plaster on my head, a souvenir of failure. In some way I was a little older.

'All right, that's the head, now the arm.'

I had been holding a wad of cotton wool to my left arm to stop the bleeding. He removed it, washed the wound again and saw where it was bleeding from, a small blue vein or something. Then he took what looked like a small pair of pliers with a spring on the end; this clamped the vein and stopped the bleeding. Then he started to sew the arm up. He did about three stitches and took out the pliers and did another three. On my right arm and wrists they only put paraffin gauze and elastoplast and I thought to myself they were going to have a great time getting that lot off later.

He gave me a couple of aspirins and I got down from the bed, thanked him, and we went back to my cell. The total experience was pretty exhausting, but quite funny in a way. I felt less guilty about the whole thing. Clean sheets. Bandages. My arm still hurt, and my ear, too. As for my head, what a lump! But it was solid stuff. My comb was still lying on the table, the cotton still red with blood but beginning to dry almost black. I got into bed and smiled—at least I tried to—maybe life was not so very bad. I fell asleep. This time the light was left on.

CHAPTER EIGHT

I awoke like a child recovering from illness, bored and lazy. Last night was far behind. Now I had everyday problems again. I got up, reached for my comb, took the dried blood off, unwound the cotton and combed my hair very carefully. I felt the stitches with childish pride, looked at my arms all bandaged up, and smiled. I heard footsteps; my spy-hole moved; the door was unlocked; the sliding bolt slid across; the door opened.

Slim, 'the kind one' I'd been introduced to by my police interrogators the night I arrived, was standing there looking like a very angry scoutmaster.

'Why did you do that, you bloody bastard? Huut, man, you got me into a lot of trouble!' He came over and pulled my hair.

'I'm sorry, but it's my life. And will you leave my hair alone!'

'So you're bloody sorry, are you? What about me and my job?'

'I've said I'm sorry, but I don't want to live any more.'

'You're always sorry.' He hit me on the side of the head, but it was more a gesture than a blow. 'Where did you get the blade from?'

'I found it in the other jail.'

'But how did you get it in here?'

I pointed, rather tentatively, at my jacket. 'The label. I hid it in the label.'

He went over and put his finger in behind the label. 'I searched that jacket myself completely and there was no blade there.'

'There was.'

'No, there wasn't. Do you hear me. You found that blade in this cell. Where did you find it?' He looked around. 'Ah, yes, that's it. Up at the window.' He got on the chair and stood by the window.

Someone else came into the room, a small, grey-haired

man in civilian clothes. Slim reached up to the broken window and removed the loose piece of glass, then put his hand outside. Turning to the other guard he said, 'He found the razor outside the window.'

I sighed and breathed heavily. I didn't want to start an argument with Slim.

The small man said, 'I want a statement about the suicide attempt.'

He gave me a pencil and a sheet of paper and I sat down at the table. I wrote a short account of what had happened and then, as he asked, signed it and put along the margin that I had made the statement completely voluntarily and under no stress. As soon as I gave him his pencil and the statement back, he danced out of the room as happy as a sandboy.

When he had gone, Slim sulked around talking to himself. 'You didn't have that blade; you found it here.'

'Sorry, but you'll just have to accept the fact. I mean, it's very little to me either way. I couldn't care less where I found it.'

'Where's the other half?'

'I don't know. I only had one half.'

'Well, we'll have to search the whole place again, and take the furniture out. You know, you are a bloody nuisance.'

His young fat friend came in and together they went through every stitch of my clothes. Then, when they were satisfied there was nothing there, they began to take the furniture out. There goes the beautiful hospital bed, my boy scout's table, and the chair. The mattress was left on the floor with the blankets piled on top. Then breakfast came, a plate of cold porridge, a lump of stale bread and a little tin lid of sugar and a mug of black coffee. I moved it over to the bed, crouched down and started. It wasn't as good as the modern jail but at least there was no hurry. Slim came back to get the plate and gave me two pads, a scrubbing brush and a broom.

'Every day this cell has to be cleaned. Polish the floor first, then sweep it.'

'Yes, sir.'

He didn't like the 'Yes, sir'. He thought I was pulling his

97

leg—but I'd got into the habit in the other jail.

I put the pad under each knee and started to scrub. It's good exercise for the stomach muscles and doesn't do the floor any harm, either. My arm hurt a bit and the bandages started to stick together. When I'd finished, I swept up. It was surprising how much dirt there was. I think most of it came through the window or under the door. I finished and did a little walking. Slim opened up, looked at the floor and didn't think much of it. He shouted, 'Bonius!' and again, even louder, 'Bonius!' Any second I expected an enormous dog to come at me. The patter of feet grew louder and louder and suddenly a small black boy appeared, wearing grey shorts down past his knees. His shaven head was beaded with sweat.

'Yes, Baas.'

'Floor,' Slim said in a whisper.

Bonius leapt for the brush and, pad under each knee, started to polish, not back and forward as I had done but sideways. I stood on my mattress, feeling helpless.

'I'm quite capable of doing the floor myself,' I said.

Slim didn't appear to be listening, he just stared at Bonius, his pride and joy. When Bonius reached the doorway he stopped, then took down the water-tank and polished under that, put it back, said, 'Thank you, Baas,' and crawled away.

Slim said, 'That's how it's done—sideways.'

'Yes, sideways.'

They left me, but a little later Slim opened up again. I always heard him before the door actually opened, and I stood at attention.

'Put your trousers on. You've got visitors.'

'Shall I put on my shoes as well?'

'Yes, shoes and jacket.'

Wondering who it could be, I dressed excitedly and followed him along the passage, shoe-laces flapping. We only went a few yards and there I saw Two-Faced Bouwer and Uncle Ferrara.

'What do you want?' I said.

'You asked to see us.'

'No, I didn't.'

'Yes, you did.'

'Look, I don't want to see you.'

'So you've got nothing new for us?'

'Nothing. In fact I don't see any point in living any more.'

'Why's that? We haven't done anything to you.'

'That's just it. You've done nothing. I've done nothing. And I've got nothing. This whole thing's a complete non-event. Why don't you charge me? Then, at least, I'd know what I'm supposed to have done.'

'We don't know if we're going to charge you yet. It depends on the D.A.'

'Well, how long are you going to keep me here? I've got to know something.'

'We want to check a few things.'

Just a little way along the corridor and up a few steps was a small soundproof room. It was a little stuffy but opening the window only made it worse. It was very hot outside. Bouwer and Ferrara sat down on one side of the table and I sat on the other. Bouwer took a newspaper cutting out of his case.

'I've got a cutting here from an English Sunday paper. It's an interview with your brother. It says that you went to school with Timol at Leicester University where he and you often talked politics. Timol was a sociology student there and you were, too. You used to sympathise with the black cause and so did he.'

'Let me read it.'

'No, I can't.'

'Why not?'

'Because, under section 6 of the Terrorism Act, it says you're not allowed to read the paper.'

'Does that mean I'm charged?'

'No, you're only detained at the moment.'

'What paper is it?'

'The *Sunday Express*, November 14th.'

'It's nonsense. Henry went to Leicester, not me. Did Timol go to Leicester University?'

'That's what it says in the paper.'

'Let me see it.'

'No, I can't.'

'Well, it's simply made up. I was born in Leicester but I

99

never went to university there or anywhere else. Henry did, not me.'

'So, you're saying it's a lie.'

'Of course it's a lie. And there's no reason for anyone to say it.'

'Well, there it is. In our country we protect our awaiting-trial prisoners. Nothing can be published about a man unless it comes out in court.'

'It's the same in England.'

'Well then, why has this come out?'

'I don't know, but I don't really believe it, because of the way you read it. You weren't really reading from the paper.'

'Look, Quentin, I've got nothing to hide.'

'Well then, let me read it for myself.'

'Sorry, I can't.'

'Well, I'm sorry but I can't believe that's what it says. It's totally illogical. Ask Martin and Dave. I know Australia. I know Australia better than they do. I went to Australia. Henry went to Leicester.'

'Anyway, there it stands.'

There was a pause which I broke. 'Look, can I please have something to read? It's completely suicidal, being stuck in here with nothing to read.'

'Why did you try?'

'Because it's hopeless. I'm going to be stuck here for ever and I can't take solitary. I've got to have something to do. I can't do nothing.'

'If you try again, it's the strait-jacket for you. If you can't be trusted with the furniture and if you start messing around, it's as simple as that. We don't want to, but you make us.'

'What am I supposed to do all day?'

'Try and remember every little detail, everything.'

'I have.'

'Well, can you explain a letter that Ebrahim sent to Timol, saying, "Be careful of Quentin and Henry. Don't trust them."? What about that?'

'I know nothing about that.' I didn't, but it was just possible that Ebrahim had written to that effect. It's one of the awful things about the situation there that nobody trusts anybody.

Eventually Ferrara said, 'Well, don't do it again.'

'Do what?'

'Cry wolf.'

'I didn't cry wolf. I didn't ask you to come here.'

'Well, why did you try to commit suicide?'

'That's my business.'

'Oh, no, it's not. You're our prisoner.'

'Look, if I can get from one to ten years for having the books and get five years just for thinking about sabotage, and I've got to wait till April just to find out—who wants to wait to find out?'

'Well anyway, we're off. I go on holiday this week but I'll be seeing you after I get back.'

The guard was called and I was taken back to my cell. I was angry. That press-cutting was very odd. I couldn't understand it. There was a lot to think about. I walked and walked and the time passed quickly. I heard the sound of the door opening, walked over, and stood to attention. Food! I bent down to pick it up. Soup for lunch. Just what I thought, luke-warm. Pea soup, but not bad. I went on walking after lunch and time dragged a bit, but a lot had happened in the last few days. The noise of the kitchen sounded as though it was within feet of me but the food always arrived cold. I couldn't understand it. I walked on. After I'd been walking for a bit, I heard a sound I recognised. It was a sneeze, and a sneeze I knew. That was Dave's sneeze. I immediately sneezed back though it was a poor imitation of his. So, Dave was somewhere very near. Good on you, Dave! Or, as he would have said, 'You little beauty!' I wondered if Martin was here too. I felt so much the better for that sneeze. The sky outside was getting darker. I stood on my slops-bucket and had a glimpse out of the window. There was a tree and the sunlight was red on it. Not long now till night. Right from the start I had made it a rule not to go to bed until sunset, otherwise the whole system would fall apart. I got up on the slops-bucket again. The tree was now dark green. The sun had set. I'll leave a little bread for the morning. Now I can go to bed. The light was on, of course. It always was except for that one night when I needed it. But I managed to go to sleep. A bell woke me and Slim opened up.

'Bucket out, plate out, broom in, pads and brush in.'

'Thank you.'

I heard my porridge go down outside, had a quick look under the door. That's it. I started walking. Exactly on the dot of five hundred lengths, they opened up. I didn't see why they had to leave the porridge out there for twenty minutes, but there was no point in complaining. I put the broom out and picked up the cold porridge, finished it and went back to walking.

The next day a visiting magistrate came. I said, as I had said before, that I couldn't complain till I was told what my rights were. I'd had no exercise, but I didn't know if I was entitled to any. I'd got nothing to read, but again I didn't know if I was allowed anything. I'd tried to commit suicide. The police had told me I could get at least five years, and on top of that I'd be in solitary till April before I could go to court.

'Are you all right otherwise?'

'Well, what do you think?'

'Fine,' he said, ticked me off his page and went on to the next cell.

The next thing I knew Slim was opening up in a rage. 'God, man what do you want exercise for? Isn't the walk to the shower long enough?' He grabbed me by the hair and pulled me outside. 'Come on, you bastard. You can get your bloody exercise.' He finally let go of my hair and I followed him apprehensively down to a big, flat-stoned courtyard.

'Walk, go on, bloody well walk!'

'Fine, just what I want.'

It was good: sky, wind and space. This was exciting. I hadn't felt the wind for weeks. I walked about twelve times round the big yard before Slim shouted 'Time!' I retrieved my shirt and thanked him. My eyes took time to get used to the light. Everything looked black. I followed Slim back to my cell and thanked him again. He swore in Afrikaans and locked my door. I resumed my walking but things were looking up. Exercise, that's good. Three meals a day, a shave and now exercise. Who knows, I might even get a bible.

The next day when I went up for a shave Slim looked at

my arms. They were beginning to smell a bit and pus was coming out.

'We'd better change the dressings,' he said.

I had a shave and saw that my spot was doing just great; it was about the size of a cent piece by now. I went back to my cell a bit depressed. Slim came up later with some new dressings and I ripped off the old elastoplast, hairs and all. The stitches looked all right. My head was fine, though my ear was a bit scabby, but my arms and leg weren't healing at all well. I could see in Slim's face he wasn't happy either. Anyway, more elastoplast was applied. Slim liked putting on great lengths of it.

'Jesus, man, you're a bloody sadist.'

'What's a sadist?'

'Somebody who wastes bandages the way you do.'

'A job worth doing...'

'Is worth doing well,' I finished it for him. I put the old bandages in the slop-bucket and went on walking.

Next day there was suddenly a shout of 'Bonius! Here, boy! Bonius! Come here!' Bang, bang, bang. What the hell's happened now? There was complete silence, then sudden laughter. Later I heard more bangs and more laughter. I had thought Slim was too old to play with cap guns! Later he came in with more dressings. I tried to appear enthusiastic about the progress the cuts were making.

'Look at my leg,' I said. 'It's completely healed up.'

I pressed the old wound and suddenly pus squirted across the room and hit Slim's trousers.

'Huut, man, stop it!'

Fatty rolled with laughter, but Slim was angry.

'Stop fiddling with it!'

'Sorry, I really thought it was all right.'

'No, it's not.'

Slim had brought in his cap gun with him and laid it on the bed. 'Next time, why don't you try with one of those?'

I smiled at him, looked him in the eye and thought to myself, 'He's not so bad really, just warped.'

CHAPTER NINE

It must have been about the 10th of December when I got a bible. The short, fat boss of the jail tottered in around mid-day.

'Here's your bible. You will not fold, dog-ear or mark the pages in any way at all. Is that understood?'

Things were looking up! I might be getting mail by Christmas, maybe even a lawyer in the New Year.

The red paper dust-jacket said, 'This bible is made by the British and Foreign Bible Society which produces one bible every two seconds of working time. It is issued in 100 countries in 900 different languages. Sow the seed.' There was a picture of a man sowing.

Now, where to start? I think it would be nice to start with the New Testament. There's not much of it. It's only about a third of the whole book. 'The book of the generation of Jesus Christ the son of David, the son of Abraham . . .' I curled up on the bed and read on. 'From that time Jesus began to preach, and to say, "Repent; for the Kingdom of Heaven is at hand."' But how can I repent when I haven't done anything yet? I did a good whack. It's communist, of course. I'm going to have to watch that side of it, but it doesn't appear to be actually terrorist. I don't want to finish it all at once, so I'll do a thousand turns between meals and spend the rest of the time reading.

Sometime during the next week, when I was combing my hair, a stitch came out with the comb but my arm was still quite painful. It felt as if the stitches were too tight, but Slim's only comment was 'That's fine.' The hole in my arm looked more and more like a belly button but it was beginning to smell less like one. Then, on the following Monday, sixteen days after the suicide attempt, the stitches were taken out and it felt much better. We couldn't find half of them but I think that was because they had dropped out already. It meant, anyway, that I could now wash myself properly under the shower.

One day after a shower, when they weren't looking, I began to cut my hair with the razor.

'Hey! Stop that.'

'But I want to.'

'Rules say, no haircuts.'

'It's my hair. Why can't I?'

'Because of identification. That's why.'

'I haven't seen anybody for identification.'

'It doesn't matter. No haircuts.'

'It's silly. If my hair gets any longer, I won't have any face to recognise.'

I gave them back the razor and finished combing the loose bits out of my hair. Then I asked the guard about Christmas.

'Just like any other day. You might get jelly if you're good.'

'Real jelly? Roll on Christmas!'

One day about this time, Slim came in. 'Get everything together quickly. You're off, man!'

I thought fast. It would certainly be a Christian gesture to release me before Christmas. But no, this was a trick. I'd had this before in the Jo'burg jail.

'Shall I put on my shoes?'

'Yes, put on your shoes. For Christ's sake, get your things together.'

'All right. I'm ready. Where do we go?'

'Follow me.'

We walked two doors down the corridor and I was put into a new cell. Well, it wasn't new, just different.

'I don't need shoes to walk twelve feet.'

'Oh, stop arguing and get in.'

The door slammed and I could feel the pain creeping across my head. Why did they have to do that to me? I could see it coming. I'd got a migraine. Shit, I'm not going to bed; that would be fatal. I'm not breaking my system because some sod's pulled my leg. In just one minute my complete faith had been lost. The noise from the kitchen was shattering. I just sat down on my mattress and cried. No, I've got to walk till it's absolutely dark. It's the only thing. I can't read. My eyes hurt. I've got to walk till I drop, till my head stops pounding with self-pity.

Then, three days before Christmas, I got my first batch of letters. Two security policemen came in and I asked them what was happening. Captain Gloy, I think it was, said, 'Who knows? We might not even charge you.' Indeed, who did know? He went and I was left with my letters. There were three and a Christmas card. I decided to look at the card first. I tore open the envelope rather apprehensively. It was like getting a telegram. 'With love from Mum, Dad and Henry.' It was the Adoration of the Three Kings. I found it beautiful but the perspectives were all wrong and the colour reproduction running far too warm. And oh, Mum, you shouldn't have sent that! One of the three Wise Men is a coon! Looks just like Buki. Now the letters. On each envelope was my name in Mum's writing and a red stamp with the date, 22. 12. 71 and *Die Kommissaris Von Die S.A. Polisie.* I opened one of the letters and stared at it through a prickly haze of emotion. It read:

Darling Quentin,

I write so many letters to you in my head that when I sit down, I feel I've said it all already and at the same time that anything I say must seem very remote and unimportant to you, but I hope it helps to distract you and send you off on old memories and just reassure you of a great fund of love and good-will.

There isn't much real news, it's been a quiet week, but I did go to dinner with Tommy Wilson in their nice, little, new flat attached to the business school that actually overlooks Regent's Park.

Stephen Hall has been terribly ill, kept alive on blood transfusions, but beginning to pick up, thank God. Old Mr Riche is dead but that on the whole is a good thing. As for Faith, I hear she's had a third stroke and is in a nursing home and quite comfortable but largely beyond human contact. Her very old friend Teddy Ashcroft went to see her and she thought he was a general who used to live next door about thirty years ago, so I don't think there's much point in making the effort to go and see her.

Henry's working to-day for Tony. They did a cover for Harper's but there won't be much work after Christmas and he is to start looking for something else. He had dinner with Brenda's mother last night. Brenda and Charles have gone to North Africa, other routes being closed by the war in India. I'd lunch with Nick at Amalfi yesterday. We go to them on Christmas Day. I've made mincemeat and puddings.

We're doing all we can to help. I only wish it was much more.

With love and a big hug,

Mum.

I wondered what Mum meant by no real news. Everyone seemed to be dropping off like flies. Well, the world's still going. Nothing about my case though, but Mum doesn't seem too worried. That's a relief. I really would worry if she did. It's all good. I'll read it again later but I'll look at the others first. Why on earth have they all come at the same time? This next one was dated December 1st ... nearly three weeks ago.

My Dearest Quentin,

Here's a weekly letter again though it's hard to write without really knowing if you even get them but I wouldn't for worlds have you expect one and be disappointed. If only there was some possibility of response or some news but we have none, unless the name of your solicitor. We have written to him and hope to hear something soon.

So, I have a solicitor! And 'Here's a weekly letter again' can only mean Mum's written before. I quickly opened the last letter to see the date on that. December 17th. No, that definitely means I haven't got all my letters. If I had had them, I bet I wouldn't have tried to kill myself. Why couldn't they have given them to me? Now for number three.

Dearest Quentin,

I think this will be the nearest to a Christmas Letter for you, though it scarcely seems possible. I do hope you will not be too unhappy on Christmas Day and that the New Year will bring you home to the warmest welcome anyone ever had. You will be in a great many people's thoughts and we will drink a very special toast to you at

Nick and Mary's. I only hope you can make do on the memories of Christmas Past. They have been very good in their time. Think of all that roast goose and red cabbage, and running round the block at Blenheim Road before the pudding, and opening presents under the tree.

I'm trying to send you a card as well as this letter. I tried to get you some of your Pre-Raphaelite girls but they don't seem to make them into Christmas cards. I went round all the galleries and bought it in Hampstead in the end. Everywhere I go I'm haunted by your ghost, but it's always a very cheerful ghost, in a hurry. The thing is, you were always a good son about taking me with you on your various ploys. I miss it very much but I'm doubly glad now.

Meanwhile your father is coming here in about an hour, mainly to discuss finances, which is a pretty unnerving thought. See what you land me into! I do hope Henry will be home in time.

I've got the little portrait I did of you in the summer on the desk as I write. It's terribly like you but I wish it wasn't so serious.

Darling, be of good heart and keep well,

Love,

Mum.

It was quite a rush of concentrated news. I was left wondering why I had a lawyer who needed money. I hadn't seen him yet. And 'Look forward to the New Year' and that warm welcome home! It's good that Mum doesn't seem too worried. That in itself is a great relief.

Every night before going to bed, I would read these three letters and pretend they were new.

Christmas came. I knew this because a small man in a green springbok jacket with kangaroos on his tie came and said, 'Happy Christmas.' No presents, no letters, and so far, no jelly. Maybe in South Africa Father Christmas wears a green blazer with 'South Africa Olympic Team 1934' on it.

Lunch came eventually. I looked under the door and saw that there were in fact two bowls, so jelly might still be in the offing. After the usual wait for them to open up, I found, not jelly, but lukewarm trifle reeking of vanilla essence. Clearly it had been the first time the cook had ever used vanilla.

Drops, not teaspoonfuls—even I knew that. I hid the trifle over at the other side of my cell and tried to concentrate on my lunch: quite a slab of meat, a few roast potatoes, even a piece of pumpkin and some very dead cabbage. The stink of vanilla made it difficult not to smile. I looked at my 'Adoration of the Three Kings' and thought of frankincense and myrrh.

The smell lasted into the New Year. At weekends we didn't get exercise and so over Christmas we lost four days of it. On top of that my jaw developed an odd pain. I'm sure it was psychosomatic, but a lump came up under my ear and it hurt when I ate. But by the time the medical man had come back after Christmas it had gone. My spot was more patient; it was definitely staying to see the New Year in. Then, on the 29th of December, the two security men came in with books. The two I got were *Everywoman, an Edwardian Love Story* and a book of Afrikaaner tales. They were both ex Pretoria library and very moth-eaten. But they meant a lot to me. I got a sense of character and started to identify with people again.

The next day after breakfast, the guard came in and told me to get dressed.

'You've got a visitor.'

'Do you mean it, or is this just another move?'

'No, you're going down to the police station to meet somebody. You must wear suit, tie, the lot.'

'They're in my suitcase. I'll need my suitcase.'

'I'll get it now.'

He closed the door. I wondered what this was all about. Could it be a deportation order or were they going to charge me? I was terrified of being stuck where I was and terrified of any change. What little security I had was in familiarity. I didn't want to lose it with cell-changing and empty promises. The guard came back.

'Wally's got the key. I can't do anything.'

'Well, I'll just have to go like this.'

'No, you can't. I'll get Bonius to wash and iron that shirt straight away.'

I took it off and gave it to him. I couldn't understand why it should be so important to look clean. These interruptions threw one into confusion and fear. My shirt came back, warm and damp. Slim was worried about me not having a suit to wear.

'Your problem, not mine. I don't care how I look.'

Again I was left on my own. These long periods of waiting inside—a permanent state of waiting—were unbearable. Something was going to happen but they would never tell me. Eventually two police officers arrived and I walked with them very apprehensively. They wouldn't tell me, either, what was happening. I was breathing deeply and felt dizzy. I got into the back of a car and was handcuffed to the second policeman. Not a good sign; they'd never done that before.

'Where are we going?'

'Down to the station.'

'Why?'

'Well, you've got a visitor.'

The speed of the car upset me, too, physically. I was distressed by the speed of the traffic and all this space flying past. I'm not going to make it. Either I'm going to be sick or I'm going to scream. But we arrived at the police station, my teeth exhausted with grinding. The handcuffs were unlocked and I was told to sit down in an office I hadn't been in before. I recognised the policeman. I thought, 'I'm not going to talk to them till they tell me why I've been brought here.'

'We're giving you a great privilege. Your consul has been asking to see you for some time, so we arranged a visit. It is important that you do not speak about the case or about prison conditions. Is that understood?'

I stared at him. I was frightened. I nodded.

'Yes.'

Again there was a wait and at last the consul came in.

'How are you?' he asked. 'Are you managing all right?'

'I don't know. I don't think I'm managing very well,' I said slowly.

'I see. Why's that?'

I looked at the policeman and then back at Biggie, the consul. My breathing got heavier and heavier, my scalp tightened, the words stuck in my throat. I couldn't look at him. I looked under the table.

'I can't do solitary.'

'Why's that?'

'I don't know.' I felt my face dissolve in shame. 'Maybe because ... I don't know. Because I'm a twin.' I swallowed and clenched my teeth but I felt my body drift. I couldn't face anyone. I stared at my feet. My nose clogged, the lump in my throat finally stuck as I got the last word out. 'Mr Biggie, I haven't a hope.' My fingers interlocked. Then I gave up. I hid my face in my hands and blubbered. When I eventually stopped heaving, I managed to say, 'I don't want to live any more.'

There was a long silence. I was terrified he would tell me to remember I was British and keep a stiff upper lip. Thank God, he didn't.

'I tried to kill myself,' I said between snivels.

'Oh, I see. Well, try to tell me about it.'

'You mustn't tell my mother.'

'If you say so.'

'I can't let my mother know. It would only make it worse.'

'I understand. Well, do you want to talk to me about it?'

I thought for a while. 'There's nothing much to say.' But I went over the suicide bid and waited for his comment.

'Well, three people have been charged. They are nothing to do with your case, but things are definitely moving.'

'But why am I still held?'

'The authorities have assured me they are doing everything they can.'

'Have you any idea when things will happen?'

Mr Biggie finally got his pipe alight.

'I've been promised the end of next month.'

'The end of January?'

'Yes. Things are moving so you must promise me to, well, not to do anything. You must hold with us, Quentin, we are doing everything we can. Have you got books yet?'

'Yes, I've got books.'

'And your mother's letters? I've got another one here but I'll have to give it to the police first.' He handed it over to the policeman who tapped it on the desk. 'Now, I may not be able to see you for a fortnight, but I've been allowed to get you some books. Offhand, what would you like?'

'I haven't really thought. I did ask for *Lord of the Rings*.'

'Isn't that a children's book?' Biggie puffed madly.

'I don't know. I haven't read it yet.'

'And what else?'

'Well, I had thought of *Romeo and Juliet,* but if you could run to the complete works, it would be good.'

'Yes, I see. Do you like Shakespeare?'

'I don't really know. I read some long ago at school. I saw the film and liked that.'

'Oh, which one was that? Was it Japanese?' I felt we were at cross purposes but let it be. 'Well, Quentin, I've got to see Dave now. But do bear with us. I've been promised that they've almost come to the end of their investigation, so promise me you won't try anything and I'll get those books sent up and see you in a fortnight.'

'Yes, I can manage. The books will help. Thank you. Thank you.'

The police led me into another room where I waited till they got enough police to escort me back to jail. Two came and a black detective ran after us, obviously wanting to come for the ride, but Colonel Ferrara called him back smartly. The black policeman took off his hat and apologised. Outside summer had come; girls were brown, in short white dresses. The grass was long and very green. The driver told me there had been too much rain.

When I got back to my cell, I just had to walk. It was pointless to try reading. My mind wandered. So three people had been arrested. What for? Anyway, something should happen at the end of January.

CHAPTER TEN

On New Year's Eve my two books from the consul arrived, plus one other, a spy thriller. At first I was very excited and wondered how I should read them. I thought one Shakespeare play a day as 'work' in the morning, then my Edwardian rubbish in the afternoon, and *Lord of the Rings* to end the day on a light touch.

The volume of Shakespeare included a biography and an account of when and where he wrote everything. This I found very interesting but as I got down to the plays, I was sadly disappointed, mainly with myself for not having the patience to understand and enjoy them. If all those awful American tourists can enjoy Shakespeare, why can't I? More and more I put him into the 'hard labour' class, and quite often I didn't feel like work at all. The Edwardian rubbish tended to be more emotional and I needed that. If Lady Macbeth wants to knock off Duncan, so what? And *Lord of the Rings* began to do the same thing to me. I couldn't identify within the situation. By the time I got a third of the way through the book, I wished Frodo would throw in the towel and put it all down to experience. It is extremely difficult to choose a book you haven't read. *War and Peace* I'd heard on the radio and enjoyed, but I was afraid to ask for it. I was in a bad state. I couldn't concentrate on the classics and at the same time, Tolkien didn't hold my interest either. The other book Biggie sent was much more sensible—a spy story set in Switzerland. It had everything I needed; the hero even got the girl. And on top of that, I thought, how could they let me have a spy book if they considered that I was a spy myself? It was a good sign. One tried to read omens into everything. At about this time the fat, bald warden came round, wearing his usual baggy shorts and medal ribbons.

'How are you?' he asked.

'Well, I've got some books now. Things aren't too bad.'

'I don't understand you. Not one of you says "Good morning". You don't know the complications you cause. You're such an ungrateful lot! Good morning.' And he closed the door. This to me, could only be taken as a good omen. So it's 'Good morning' from now on.

I couldn't put the spy book down. After reading it once, I went straight back into it again. I used the Shakespeare for my sugar. It had a polythene cover, so if the guard wanted the bowls out, I would tip the remaining sugar on the portrait of Shakespeare and as the day grew on I would dab my tongue at him and more of his face would appear with each lick till, sadly, he was complete and I had run out of sugar. It was an odd relationship, but his was the only face I had. When I gave *Everywoman* and the Afrikaans book back I was given two more, not quite such old ones. *The Sergeant* by Murray Murphy, which I thought brilliant and *Love is a Many Splendoured Thing*, which had a few pages missing.

When I see Biggie in two weeks' time I must try and get some books on anthropology or psychology. None of this is really any good to me. Half the books I want to read are banned and the other half I haven't heard of. I made up my mind to finish the Tolkien and try and do the Shakespeare tragedies; the comedies I just couldn't make anything of at all. I found the tragic Edwardian love stories much funnier. 'He was a brute but she loved him, loved him for his very brutality and superb animal strength.' And he was an Arab! There goes apartheid! I'd heard *Black Beauty* was banned —how on earth this one got through I don't know. I almost felt it was my duty to complain. I didn't like to reject Shakespeare but I realised I had bitten off more than I could chew. On the other hand, I almost felt they might test me on it, just as I felt they might test me on the bible. A dictionary would have been a better choice. I didn't know half the words. It defeated me. When I see Biggie next week, I'll ask for a dictionary and a book called *The Territorial Imperative*. I'd heard a lot about that one but I forget who wrote it. Even with quite ordinary words like 'vapid' and 'red-letter day', I didn't really know what they meant.

On rainy days we got exercise in the corridor which ran along the cells to the bathroom. There were two large fire-taps at each end and I walked between the two. The warders —two, sometimes three, but never one—would sit playing cards, smoking, fighting, or reading comics. Sometimes they would get Bonius to polish their shoes. I might walk thirty times the length of the corridor, which had twenty-five empty cells standing ready with their doors open waiting for the revolution, and in that time Bonius would have done only one toe-cap. He would kneel on the polished floor and do half a shoe in the time it took me to have a day's exercise. The guards would laugh and joke together, read, change their position, recross their legs and Bonius, I'm afraid, like a good dog, would never fail to follow the scent.

The two weeks are almost up. I've fired William S. and Tolkien's dead, finished. I never want to see him again. Biggie's my only hope. I'm in a rotten state. I had thought once I got books I'd be all right but I'm falling apart again. No sooner does one have something than one wants more.

Eventually Biggie came again and I went down to see him, not at the police station but in a small room in the jail.

'How are you? Better?'

'I don't know. Things haven't changed.'

'I know. They still won't tell me whether they're going to charge you or not.'

'Does that mean I might still be deported?'

'Well, they haven't actually suggested that. All they'll say is that they are coming to the end of their investigations.'

'They said that last year.'

'I know, but I wouldn't be discouraged about it. It doesn't help to get into a state. I've got another letter from your mother.'

There was a pause.

'Shall I go now?' I asked.

'No, there's no need to go yet. I thought you might like just to sit and talk.'

'I do, but, it's hard to know what to say.'

'Shall I say you seem a little better than when I saw you last?'

'I don't know.' I stood there.

'The books, how were they? Did you get the spy one? I thought you might like that.'

'Yes, I liked it very much. Thank you.'

'I gave Dave another by the same woman. She seems very good. Are there any other books I can get you?'

'I would like a dictionary.'

'Oh! Are you sure you'll find it interesting?'

'I need a dictionary. And a book called *The Territorial Imperative*. I don't know who wrote it, but I would like it, or—or a book on psychology or anthropology.'

'I'll see what I can do. Do you like travel books?'

'I've travelled a lot but I've never read travel books.'

'Tell me, have you been to Kuwait?'

'Yes. I sold my blood there.'

'Seems a little odd.'

I couldn't understand why he was asking me all those questions. Somehow I couldn't take in that this was a social visit and that he wanted to be friendly. I started to go out. 'Can I go now.'

'Well, I do have to see Dave but there's really no hurry. Tell me, is the food all right? What do you actually get?'

I explained what we got but I was sure that he knew already.

'Would you like me to bring you anything?'

'It's not important. I get enough.'

'No nuts or anything like that? I'll see what I can do. I'm sure I'll be able to get the books anyway and if I can't get that other one, what else?'

'The police talk a lot about G. K. Chesterton, short stories 1 think.'

'Yes, I see. Well, I'll get the police to look at the letter. I'll probably be able to see you again next week so do keep your spirits up. It's not much longer now.'

'Longer than what? Longer till what?'

'I can't say. I might know more next week.'

I plodded back to my cell. Another week. Two and a half months, and I still haven't a clue what they're up to. As always after a visit, it was hard to concentrate on reading. I had to walk and think. I couldn't understand why he had asked me about Kuwait.

Next day the books arrived. He'd managed to get *The Territorial Imperative*. After reading it for a bit I was glad I'd also got a dictionary. I dog-eared the pages for certain words that kept on recurring, like *amity, enmity* and *animosity*. I'd read *The Naked Ape* in Ireland. I remember I had hit a donkey on the head with it when it wouldn't get out of the way of the car. I thought now a lot of it had been cribbed from Ardrey's books, and my views on aggression expanded from this point on. Amity equals enmity plus hazard. Where hazard becomes very high enmity drops in proportion. I've always been accused of making dogmatic statements but I think on this occasion Ardrey wins hands down. I wasted a good four days on that. Maybe it wasn't entirely wasted. I might be able to use some of it. Being stuck in this position, one is vulnerable to ideas. I did tend to agree with him about many things. It was the first solid piece of writing that took me away from jail. Even when exercise came up, I was almost annoyed to leave it. On one occasion we went down to the yard and found it chock-a-block with African prisoners washing their clothes, scrubbing away on the flagstone.

'Don't worry,' I said to the guard. 'I don't really need exercise.'

'Oh, no. Just you hold on. My orders are to give you exercise.'

'But the yard's full. I can easily have it later.'

'No, stop worrying. This won't take a minute.'

I would have felt much better having it later but the guard, with obvious pleasure, whistled, then shouted a few words in Afrikaans and raised his right arm to point. Within seconds the whole place was cleared. Some, who were washing the only clothes they had, ran naked with the others into three small communal cells about twenty foot by ten, the centres of which were already piled with blankets. As they ran past, the guard conked them on the head with his bunch of keys. I realised now why Bonius always held his arm up. I tried not to look upset. It's all part of their system, not mine. When I'd finished my fifteen minutes I walked back past the ventilation grating and the heat poured out. They were packed like sardines. ('When hazard is high enmity drops proportionately.') At least half of these African prisoners would be there simply for breaking the pass laws, which, basically means, being in the wrong place at the wrong time. The whole pass system could be considered a hazard in Ardrey's sense.

Biggie came about a week later. His visit went much better this time. We did a lot of talking, and though the future seemed just as non-existent, I didn't mind so much. He said he would try and see me the next week but thought something might have happened by then. I'm certain he knew but felt it better not to tell me. He did make one slip, however.

'Don't worry, you won't be needing any more books.'

I went back to my cell and went on with my reading. Next week, is it? Well, next week I'll be twenty-six.

On my birthday, a Sunday, Bouwer came in with a big map of Johannesburg and asked me what certain marks on it were. I denied all knowledge of it and insisted on keeping my paws off it.

'If you want fingerprints, go and get someone else's.'

'And the dagga in the studio?'

'Haven't a clue.'

'Well, see you tomorrow.'

'Why's that?'

'We're taking you to Jo'burg.'

'What for?'

'Don't worry. You'll see.'

It must be deportation.

The next day after lunch Bouwer turned up.

'Everything ready?'

'Not quite. I need my case.'

As I packed my books, Bouwer said, 'Do you need the Shakespeare?'

'I can't really recommend it but you can certainly have it.'

'No, it's not for me. Martin wants it, actually.'

'What the hell does Martin want it for?'

'Oh, he's staying here.'

Why? I wondered.

We got into the car. I was put into the back and hand-cuffed to my suitcase. Well, at least I wouldn't lose it. The drive was quite pleasant, no hurry, nice and easy. Bouwer told me about his holiday. 'But I had to cut it short, Quentin, so much bloody work on. We're very busy, you see.' He paused and shook his head. 'Quentin, can I give you some advice?'

'Go ahead.'

'If you ever get to another country, don't bloody tell them how to run it.'

'When have I told you how to run it?'

'You haven't, but I'm warning you. You can't do it here. This is our country and always will be.'

At John Vorster Square police station I went through the usual signing in, money out, and followed the guard upstairs.

'One mattress and four blankets each.'

It was very good to be with people again. There were three men in the cell.

Someone asked me, 'What are you in for?'

'I think terrorism, but I haven't been charged yet.'

'Here, Jack! This bugger's in for terrorism. Remember?'

'Oh, yes, I read about you. Photographer.'

'Yes, a studio in Pritchard Street.'

'That's the one. Oh, I read a lot about you.'

'Well, what did it say?'

'Ah, Jesus, I forget.'

'It's a long time ago, before Christmas.' I paused. I did want to know. 'What's your problem?' I asked the big one.

'My problem? He's my problem,' with a jerk of his head towards Jack.

'Aw, knock it off, Bill.'

'Jesus, I didn't know you had a bottle.'

'But you bloody drank half of it before they came.'

'No, I didn't, True to God, I didn't.' He turned to me. 'You see I'm in the park and meet Jack and then the police came. He's so pissed he drops his bottle and here we are, put inside. True to God, I didn't drink any.'

'You're a bloody liar, Bill.'

'Aw, don't listen to him.'

'What will you do?' I asked Bill.

'Pay admission of guilt, ten rand. It's either that or a ten rand fine or ten days.'

'Well, that's not the end of the world.'

'No, it's not bad. What about you?'

'Well, I don't know, but I hope tomorrow either to be deported or charged. Anyway, something. I've been three months in solitary.'

'What do you mean, three months?'

'I mean three months.'

'Let me just tell Bill. Bill, wake up!' But there was no response. 'Aw, he's pissed. What was it like?'

'Doesn't matter any more. It's over.'

'Bet you're glad?'

'Oh, yes. It's good to meet you and Bill.'

'Bill's all right. He's just had a few too many. He's not bad, really.'

Next to come in were two very excited youths. One, wearing a leather jacket, was called François.

'My father's a millionaire. He'll get me out of this,' he said.

'What's all the blood in your hair?' I asked him.

'Where?' He ran his hand over his forehead. 'I didn't even know I was cut.'

'What actually happened?'

François stopped pacing and sat down on his mattress. 'Well, we'd been up at a friend's flat in Hillbrow and had a few smokes and then went on to see this other friend in hospital and something happened. They wouldn't let us in so I hit him and the police came.'

We talked for ages, then a guard came asking for François's friend. He got up, very excited and said, 'Don't worry, François. I'll return with some money.'

'I hope he does. I mustn't get stuck here.'

I talked to François. 'If I'd been awaiting trial like you,' I said, 'I'd have skipped the country.'

'I can't. The police have my passport.'

'Get another one.'

'I can't do that either. Interpol are after me.'

'What for?'

'A smuggling charge in France.' There was a pause. 'Look, I know what I'm doing. I can get ten years in France. Here, at most I'll get four, and if I have the choice between French prisons and South African prisons, I'd have South African any day. Let me tell you I've been in more prisons than I've had birthdays and the best is Pretoria Central.'

'What? The new one?'

'Yes, the new one.'

'Well, I've been there. First the Pretoria New and then Pretoria Old—that's the remand one—and I thought the worst was Pretoria New.'

'You must have been somewhere else, because they've got clubs, darts, billiards, football. You can even work if you're silly enough.'

'Work! God, I would do anything for work.'

'Look, if my friend doesn't come back, can you lend me five rand? Then I can pay admission of guilt.'

'We'll see if your mate comes back.'

He still had his watch, I saw, an expensive one, square and gold with a lizard-skin strap. He was built for the job, the absolute confidence man. I thought he deserved five rand.

'Hey, Quentin, if that guard comes back, we'll ask him if we can get your money. Is that all right?'

'I suppose so. I don't know what money is any more.'

'Good. Thanks. You have some sleep. I'll wake you if he comes.'

At three o'clock in the morning François woke me. 'Hey, I've got a guard. Where's your slip? You'll have to bring your slip.'

When I got up I found it was my old friend, the guard who had started his job on the day of my arrest.

'How are you?'

'Fine.'

'Where's your Australian friends?'

'I think they're still down in Pretoria.'

'Well, what's this about money?'

'Oh, yes, I want to lend François...'

'That's me.'

'Er, lend him some money.'

'All right. Let's do it now.'

We all walked down to the lifts. I took all my money out, re-signed the slip, gave five to François and we all went up again.

Morning came and a guard woke us. 'How many are there of you in there?'

'Four.'

'I can only see three.'

'One's asleep over there in the corner,' I explained. 'You won't be able to see him, he's in the corner behind the wall.'

'Bring him out.'

'I can't. He's asleep.'

'If I can't see him, it means there's only three.'

'Well, when he wakes up I'll tell him that.'

Over breakfast they all tried their hard-luck stories on me, and to cut a long story short, they cleaned me out between them. François's fine was twenty, so I gave him another five and Jack and Bill needed the rest.

Finally, after they had all left, the police came for me. I went down with them to get my case.

'What about your money, Quentin?' Ferrara asked.

'Oh, that. I've had it already. Spent the lot.'

Colonel Ferrara went purple. 'What do you mean? You can't have spent it, man. Where is it?'

'I didn't actually spend it. I lent it to some guys I was in with.'

Colonel Ferrara turned to the warder. 'Which of you buggers locked him up with other people? I bloody told you he was in solitary. Three months I had this guy in solitary and you bloody wreck the lot! Jesus, you can't leave a terrorist with the others. How did he get his money out? Terrorist's written on his bloody slip. Can't you read?'

'I wasn't on last night,' the guard said. 'Nobody told me he was a terrorist.'

The colonel turned to me. 'Why didn't you tell them?'

'Tell them what?' I thought he was going to scream.

'Jesus, man, get your case and get out of here.'

We went down to the ground floor, out, around, and in the express lift up to the dreaded tenth floor. The old man opened the steel door and I followed Ferrara into a room full of my equipment. They must have got it back from D.L. Studios where I had left it. Most odd. The colonel grabbed some papers and said, 'Come on. We're off.'

I followed him downstairs and into the street.

'Do you know that building, Quentin?'

'No, I can't say I do.'

'Well, you will soon. I can tell you that for nothing.'

We went up the steps into a hall. The notice on either side gave the show away. 'Courts 1-10 on the left, 11-20 on the right'.

'Now, do you know where you are?'

'Yes.' I nodded.

'Didn't I tell you you were in trouble, deep trouble?'

'Probably. You've told me so much crap I should think anything's quite likely.'

We walked down the hall and I saw François. 'Hi, how did it go?'

'I got off.'

'Who's that?' Ferrara snapped.

'Just the bloke I lent money to, that's all.'

'Get him. Here, you come with me,' he said to François.

'Sorry, I've got to go to the toilet.'

'Jesus, man, I'm a policeman.'

'Sorry, I can't hear you.' François was a little bit more agile than Ferrara.

'Don't worry, Quentin, I'll get him. You're more important at the moment.'

'I wouldn't bother. He's only a car thief, a fraud and what you would call a drug addict.'

'I'll get him later, don't worry.'

Halfway down on the right Ferrara signalled me to go down some stairs at the bottom of which was a vast great cell. There must have been about forty people in the large polished hall. Pairs of well-suited gentlemen marched up and down, hands in pockets, discussing something with great concentration. I slid my case over to a bench, sat down and just looked at the whole thing. A man, who looked about thirty, hobbled over and sat down beside me.

'What's up with your leg?' I asked.

'It's artificial. It needs adjustment.'

'Sorry. How did it happen?'

'I was a mercenary in the Belgian Congo.'

'What are you in for?'

'Nothing much really. Fraud. Forty thousand rand.'

'What's that worth?'

'Two years after remission and good behaviour.'

'First offence?'

'Well, let's put it this way, first in this country.'

'Twenty thousand pounds. How did you manage that?'

'Quite easy, really. When the boss went on holiday, I quickly signed a number of cheques to a company I own and transferred the money to England.'

'What did the boss say?'

'Oh, he didn't mind. I'd taken out an insurance policy for his company against fraud, so he doesn't lose a thing. It's the insurance company in London that's annoyed.'

'So, what went wrong?'

'Nothing.'

'Well, why are you here?'

'Gave myself up. It's the only sensible thing to do.'

'Why's that?'

'Well, if you give yourself up and plead guilty you only get three years and you get a third off for remission and good behaviour.'

'So?'

'I've just made £20,000 tax free in two years. What are you in for?'

'I don't really know. I haven't been charged yet. I'm hoping to be deported.'

'Why's that?'

'It's a long story. Three months ago I was arrested for having subversive material in my studio, so they clapped me in jail. Been in solitary ever since.'

'Oh, yes, the photographer from Pritchard Street. Excuse me, let me just tell my friends.'

I went over to buy some chocolate from a black girl on the other side of the bars and when I got back to my bench, quite a crowd had gathered. They all seemed to be English accountants, like the man I had been talking to.

'Congratulations,' another one said, 'it's very good to see you. Glad you came through.'

'It was nothing. I haven't done anything.'

'No, no. Your case is going to be the main subject of conversation for weeks. Isn't that right?'

There was a chorus of agreement.

I was so excited by this contact with people that I completely forgot my own court appearance and then suddenly my name was called.

'Good luck,' several people said.

'Thanks. I'll be seeing you. Goodbye.'

A young guard led me round to a door under the court. 'Wait in there till the other door opens, then go up when it does.'

It was a little like a race, my heart pounding away waiting for the door to open. Minutes passed. Come on, let me go. The door opened at last. We're off, up the stairs with my case to a very poor start. The case is too big for the stair, I'll have to hold it in front of me. The noise upstairs was unbearable. Finally I made it, exhausted, frightened shaking. The court was packed. A man came over and said in a rush, 'I'm Zimerman, your solicitor. Just sit down and shut up.'

'Yes. Do I have to do anything?'

'No. When the judge comes in, just stand up and shut up. Is that clear?'

'Yes.'

I was absolutely speechless, anyway. Down both sides of the court were Press people, looking at my dirty shirt and my long hair, all madly taking notes.

'That's the judge. Get up!' Zimerman said.

'I am up.'

'Well, shut up.'

I looked round gulping. Then a big, fat man in a black gown started speaking.

'I now charge Mr Quentin Charles Bulow Jacobsen, aged 26, a European male, formerly of 57 Pritchard Street, Johannesburg, the Transvaal, under Section 2 of the Terrorism Act number 83 of 1967 and alternate counts under Section 11 of the Suppression of Communism Act, No. 44 of 1950 and Section 12 of the Suppression of Communism Act No. 44 of 1950.'

Mr Zimerman asked where I would be detained pending

the trial and the prosecutor, Mr van Lieris, said, 'At the Johannesburg Fort.'

And that was that. Notebooks were snapped shut and people rushed out.

Zimerman came up to me. 'Go back down there. Biggie and I will see you later.'

CHAPTER ELEVEN

Down in the depths below the court I met Mr Zimerman again with Biggie. Zimerman was a short, square, energetic man with grey hair and a strong South African accent.

'Don't worry,' he said. 'On the face of it it's not too bad. The mere fact that they've charged you on three counts means they're not certain of the main count.'

We walked into a small room with just three chairs and a table. I wanted to say to him that I was entirely in his hands, that I respected his position, and that I really did have a great respect for the law. I wanted to say 'Please help me and I'll do anything.' But I didn't somehow get the chance—

Biggie interrupted. 'What I don't understand Mr Zimerman, are these sections. I was in on the Dean's case. Tell me, is this under the same sections of the Act?'

Zimerman answered him pretty brusquely, 'I think so. I don't really care. What I want to know is what really happened. Why are you charged?'

It was a bad beginning. I was still suffering from the shock of the crowded courtroom and I really didn't know who he was.

'All I did was to take a couple of books into South Africa. One was the *Anarchist Cookbook* and the other was a *US Army Handbook on Sabotage and Demolition*.'

'Yes, but I'm telling you they wouldn't just charge you under Terrorism for bringing in a couple of banned books. I want you to be as objective as possible. I'm not here to give sympathy. I'm here to find out what your case is really about.'

Biggie interrupted again.

'Please Mr Biggie. This is my client. Will you shut up for a moment?'

Biggie went back to filling his pipe.

'Now, Quentin, tell me, why have the police arrested you?'

'It's just these two books.'

'No, it can't just be that.' He became quite angry. 'It must be something else as well. What is it?'

I felt terrified. I hadn't been introduced to this man, he didn't get on with Biggie, and now I thought he was trying to fix me.

'I don't know.'

'But you must know. They wouldn't charge you on the books alone.'

'I haven't done anything.'

'That's not the point. I've been a lawyer in this country for almost forty years, and I know you must have done something.'

'I haven't done anything.' We looked at each other. 'Anyway I don't care what they do to me so long as I'm not left in solitary any longer.'

Zimerman smiled. 'Well, don't worry. That's over. You're now an "awaiting-trial" prisoner like any other at the Fort.'

'What . . . what if I'm found guilty?' I managed to say.

Zimerman smiled. 'The court's in two months' time. There's no hurry. There will be plenty of time to talk about it. I don't think they would hang you over a couple of books but I'm afraid the least they could give you is five years without remission or anything.'

'Five years?'

'Five years, but, judging by what you say, it looks very easy money to me.'

I couldn't make out if he was trying to be funny or not.

'Look, I've got another case this afternoon,' he went on. 'I'll see you tomorrow afternoon. Don't talk about the case to anyone, and from now on it will be all right. You'll be just like any other prisoner.'

'Yes, I understand.'

Biggie asked if he could give me some letters or if they should go to the prison authorities. Zimerman closed his briefcase.

'Come with me. The court sergeant out here is someone I've known for years. I'll ask him to read them first.'

We all left the room together. Zimerman talked to the sergeant and they laughed together. The sergeant read the letters, though I wasn't convinced that he could actually read, then nodded to me to take them.

'I'll see you tomorrow afternoon then,' Zimerman said, 'or,

if I can't manage it, Thursday. All right? So don't talk about the case with anyone. Understand? See you Thursday.' And he left.

Biggie said, 'Look, if Zimerman's coming on Thursday, I'll see you on Friday. Is that all right?'

'Fine,' I said, adding to myself. 'I'll be sure to be in.'

When he had gone, I was led back into the big hall again where the other prisoners were.

'Well? Well? What happened?' The group of accountants surrounded me.

'I got charged, not deported.'

'Under what?'

'Terrorism and Communism.'

'Oh, I am sorry. But don't worry. You'll be able to tell us all about it.'

'No, I can't. My lawyer says I'm not to talk about it.'

The man who had done the talking laughed and said, 'Who is he?'

'Small, grey-haired bloke called Zimerman.'

'Never heard of him. Where's the case coming up?'

'Johannesburg. Supreme Court. March 20th.'

'Well, if it's the Supreme Court, you'll need an advocate as well.'

'What does that cost?' I asked.

'A good one like mine costs between 150 and 200 rand a day and then you've still got your lawyer's costs on top of that.'

'And how much are they?'

'The same, sometimes less. Depends how good he is.'

'So that's at least 300 rand a day.'

'I know. You see, Terrorism in the Supreme Court, that doubles the price straight away.'

'Well, I don't have that sort of money. I could do about 1,500. That would be what? Five days. How long do you think a case like that would last?'

'It depends. If you've got the money, you can try and break down the witnesses. But it takes time. How many witnesses do you think there will be?'

'I don't know. Martin, Dave, possibly Ian and maybe the two Africans. I really don't know.'

We went on talking about lawyers and I found myself saying, 'I'm not very happy with mine.'

'Oh, why's that?'

'He looks, oh, I don't know, he looks like a policeman.'

'I wouldn't worry. He's probably all right.'

'Is the Fort that jail up near Hillbrow?' I asked.

'That's the one. If they don't collect us soon we'll miss dinner. There it goes!'

The gate opened and I followed through with the others up some stairs and along to a grey truck, past the driver and his mate, who counted us as we went in. The door was padlocked and bolted and we were off.

Eventually someone said, 'Well, here we are! Home, sweet Home.'

The inside of the Fort is very different from the outside. From the road all one sees are grassy slopes with vast beautiful cactuses and a few guards with rifles patrolling the top. It could almost be a Middle Eastern embassy or the private residence of some crank. But the inside has castellations, dripping tunnels and wooden floors. It is, in fact, a 'protected' monument but the people who 'protect' historic buildings obviously never live in them. None of the cells had water or lavatories. All in all it was a little like Colditz; we even had our tin-leg man.

I was given a blue card with a number and we all went on to the next department. We all stood in a line and laid our luggage out in front. Mine consisted of my case and a comb. Most of the others had brought stocks of tobacco and boxes of matches but all I had was my comb. They checked through my case, liked the photos, called a few other guards out to have a look. One of them said, 'Better check for porn.'

'I'm in on a Terrorism charge and I've been in for three months already. I have no porn.'

'Where are all your cameras and stuff?'

'The police have got them. Look, I don't want the case in my cell. Can you look after it?'

'Yes. We wouldn't let you have it anyway.'

I gave them the case and walked in. The building is two storeys high. Prisoners were swarming everywhere, running back and forth with buckets and tins. I wandered around till I found an empty cage. There were about five corridors each with a good twenty cells and I suppose the same number upstairs. The cages were about seven feet high, seven feet long and four wide. Inside was a bucket, a three-quarter inch felt mat and four blankets.

'Lock up in five minutes,' someone shouted. 'If you want supper you'd better hurry up.'

'I haven't a plate or a spoon or anything.'

'Ask in the office. They'll give you them.'

I rushed over to the office and managed to get an old coffee-tin and ran to a door where someone was serving soup. He put some in my tin and I ran back to my cell.

'All right, everybody in. Inspection and lock-up in two minutes.'

Two minutes. Must get something to read.

'Hey, you! Have you got anything I could read?'

'Do you want this?'

'What is it?'

'Magazine. It's got Liz Taylor and Richard Burton's romance.'

'Fine.'

The bulb was on the ceiling, a few feet above the wire-mesh roof of the cage so that the light broke up into a pattern of shadows.

'Lock up!'

Everybody rushed round and got into their own cells. The warder went down my side slamming all the doors and then up the other. With the door shut the cell is bloody small; the bucket stinks and the light is so poor I don't think one can do much reading. I shouted to the man across the corridor:

'What time do they open up?'

'Six.'

'Then what?'

'Breakfast.'

'And then?'

'Well, you're out till eight then locked up till ten. Out again till twelve then lunch, locked up till two, out again till four or four-thirty.'

'So that you're locked up for roughly six hours a day and twelve hours a night.'

'That's right. Eighteen hours.'

I said good-night.

Waking up was a very slow process. Sounds first of coughing and other prisoners going to the lavatory, then of conversation. About an hour later when everyone was yapping like mad, the doors opened up. For half an hour you cleaned the cell, which means rolling up your mat and putting your four folded blankets on top. There should be two small pieces of old blanket left in the cell which you put under your feet and skate around, generally with your hands in your pockets, doing the floor. It doesn't do the floor much good but it does give you an opportunity to meet people, since the door is open and you do the corridor outside your cell as well.

After that we joined a long queue for breakfast. This part was very civilised—a dollop of porridge, lump of bread, piece of butter, some sugar and coffee. The sun was out and many of the men had their shirts off. I met Tin-leg.

'Sleep well?'

'Not too bad. And you?'

'Fine. Where are you?'

'I'm in the third corridor on the right.'

'Well, after breakfast I'll turf one of my lads out and you can come into our corridor. All English in our lot, none of these foreigners.'

I finished my porridge, which was nice and hot for a change. All the benches were full so I sat in an empty sink. Tin-leg ate from the next one. I liked this—no hurry and plenty of people.

I chatted to another Englishman. He was in for car theft and the usual fraud. When I said I was in for Terrorism he said, 'What do you want to do that for? I shouldn't think there's much money in it.'

'No,' I said, 'you're right there. I used to be a photographer. Good money in that.'

'Plenty of skirt too?'

'Yes, plenty of skirt.'

My name was called. I was wanted at the office. There the warder told me I was going over to D Group.

'What's D Group?'

'Hard Labour.'

'Well, as long as it's not solitary, I don't mind anything.'

But when I came back I was told there had been a change of plan. I was to go for a medical first. I didn't like this. I could smell a rat.

'All right. Follow me.'

There were about ten of us. We followed him over to the medical examination room and waited outside. There was a big palm tree in the middle of the courtyard and lots of cats wandering around. Eventually a small Turkish-looking doctor staggered up to the door. He wetted his moustache as he walked by. I felt rather sorry for him; even the guards joked, 'Pissed again'.

I was first in line.

'What are you in for?'

'Terrorism, sir.'

'It must be Terrorism and Communism. You can't be done for one without the other. Any peculiarities? Any problems? Any complaints?'

'Yes sir, my teeth hurt.'

'I'm afraid I'm not a dentist. You'll have to wait for that. And get your hair cut. I don't like seeing prisoners with long hair. It's dirty.'

'Yes, sir. But are you sure I'm allowed to?'

'I'll bloody well make you. Now is there anything else?'

'I do occasionally suffer from a collapsed lung. And in the last jail I tried to commit suicide. These are the marks on my arm and wrist.'

He looked at them cursorily. 'Well, they seemed to have healed quite well.'

I made no comment.

'Put your trousers on and tell the next one to come in.'

I went out and called the next one in. Then I told the guard I must have a haircut. Doctor's orders.

'No, you don't. He's a bit of a drinker, our doctor.'

'But I want a haircut.'

'Well, when you're over in D group, you can.'

When the last prisoner had been checked, we made our way back to the Awaiting Trial group. There I was given my case and escorted to D Group. I felt as though I were going to the gas chamber. I wasn't told I was going back to solitary, just that I was going to Hard Labour, but I knew there was a catch. We went through a kitchen and across a hall where other prisoners were doing a slow waltz with bits of blanket under their feet. They all looked like Biggles characters. In D Group they wear prison clothes and look like POWs. They were passing cigarettes to each other as they slogged around.

The warder called me in.

'Jacobsen, what are these photographs? Did you steal them or something?'

'No, I'm a photographer, I took them myself.'

'They're very good. I like them. These must stay here in the office. The rest of your clothes you can have in your cell.'

I didn't need to ask how many others were in my cell.

'You're very lucky. We managed to get you a room to yourself.'

'I don't want a room to myself.'

'I can't do anything about that. If you want to see the boss he'll be here tomorrow afternoon.'

'Look, I've been in solitary for almost three months. I can't do any more.'

'This is not solitary. It's solitary when you are on Spare Diet. This is not Spare Diet. I've been told to do this for your own safety. You can ask the boss tomorrow.'

'My lawyer said I'd be like any other prisoner now.'

'Get this clear. I can't do anything. It's no use complaining to me.'

'I don't want to go. *Please* don't leave me alone again.' I was desperate and showing it. 'Please, I'll polish floors. I'll do any sort of work. But not solitary.'

'I can't help it. This is not solitary. It's for your own safety.'

My new cell, twelve by ten, had three tomb-stone shapes painted on the floor, I suppose to show where mats should be spread. I unrolled mine on the last one, and wished I wasn't alone.

CHAPTER TWELVE

The next day my name was called and I was told I had a visitor. I dashed over to get into my trousers, shoes and socks. The warder closed the door behind him and I followed him down. At the bottom of the stairs he had to call another guard to open the door. Then through the kitchen, outside along by the castellated wall and left into a small room where Zimerman was waiting for me. My guard was more excited than I was and even asked for his autograph. When he'd finally gone, I asked Zimerman what their conversation in Afrikaans was all about.

He smiled. 'A good many years ago I was a Springbok Rugby player and that guard you've just seen, well, he and some other club members are starting up a museum and they want me to autograph old photographs of the team for them.'

'How did I actually get you?'

'Well, Quentin, it's like this. Dave's father flew over here. He asked his company's solicitor to handle it but you know what those big firms are. As soon as they heard it was a political charge they wouldn't touch it.'

'So what happened?'

'They rang around town and eventually got me. Nobody else wanted it.'

Most encouraging.

'I must start by saying I've never been in court before,' I said. 'I haven't a clue what happens.'

'Well, what I always say to my clients is, in the words of my old teacher, "A lawyer is like a taxi." You hire me and you fire me. And if you want to change taxis when you're halfway there, why that's fine by me.'

He sat there with a big grin on his face. He was certainly a character. Then he pulled out a big, clean notebook, suspiciously like a police one. 'I want you to remember everything you told the police, everything, you understand. Now how did it begin?'

'It began—it began very much like this, only there were two interrogators, not one, and they sat, just as you are sitting, across a table. One would ask questions and the other would write.'

'Yes, and what did they write?' Zim grinned widely.

'Well, for the first forty-eight hours I told a pack of lies. I said the books belonged to Henry.'

'Who's Henry?'

'Henry's my twin brother. He's in London.'

'Double trouble,' and another big grin.

'Then in the next interrogation they said that was a load of rubbish and they knew I brought the books in. They knew everything. I couldn't tell them anything they didn't know already.'

'Well, tell me about the books.'

'The books were about explosives and how to make bombs?'

'Did the police ever ask you how to make bombs?'

'Yes.'

'And what did you say?'

'I told them.'

His face screwed up and I thought he would explode. He hit the table with his fist.

'Listen. Listen very hard. If anyone asked me how to make a bomb, I would say "I don't know and I don't want to know".'

'Yes, but I do know,' I said softly.

He hit the table again.

'You're not bloody listening, Quentin. I was in the army and I still don't know how to make a bomb. Now, I'll ask you again. How do you make a bomb?'

'I think you get some fuse and then...'

Zimerman shouted, 'No, no. You bloody well don't. You're not listening, Quentin.'

'But I don't understand what you're trying to do. You start saying one thing and then something else completely different. I think you're horrible. For one thing, you said I'd be just like any other prisoner. Well, I'm not. I'm still in bloody solitary. You told me to say nothing in court but I'm going to be stuck in solitary. I just don't want to live any more. I wanted to ask the judge if I'd still be in solitary if I was charged.'

'OK, Quentin. I'm sorry.'

'You're not sorry. You hit the table and shout at me. I've had enough. And as for your cab-driver, I don't want a cab-driver. I want a friend.'

'Look, really I didn't know you were still in solitary. I'm sorry.'

Well, I am and I can't think. I haven't got a chance.'

His expression changed. For the first time he looked concerned. 'I tell you what. Let's go and see the Commandant and see why you're still in solitary. Come, blow your nose. Here's a hanky and we'll go and see the boss. All right?'

'And you promise not to shout?'

'I'm sorry. I won't shout any more. I promise.'

I pulled myself together and we went round to the main office. There all the lettering above the doors was in German script and they had pictures of past Führers on the wall. Zim spoke to the Commandant first.

'This is my client, Quentin Jacobsen. He tells me he has been put in solitary. He's already been in solitary for three months. I can't have proper access to my client when he's in this state.'

'I'm sorry, but he's not in solitary.'

'He's just told me he is.'

'I'm in a room on my own and I'm exercised alone,' I broke in.

'That's not solitary. Solitary is when a prisoner is on Spare Diet.'

'If a man's in a cell on his own, surely he's in solitary,' Zimerman said.

'No, he's not. Solitary means when he's on Spare Diet, rice water. He gets food like any other prisoner. He's not on Spare Diet.'

Zimerman began to shout again but this time I didn't mind. The argument finished with Zim and me storming out of the office.

'It's not finished. I'll do everything I can. You have certain rights as a prisoner and one of these is legal access and if you're in a state where I can't get your confidence, then you're not getting proper legal representation. I'm seeing the Attorney-General in Pretoria about the possibility of bail. I'm not hopeful but I'll try, and I'll ask about solitary too.'

'Try anything you can. And can you get me some food? Fruit or biscuits?'

'Certainly, and I'll get you books too. We're not finished. You'll be all right, so don't worry.'

'What do I do now?'

'Well, it's almost four. I've got to go now but I'll ring the consul before he comes tomorrow and I'll get him to bring something to eat.'

We went back to the office and he got his briefcase. And I went back with the guard to my cell. That night was hard.

Next morning while it was still dark, I heard the warder come upstairs. I got up immediately and had a look out of the window. It was not quite pitch black. It must be shower time. I always tried to have my blankets folded before he opened the door. In this jail you put your plate on the bucket and took the lot downstairs. I emptied the bucket and washed the plate and was given a razor.

'I don't think I'm supposed to have a razor.'

'You've got to have a razor.'

'But I don't know that I want it.'

The guard didn't understand, and once in the shower room I could see why. Littered everywhere were used razor blades. Well, I thought, while I'm at it, I might as well cut my hair. The guard saw me and said, 'No need to do that. We've got a good barber in Hard Labour.'

After breakfast the guard opened up and I went down for my haircut. A young prisoner with very short hair was standing holding a pair of scissors.

'How do you want it?'

'I want to look as normal as possible, sort of short back and sides.'

'And the parting?'

'Put it on the left.'

He started snipping away. I wanted to talk.

'Have you read *Lord of the Rings*?'

'What's it about?'

'It's a sort of fairy story. Do you want it? It's pretty big.'

'No, I don't think I do.'

'What are you in for?'

'Fraud.'

Later Biggie came in to see me.

'I heard from Zimerman ... sorry, but your hair's quite different.'

'Yes, I know, but the court's in two months. It will have grown again by then.'

'I heard from Zimerman that you're still in solitary. I am sorry about that. Shall we go to the Commandant?'

'I don't know if it will do any good.'

'Well, I think we should at least try.'

I had to admire Biggie's courage. He and I stood in the Commandant's office while he took out great textbooks on the definition of 'Solitary'.

'I only do it for the prisoner's safety,' the Commandant repeated.

'Well, he says he's got a razor in his cell.'

'I can't help that.'

'But he tried to commit suicide in Pretoria. Don't you think it's a little odd to leave him in solitary with a razor?'

'I've told you, it's not solitary. You've seen the books.'

'All right. If you can't understand me, who's above you?'

'There is no-one above me. I'm in charge of all the prisoners here.'

Biggie and I just looked at each other with a how-on-earth-did-he-get-the-job expression and walked out.

'Not much else we can do. It's been raised already in the English parliament. I've done all I can.'

'I know. It's only two months till court. I'll just have to hold out till then.'

'Well, perhaps papers will help, and letters and food.'

I couldn't reply. I just shook his hand and walked back with the guard.

Half an hour later, Biggie's parcel arrived, with coffee, sugar, condensed milk, biscuits—savoury ones at that—and a good old English *Sunday Times*. News, even last year's, was fascinating.

On the Monday I saw Zim again. He seemed a little surprised.

139

'You know, they've let Dave out.'

'No! Fantastic! Who's left in?'

'Martin, Seadom and Buki. I think Martin's to be a state witness. I don't know about the others. It seems to me that Martin's to be the problem. Does that sound logical to you?'

'Seadom knows more, but he's a stronger man. Martin, well, Martin's got a degree in maths. He's not so physical as Seadom. Have you got the charge sheet yet?'

'No, no charge sheet. I've been told I'll get it in a month's time. I've asked for the interrogation notes from the police. It'll save a lot of time and I can get some idea of what they think you've done. Let's talk about those books. If the judge asks you what was in them, what would you say?'

'I would say ... I would say ... I would say, "I can't remember." '

'Well, do you know what I would say? "My Lord. I haven't read these books." '

I bit my lip and repeated, 'My Lord, I haven't read these books.'

'Now, Quentin, listen. If the judge asks you, "Why did you bring these books to South Africa?" '

'Why did I bring them to South Africa?'

'Yes, why?'

'Shall I deny it?'

'No. How can you? What about fingerprints?'

'It's a difficult question.'

'I know. But it's important. Now I want to go over the arrival. What happened, right from the start? You know: why did you come to South Africa? Everything.'

'Why did I come to South Africa? I've been thinking a lot about that. I think it started in Ireland. I was staying at a friend's place in Galway and I borrowed a book called *The Autobiography of Malcolm X.*'

'Yes?'

'Well, I read it.'

'So what? I've read it too. It's a silly book.'

'In a way, but I was influenced a lot by it.'

'And then what?'

'Well, after I had gone back to England I had quite a lot of work on, and I met Martin Cohen.' Zim looked up. 'I met him at a party and asked him if he would like to work for me. There was a lot of work and I needed an assistant. Then when my twin brother Henry came back from India I asked Martin to go because I wanted Henry to take over.'

'Does Henry know any photography?'

'No, not then, but neither did Martin.'

'Go on.'

'Well, Martin went off on holiday and Henry and I went on with the work in London but things tightened up a bit there so we decided to go to Paris.'

'When was that?'

'About November 1970. While we were in Paris, one evening Henry and I and another photographer friend, Tony Horth and his girl-friend, and a French photographer and his girl, a South African model called Claudia Duxbury...'

'Yes, I know the girl you mean.'

'Well, we all went to the cinema to see an old American film called *Wild River*.'

'And?'

'It's a bit odd, but while I was watching the film I had a "vision".'

'I'll write it down but I don't think it was a vision. And?'

'It told me I should come to South Africa to help the black man.'

Zim put down his pen and looked at me.

'Did I say something wrong?'

'I don't know yet. Go on.'

'This thing, the "vision", was so strong I was certain the others must have felt it too, so ...'

'Hold it. I'm not up with you.' Zim was scribbling away. It looked totally illegible to me. 'And?'

'And so I lent the book to the model, Claudia, to see if she'd had any ... any idea like mine.'

'You mean "vision"?'

'Yes, vision. Anyway I told her I thought of going to South Africa and waited for her reply.'

'Well.'

'She didn't reply. She hadn't ever thought of going back to South Africa.'

'Hold it. Let me finish.'

'So I tried my brother. I asked him if he would like to come, and he said he would.'

'What does your brother do?'

'He used to be a student at LSE, that's the...'

'I know, the London School of Economics.'

'Then he got kicked out of there and went to Leicester.'

'Where were you when he was at University?'

'I was in Australia. Then I came back and did a year at Guildford School of Art.'

'So, it's Christmas 1970.'

'Yes. Then sometime in January I met Martin again and asked him if he would like to come and he said he would. He sold all his cameras and things and joined us. About two weeks before we were due to leave, Martin introduced us to Dave who'd been at school with him in Sydney, and Dave decided to come as well. I suppose our original reason for coming was to try to make a film about conditions in South Africa and possibly to train a black photographer to help shoot stuff in the Homelands.' I waited till Zim finished his line. 'But, after being here for four months, I was convinced that a film would have no effect, so I went back to London to try and get money for, shall we say, "research" into sabotage methods. I approached the ANC and asked to see Dr Dadoo.'

'Don't worry. I know about Dadoo. You don't have to explain. Has he still got his pipe?'

'Yes. Anyway, they weren't interested, so I bought some books that Aziz of ANC recommended, the two the police have got, and flew back to Jo'burg. Seadom, Buki, Henry and I wanted to print the books and distribute them, but Martin and Dave were against it, so I left it because there had been a bit of a rift in the studio and they were leaving anyway. Then we got busted a week before they were due to go. I feel sorry for them.'

'I wouldn't feel sorry for them. They're going to run you down, I can tell you. And Henry?'

'Henry left to go back to England on the 25th of October to see a girl-friend, a week before we were busted.'

When he had finished writing, Zim thought for a bit and said, 'Well, it doesn't seem much. I'm sure there must be more than this. Do you know why you brought the books?'

'I've thought about it. Shall we say for "kicks"?'

'The judge wouldn't understand that. Go on thinking about it. Now, what was this rift between Martin and Dave on the one hand and the studio on the other? They were part of the studio weren't they?'

'Well, in a way we had two studios. One was the photographic studio, the other was our organisation, if you can call it that, to help the Blacks. We'd felt it was safer to refer to this side of our interest simply as the other studio, Studio, in quotes, as opposed to studio without quotes. Its principles were to be the advancement of democracy, equality and liberty for South Africans.'

Zim grinned. 'Didn't get you very far, did it?'

'I know. If anything we've gone backwards, not forwards.'

'Who was in this second "studio"?'

'Originally, just the four of us from England—that's Dave and Martin and Henry and me. Then we met Seadom and Buki and Ian Hill—Seadom, a black student, at Wits University and Buki at a play called "Puri". Ian Hill's a medical student at Wits.'

'I did my law degree at Wits.'

'Good place. We used to go to the cinema there, all of us together.'

'Did you ever talk about politics?'

'No.'

'I just can't believe that Quentin. I'm sorry.'

'Well, we did talk about what we could do here.'

'And?'

'Well, one of us might have mentioned sabotage as a hypothetical idea.'

Zim took off his glasses. 'I know. This is very common. I've said it myself. "If change does not come soon in South Africa, then violence is inevitable." I've said it myself. It's not illegal.'

'The police said it was.'

'Don't worry about what they said. I'll tell you what's legal or illegal. That's what I'm paid for.'

I thought for a moment then asked, 'Do you think I've got a chance?'

'Judging by what you tell me, I think the police have got

a very slim chance. But I don't think you're telling me everything.'

'It's very hard, because I don't know the law. I don't know what your duty is.'

'I'm here only in your interest.'

'But if I tell you everything, are you under an obligation to repeat it?'

'Yes, but we can interpret it as we think it best suits our client. I'm here only in your interest. Now, you may talk about sabotage but, in a sense, your film would have been sabotage wouldn't it? I mean it was designed to discourage foreign investment and hence sabotage our country financially, wasn't it?'

'I see what you mean.'

'Look, I've got to go now. I'll see you on Thursday. Think about what I've said. All right?'

'Yes, I will. And don't forget the milk and some fruit.'

'No, I won't forget.'

CHAPTER THIRTEEN

'Jacobsen, visitor!'

I got ready. The door was opened and I went down. I couldn't think who it could be. I soon found out. Colonel Ferrara and another policeman were waiting for me.

'What have you done with your hair, man?' Ferrara said.

'What does it look like?'

'It looks like the newspaper photo of Henry.'

'That's what I want.'

It didn't please them at all.

'Here, we've got a letter for you.'

'Can I have the stamps?' the other policeman said.

'Yes, take the stamps.' What a bunch of overgrown kids!

'You see, we're not so bad, are we?'

'What do you want?'

'Well, we've just found some addresses on your presscard. What we want to know is, did you ever contact the ANC from here?'

'Do you really think I would tell you?'

'We're only asking.'

'I don't know where you get the nerve. I was your prisoner for three months.'

'Well, we've only just found out.'

'I don't have to answer you. You know that.'

'We're trying to be friendly.'

'Friends like you, I don't need. Keep the stamps.'

'See you in court.'

When Zim came I told him about this.

'They can ask you but you don't need to answer. If they come again try to be polite but don't tell them anything. And don't write anything down that might incriminate you.'

'Fine.'

'I've brought you milk and stuff, so you'll be all right for the weekend. Now let's get down to interrogation. This model, Claudia. She's an attractive girl, isn't she?'

'Well, sort of. Bit overweight.'

'Now, I'll tell you this. It was her that attracted you to South Africa. Not the book, or the film. They've got nothing to do with it. It was the girl.'

'I don't quite understand.'

'Look: this "vision" ... it's a silly word for whatever it was. If you tell the judge you have a vision, he won't understand. Now, as I see it, you went to the cinema with an attractive model and during the film you thought that if all South African girls were like this, it must be a good place to go to.'

'But they're not.'

'That's not the point, quite apart from the fact that it's rude. Listen! If you use words like "kicks" and "vision", the judge will think you're mad. You've got to make him understand what kind of person you are and that it was just a lot of silly nonsense talk, that's all.'

'So. So I never had a vision.'

'Of course not. It was the girl. Do you understand?'

'But what if they call her as a witness?'

'I don't think they will. She's abroad, but if they do, what does she know?'

'Nothing.'

'Do you understand now?'

'Yes, I think I do. I'm beginning to get the hang of it.'

'Good. What do you think the other witnesses are likely to say? Seadom? Buki? Ian Hill?'

'I think Ian Hill might say I intended to print the books up and distribute them.'

'If he does, what will you say?'

' "I don't remember".'

'No, never say that, because then the prosecution will say, "So it's possible". Listen! If you don't remember, you don't know, and if you don't know, then say, "I deny that".'

'Yes, but what I always feel about "I deny that" is that it sounds as though you're refusing to accept that it might have happened. I would prefer to say something like, "It's outrageous" or "Why would I want to do that?" '

'It's a good point, but you're not allowed to ask questions. You must answer their questions. Now, if the prosecutor says,

"Why should the witness lie in his statement?" what will you say?'

I had a mental image of Raquel Welch on a television interview.

'How about, "We're just good friends"?'

Zim smiled. 'Well, I hope that you are, but—I tell you, I think that you'll be very disappointed.'

'Why?'

'Well, for a start, when a Black sells out, he really sells out.'

'I think you're wrong. I think Martin will be the difficult one, not Seadom or Buki.'

'Quentin, I've been a lawyer for getting on for forty years and I hope you're right, but plain, bloody experience tells me you're wrong.'

'We'll see.'

'I think you will be amazed what people will say against you. If I've seen it once, I've seen it a dozen times. They'll try and drag you through the gutter.'

'No, I've got a lot of faith in them, especially Seadom and Buki.'

'You know, anyone in their position begins to agree with police suggestions just in order to please their captors. It's impossible for them to be objective, and you must remember that. Now, what do you think Seadom might say?'

'Well, I'm hoping that Seadom won't say anything, but he might if he was pushed to it. He might say that we intended to blow up the Modderfontein Dynamite Factory.'

'But that's ridiculous.'

'Yes, I know, but he might still say it.'

'But you haven't even been out there.'

'Well, I have actually.'

'Why didn't you tell me?' He was waving his arms about again.

'I'm trying to.' I paused. 'But if you're the only cab in town, I don't want to get dumped somewhere out in the sticks.'

'Boy, I won't dump you, but I can't take you anywhere until I know how far you've come already. I've got to know everything.'

'Well,' I said, 'shall we start with Modderfontein?'

'I think we must.'

'It was after I had been back to London. A cigarette campaign came up and I needed some glass props made. I didn't know any glass-blowers, so when a photographic rep came into the studio, I asked him if he knew any. He said, "You need my friend Mr Meerholt out at African Explosives."' I was repeating this like a record, I'd told it so often to the police.

'So?'

'I rang him first and then Dave and I went out to see him. Henry was still in Swaziland at the time. We took the combi and drove out. I saw Meerholt, ordered up the glass had a look round and drove back to the studio. Then about a week later I rang and was told the glass was ready, so I went out with Henry. This time Henry had a camera with him and took some photographs which he's got with him in London.'

'What were they of?' Zim asked apprehensively.

'I didn't take them, but I could guess.'

'No, don't tell me. I don't want guesses. If you don't know, please don't guess.'

'And then a couple of weeks later we all went out there to a party at a friend of Seadom's, the Laymans' party.'

'Who's "we all"?'

'Henry, Seadom, Buki, two other Blacks, one of them a girl, and me.'

'Did you tell the police about that?'

'Oh, yes, they loved that.'

'I bet they did. Anyway, go on.'

'After that we went on to another party at Four Ways but we couldn't find it so we drove the Africans back to Soweto.'

'How many times have you been to Soweto?'

'Enough to know it's good fun. Henry practically lived out there.'

'What else could Seadom say?'

'He might try and say I planned to blow up the bus sheds and buses, and the pass office, and the telephone exchange. He might say—I took photographs of these places, as well as various bridges in Jo'burg and Pretoria.'

'Well, did you?'

'No. The police think I have but, in view of the fact that

148

I've been arrested, I think Henry did, not me.'

'Where are the shots now?'

'At home in London.'

'You're positive?'

'Absolutely. I took them to London myself. I also took some colour shots of the usual tourist places, like Fordsburg and the Voortrekker Monument, the Paul Kruger statue and the Union buildings.'

'Could we get those back?'

'I hope so.'

'Were there any plans or maps in the studio?'

'Quite a few, including a nice big one of Modderfontein Dynamite Factory. There were no marks on it. The police have tried to ask me about another map that did have marks on it but I refused to touch it.'

There was a pause for thought.

'What do you think they'll charge you with?'

'I really don't know. We did have a lot of hypothetical discussion in the studio.'

Zim grinned again. 'You like that word "hypothetical", don't you?'

'Yes, I think it's nice. I got it out of the dictionary. "Meta-phorical". That's another word I like. "Metaphorical".'

'Have you ever heard of clemency?'

'It's funny you should say that. I've got that one dog-eared, too.'

He put the cap on his pen and lent back in his chair. 'You know, Quentin, I'm a progressive but even I think you've be-haved very badly. I think you should ... I don't know, it depends on the judge. I think you should be very careful. I think, of course, that the police have behaved very badly too, but not without cause. But it's no good making you feel guilty. When you walk into the court I want you to feel as confident as possible. There won't be anything, not anything, that you don't have to answer for.'

'Like what?'

'Well, we don't know yet till we hear the evidence. I mean we don't know yet what the charges are.'

'And we'll get that in a few weeks' time. But before that I'll get my police interrogation notes back, won't I?'

'I'm terrified of what's in them,' Zim said.

'Don't worry. It's all "if" or "might". None of it's "would".'

'As you know, this is to be in the Supreme Court, so I won't actually address the court myself. I will be instructing an advocate who will act on your behalf.'

'I'd like to see him, you know, before it starts.'

'I should think by the time we've finished with you, you'll be sick of the sight of us both.'

'What's my advocate like?'

'Mr Bizos, George Bizos. I can't speak highly enough of him. You're very lucky I've got him. If I can get him away, I'll bring him up next Friday. But he's a very busy man, very busy.'

'You remember what you were saying about me being as confident as possible? Well, do you think I could have some visitors?'

'Certainly, certainly. Only I don't think they'd come. It's frankly a danger to them.'

'Well, what about the chaplain?'

'Yes, I can get him to come. I think there's only one that's allowed, but it's a visit. It all helps. Now I can't see you till Friday and then I'll probably come up with Mr Bizos, so in the meantime you can do a little writing about everything you did, the people you met, parties you've been to, everything. Don't write anything that might be incriminating, leave that out, but everything else I want. I'll arrange about the chaplain and I'll bring more fruit and stuff when I come with Bizos.'

I went back to my cell feeling a bit more confident. It's all happening. The more I tell him the better. He doesn't seem to mind. He's all right, and I think the Springbok image might help a lot. I'll do a walk and think a little. If Biggie comes once a week and Zim once a week and the chaplain too, things are getting better. And even if I am found guilty, at least I won't be in solitary any more.

The guard came to collect me for exercise. I was always put in one yard while everyone else was put in another. They got two hours. I got half an hour, once in the morning and once in the afternoon. I was generally locked in the yard but on this occasion I wasn't. The guard instead decided to as-

sault a harmless old drunk right in front of me. I'd seen
brutality before but not to someone so pathetic. Woomera
was his name, and what made it all the worse was that I
knew him. I don't think he remembered me, but then he'd
been drunk and I'd been sober. It was a month or so before
I was busted, in a fish and chip shop in Fordsburg. Fordsburg's a beautiful old part of the town that the Indians own,
or rent. I was in this fish and chip shop eating my chips with
curry powder on top and these two white drunks came in,
not noisy or anything, just hungry, but they didn't have
enough money, so the Indian refused to serve them. I suppose
he got a kick out of it but, just so as not to start an argument,
I went over and offered to pay. He looked worse now he
was sober.

The guard and the drunk were in a corner of my yard
and I couldn't avoid walking right up to them. Then I turned
and went back to the opposite wall. I mustn't look too upset. I should think right now he doesn't want to remember
anything. His screaming and dribbling only encouraged the
other prisoners, who were watching through their mesh fence,
laughing at him. The warder, large, blond and well-tanned,
looked a bit like my elder brother which only made it worse.
He had the leather strap with the keys hanging on it round
Woomera's neck and when he wasn't kneeing him in the
groin, he was hitting him on the head with the keys. After
he'd reduced him to a hollering wreck, the guard used his
bare arm as an ashtray. But what upset me most was the
attitude of the other prisoners. They loved it. After a bit he
was pushed in with them, and between the bouts of physical
assault from the guard they would throw cold water over
him. I was on my own and so, I felt, was he. I was very sorry
for him but I couldn't do anything. As it is, I'm sick of
problems already. All I know is I don't want to be exercised
while they bully other prisoners in front of me. I'm entitled
to my hour's exercise every day. It's all I've got.

Eventually they let him go and I saw him run upstairs
into an empty cell. He wants solitary, I thought, and I don't.
He's poor and totally without friends or visitors and I, on the
other hand, have an attorney and the British Consul coming
every week. The last time I saw him, I paid for his chips. I

remember thinking that he might be offended but, in fact, he had been very polite. Then I thought he might get his own back on the Indian but he was very polite to him too.

The next day I found another prisoner in the shower.
'I say, I'm in solitary,' I said. 'I'm meant to have a shower on my own.'
'That's all right. I'm in solitary, too.'
'Oh, well, nice to know I'm not alone.'
'What are you in for?'
'Terrorism and Communism.'
'Glad I'm not in your shoes. Jesus,' he laughed, 'that's one thing I haven't done.'
'Why are you in solitary?'
'I was caught in this jail with a hacksaw blade after I'd been picked up for escaping twice from John Vorster Square.'
'I thought John Vorster was impossible to escape from.'
'So did they. That's why they're angry.'
I finished my shower and started shaving. 'What's your name?'
'Trevor.'
'Mine's Quentin.'
'Hell, man, that sounds queer.'
'Well, I've got a brother called Henry. Is that any better?'
'No. I'll tell you what—I'll call you Clinton. How's that?'
'Fine.'
While I was shaving, I noticed his tattoos in the mirror. 'Where did you get your tattoos?'
'We did them ourselves. I did my mate's and he did mine.'
'What are they?'
'I've got a Chinese dragon on my back and this here's a hawk.'
'I know what you're thinking, Trevor. You're thinking, why haven't I got tattoos.'
'Well, why haven't you?'
'It's a very big decision. A distant relative of mine, the King of Denmark, has some, but I don't know what I would want.'

I lent him my razor and while he shaved, we talked. When I saw the guard coming, I said quickly, 'See you tomorrow,' and took my porridge back to my cell.

CHAPTER FOURTEEN

It all helps. Biggie, Zim and now Trevor. Even the *Spectator* that Biggie brought. Every little piece of information from the outside world and every second I spend out of this cell, help to recondition me into being a more confident human being again. By the time I go to court I'll know the answer to every possible question they can ask me. And, if I am found guilty, I don't mind. I'll do a course in jail, probably psychology. Jail's the ideal place to study in; total isolation, no radio, no television, no visitors, absolutely nothing to distract one.

I'll start writing my thesis for Zim. I'm a very poor speller but I've got a dictionary and plenty of time. That doesn't mean I won't do any more exercise. I'll still do press-ups, but not walks. The best way to approach court is to expect the worst and, if it turns out good, why then, that's fine but if it turns out bad, don't show it. Always appear confident. I'll say, 'I am innocent of these charges.'

There was another visit from Biggie. He told me that my mother wanted to see me. This was fabulous news but Zim had said she shouldn't come until the court had started because there was no guarantee that she'd be allowed to see me before then. I thought Zim was right in a way. It was then the heat would be on and I'd be able to see her in court. It was one more reason to look forward to the trial. All movement is good. One must have a horizon, something to look forward to and recognise, even if it's ten years away. It was very moving that Mum wanted to come. Somehow I had known she would. Mum could be my public relations officer, not to increase sales, but to improve my image.

Biggie, I noticed, was wearing a black tie.

'Nothing wrong, I hope?' I asked.

'Oh, no, just regulations. Official mourning for the King of Denmark.'

'But that's terrible,' I said. 'I'm vaguely related to him and it means now there'll be no more kings. My grandfather was knighted by his father. I must tell Trevor.'

'Who's Trevor?'

'Oh, he's someone I meet in the shower. He's also in solitary.'

'Oh, God, not English, I hope.'

'No, he's fraud but not English.'

At the end of his visit Biggie said, 'Look, I won't be able to see you next week. I've got to go to Blomfontein to hear the Dean's appeal, but the vice-consul, Miss Angela Lloyd, will see you instead. She'll bring you some more coffee and sugar.'

These visits from the consul had become less and less official. He told me about his painting and his interest in jazz and, in a way, I found that the parental role that the police had acquired with me was being taken over by Biggie and Zim.

All the time I was becoming more confident. For one thing, I was now allowed to write letters home and this helped me to release something. Although I was still in solitary, life began to have some human feeling in it again and in letters one could begin to express it. I even had one or two letters from National Union of Journalist members. It seemed strange that these people I'd never met and never even heard of should care. Even visits became unpredictable. It might be the chaplain or the consul or the lawyer or the advocate, or even the police. I thought I'd finished with the police, but they came once again. This time it was to find out where the nearest post office was to my home in London, and to check my father's name. My father's first name is Bent which to a policeman may sound encouraging.

Although I had one brief visit from the chaplain which didn't work out at all well, I did start to go to church on Sundays. Service was in Afrikaans, a language of which I know nothing, but just sitting there with people was comforting. At the end one of the other prisoners would say, 'Don't worry. He didn't say anything anyway.'

Then as time went on I occasionally got exercise with Trevor. We weren't supposed to talk, but all they could do was tell us to stop and we'd go our separate ways for a bit then drift back together again. He was a few years younger than I was and had left school even earlier, when he was fourteen, and had been a hustler ever since. I think his most original crime was stealing a masonic sword and selling it somewhere in the Transkei to a black chieftain, who is probably waving the thing round now with pride and joy. He was also an expert on porn, and on rough diamond buying. He'd done a four year stretch for theft and was now waiting for more. He was clever, the best chess player in the jail. In a way he should have gone to university; then he could have flogged the chieftain a few microscopes and books. One of his stories was about an epileptic craze that swept through the prison. Originally it had started with a young, and genuinely epileptic accountant involved in a five-million-rand fraud case, who landed in the Fort as an awaiting-trial prisoner. He came from a rich background and his family would send him very expensive salamis and peaches and chickens. Trevor, of course, wangled it so that he could be near him— you know, 'to look after him' and it was when, in fact, he had his first epileptic fit that Trevor dived to protect the salami and, in Trevor's words, 'I've never seen a man stop having a fit so fast!' In jail an epileptic gets hospital food, which is fried steak and dried apricots and milk. Overnight everyone was throwing fits. Trevor, finally, even got his accepted and joined the accountant on his diet.

Most of the convicted prisoners at the Fort were either short-term drunks or long-term frauds who were waiting to give evidence on future trials, which is one of the best ways of getting remission. But at weekends, forty weekenders would come in. They looked more depressed than the ordinary prisoners because they don't give themselves to the system. Most of them are doing a two thousand hours' sentence for drunken driving or a thousand hours for dangerous driving. They just sit there and smoke and it's very hard to get any conversation with them. Trevor always conned them for matches and tobacco. I don't smoke myself, but most prisoners spent hours splitting matches and rolling cigarettes out of old newspaper. Sometimes the guard gives out prison-issue Ritz papers, but only when he feels like it. Pipes are not allowed because this is the traditional method of smoking dagga. The best way to make money in jail is by selling dagga. How it happens is quite interesting. The black police sell it to the black prisoners, who sell it to the white cook, who sells it to the white prisoners. It starts off at a pound an 'arm' and then people take a hundred per cent as it passes hands. An arm is about four ounces, a large handful put in a newspaper and rolled up. That's then broken up into 'fingers'. Both money and dagga are strictly illegal in jail, but according to your position you can get practically anything. Getting the money in is almost more difficult than getting in the grass. If you are an A-class prisoner like the cook, then you're entitled to what is known as a contact visit; so when your girl-friend arrives you kiss her and immediately you're five pounds the richer, and you know she still loves you. She has wrapped it up tightly in polythene so if you have to swallow it, no harm's done. Because of the sheer size of notes, small notes are worth twenty per cent more. Once you've built up a good supply of change, then you start sending the big notes back. The best place to hide things is in your shoes.

Most of Trevor's friends were inside and the honour among them was proverbial. He was meant to be on Spare Diet but things were smuggled into his cell all the time. I found myself doing it, too. It was a game. Bananas would slide through his spy-hole but apples had to be broken in half. At one point a very kind person sent me a marvellous food parcel including a box of very expensive glacé fruits but, by then, I had toothache and couldn't eat them, so I gave them one by one to Trevor.

It was a humiliating fact that all one's precious values got lost in the need for self-survival. The 'Black' jail is totally separate from the White and the only place I ever saw Blacks was in the kitchens or sometimes outside near the castellated wall, when I was waiting for Zim or Biggie. Then one might see a Black pointlessly cleaning a drain-cover or wiping dust off the flowers outside the Commandant's office If there were groups of Blacks waiting for somewhere to go to, they would be made to crouch down as though they were going to start a race. I've seen them left in the sun for hours, like that. They were not allowed to sit, not allowed to stand, they just waited. Blacks always had their heads shaved. Blacks were always counted in pairs, a brace of Blacks. Black prison warders would assault them, just as much as Whites.

Sometimes I had to stop and remind myself that the charges I was on were for trying to help the Blacks, but, right from the start I'd told the police that I'd come to South Africa to make money, nothing else, because that was what they wanted to hear. And I had to keep this attitude up while I was in jail. Every letter I wrote was checked, not just by the prison authorities but also by the security police, and the same was true of all letters coming in. Whereas six months before I would have lost my temper at the things I saw, now I just continued to pretend they had nothing to do with me.

'Jacobsen, visitor!'

Odd time for a visit. I wondered who it was ... Colonel Ferrara. I wondered what he wanted now.

'Your attorney asked for the interrogation. Here it is.'

'If he asked for it, give it to him. I don't want it.'

'What, are you afraid of it or something?'

'No, not afraid. It can't be used in court. It means nothing.'

'Well, now that we're here, do you want it?'

'I didn't ask for it but I'll give it to my lawyer. I know he wants it.'

When they left, I went out to have exercise. I wanted to think I could just put the papers on the ground and walk nonchalantly past them, but curiosity got the better of me. There were about fifty pages. I was a little embarrassed at first, but after a few pages my embarrassment turned to anger. I never said that ... or, more to the point, I never said it then. The whole thing had been chopped and changed round. What's Zim going to think? He'll do his nut when he sees this. I read it through. I don't know, but I may well have been watched by the police while I did so. The whole thing was a pack of lies. For a start they left out any mention of the time of day when I said things so that you couldn't tell how broken down I was by long periods of interrogation. One thing I remembered saying when it was put to me last thing in Pretoria, and they'd bunged it in right up near the beginning. I thought, as soon as I get back to my cell, I'll write explanations in the margin. I hope Zim doesn't dump me after he's read this lot.

After exercise, I frantically 'corrected' my interrogation. The sooner I got that out of the cell the better. I was terrified the police would find it. But the police had just given it to me. I felt I was locked in with stolen property; I wanted to dump the stuff before I was caught.

Next day 'Visitor!' was shouted again and I slid nervously downstairs, clutching my interrogation. Zim was waiting for me.

'I've got Bizos with me,' he said. 'He's in here. We've also received the indictment. It's ... well, it's not too good.'

I walked in and there, sitting by the table, was a short, plump man with black-rimmed glasses. He brushed his hands through his retreating hair and took off his glasses. He had an odd, rather strong, Mediterranean kind of accent.

'My name is Bizos. I have worked on many Terrorism cases, most of which I've lost. Terrorism is a difficult subject. It's quite new; indeed each case defines the law further.' He slowly put his glasses on again. 'I've read the indictment and it doesn't look good but I shall do all I can.'

I leant over, smiled and shook his hand. 'Where did you get those glasses?'

'Why? What's wrong with them?'

'Nothing. I think they're marvellous. Did you ever see *The Anatolian Smile* by Elia Kazan? It had two names, that and *America, America?*'

Bizos sat back and smiled. 'I know the film. I'm from Anatolia myself.'

'Well, do you remember the scene in the carpet-shop before he left Istanbul?' Bizos smiled again. 'Well, the man who owned the shop, I'm sure he had glasses like yours.'

'You know, Quentin, for the next month, I want to find out every little thing about you. I want to know your sex life, your politics, your philosophy, your favourite food, your favourite films, everything. By the time we go to court you will be sick of the sight of us. Now first, above all, we will not talk in a way which might be dangerous. I will write down a word and then point to it and you will reply.'

He wrote some words on a sheet of paper and very firmly

pointed to one of them. 'In your studio. Did you have any of this?'

'You mean explosives?'

He put his hand up to his forehead and slowly rubbed it. 'No, you're not listening. I want you to listen.' He lowered his voice. 'When I give you the word, you will give me the answer "yes" or "no", nothing else. Is that clear?' There was a pause. 'Now, in your studio did you have any of this?'

'No.'

'Or this?'

I thought for a while. 'No. A little. Well, not really.'

'I'll go back to that later. Or this?'

'Yes, about a bag full.'

'Or this?'

'No.'

'Fine. Now we have the indictment. I will briefly explain what you are accused of. It comes in three parts. The first is participation in terrorist activities, this includes actual acts done; then conspiracy to do more acts; and thirdly, the incitement of others to join the said conspiracy.'

'That's in a way a sort of past, present and future?' I said.

'Yes, not a bad way of putting it. Now, that's just the beginning. Now there are two alternative counts. Count one, Communism in furtherance of a common purpose shared with others, namely Henry Jacobsen, and/or Seadom Tilotsane and/or Buki Franz Monamudi, did wrongly and unlawfully obtain in the manner set out hereunder, information which could be of use in furthering the achievement of any of the objects of Communism.'

'I suppose that means the books,' I said. 'But there's no mention of politics in the books. I'm certain of that.'

I thought Zim was going to remind me that I hadn't read them but he didn't.

'In this country communism is a funny business,' Bizos went on. '"Communism" is any doctrine or scheme which aims at bringing about any political, industrial, social or economic change within the Republic of South Africa, by threat of unlawful acts or omissions. You're not charged with omissions. That's for strikes and civil disobedience. But, you see, on this there's still a minimum of five years. This is a

160

sticky one. The last alternative count is that you advocate, advise, defend or encourage the achievement of any of the objects of communism. Blah, blah, blah. I wouldn't worry about this one, because if you're found innocent of the main count then you're innocent on the last count. They're basically the same thing. So there you are. Now I'll run over the main count in detail. It says "Acting alone or in concert with Henry Jacobsen, and/or Seadom Tilotsane and/or Buki Franz Monamudi, and in furtherance of a common purpose shared with them, commit one or more of the said acts set out in Schedule 1. That the accused photographed in England approximately during the period 19th August 1971 to 9th September 1971 pages of the following books. *The Anarchist Cookbook* and the *Field Manual* nos. 5-25 issued by the Department of the Army USA dealing with explosives and demolitions and/or, paragraph 2, the accused introduced into Johannesburg in the district of Johannesburg in the Republic of South Africa, upon or about the 9th September 1971 the negatives of the photographs referred to in paragraph 1 supra and/or the accused made enlarged prints of the negatives referred to in paragraph 2, approximately during the period 9th September 1971 to 2nd November 1971." It then goes on to say that you did this with the intention of distributing them in South Africa.

'"That the accused showed copies of the photographs to Seadom and/or Buki and/or Ian Hill and/or Martin Cohen.

'"That the accused photographed the following places, approximately during the period 1st July to 18th August, with the intention to use the photographs in question for planning and preparing the destruction or damage of the places by sabotage.

'"Portion of the understructure of various bridges on the Ben Schoeman Highway in the districts of Johannesburg and Pretoria respectively...."'

Zim interrupted. 'I've asked to see those photographs. They say they've actually got them.'

I said quietly, on the assumption that we were bugged, 'I think that is impossible. They must have faked them, in which case I'm certain I can prove they're not mine.'

Zim whispered back, 'How?'

'Easy. Film emulsion number, type of scratch on the back.'
'All right. Don't say any more. Put it down on paper and give it me later.'

Bizos continued, ' "Photographs of the understructure of a bridge on the De Villiers Graff Motorway, the radio and communication mast of the Defence Department, Pretoria, the Vehicle Reserve Park of the Defence Department Fordsburg, the bus sheds in Johannesburg, the sub-power station of the bus sheds and the terminal of the oil pipeline between Durban and Johannesburg, and/or the statue of Paul Kreuger." And that you sought the assistance of Ian Hill in connection with an experiment in the construction of petrol bombs intended for sabotage purposes. Now those are acts done, although I don't think asking someone to help on the construction of petrol bombs is an act. But we'll argue that later.'

'The photographs of the places—they won't have a chance of proving that they're mine.'

'Why?'

'Well, the light will be in a different direction, the foliage on trees will be totally different. The things themselves may well have changed since the date I was supposed to have taken them. I think they would be very hard to fake.'

'Well, we'll just have to wait and see, then. "Schedule 2. Conspiracy. Bringing about a political change in South Africa or the crippling or undermining of the economy of the Republic of South Africa by means of sabotage and/or destruction of the following places. a. The Johannesburg telephone exchange and/or bus sheds in Fordsburg and/or bridges on the Ben Schoeman Highway and/or De Villiers Graff Motorway and/or other unspecified bridges." I want to explain conspiracy. Conspiracy is not, I repeat not, when I say to my wife, "If I run out of money next week, you will have to go out on the street and become a prostitute".' He smiled, and said quickly, 'That is not conspiracy. I repeat, not conspiracy. But, and listen very carefully, conspiracy is not even when I say to my wife, "I have run out of money, tomorrow you will go out and become a prostitute". That is still not conspiracy. It is conspiracy only when she actually agrees to go out and become a prostitute. Do you understand?'

'Yes, but...'

He went straight on to the next schedule. He turned the page and began to read. 'Blah, blah, blah—destruction or damage of the following.'

He ran through the familiar list from the telephone exchange to the Voortrekker Monument.

'Interesting,' I said, still thinking about his definition of conspiracy. 'But if you said to your wife, "Tomorrow you go out", isn't that incitement?'

'Depends on who incited who.' Then he went on, 'If it's any consolation to you, I heard the Voortrekker Monument's falling apart already.'

I thought for a while. 'What I find interesting is that Seadom knows I've photographed the Union Buildings, but it's not in the indictment. I took a lot of photographs for my library. I remember taking some buses in Fordsburg, some cooling-towers with a palm tree in front, some statues and some of the Voortrekker Monument. But these were definitely tourist shots.'

Zim didn't like the idea. He already knew what I was thinking.

'I think we should get them over.'

'So do I,' said Bizos. 'If you think they will help, then let's get them over.'

'I do, because, in a way, we could say that the cooling-towers were really their sub-Power Station. I mean, it might well be. I don't know. And the buses with the bus sheds.'

'But what about the Voortrekker Monument?' Zim interrupted. 'It's in the bloody indictment. And the Union Buildings?'

Bizos argued that hundreds of people had taken shots of the Voortrekker Monument. 'Quentin's just like any other tourist photographing the sights. Same with the Union Building.'

'I know these shots,' I said. 'There's nothing harmful in them except possibly a shot of a "Whites Only" park bench. Is that dangerous?'

'Not unless you're going to blow it up,' Bizos said.

'No, not a park bench. Well it's all there, isn't it? The only thing I feel is odd is that ... oh, by the way, the police dropped in my interrogation ... the only thing I find odd is that I've admitted to photographing the railway station, but it's not in the indictment.'

'I wouldn't complain. I think we have enough work as it is.'

'Do you think I have a chance, Mr Bizos?'

'Frankly, not much. As I see it, the books are the problem. The other things we can argue about. Witnesses—well, you never can tell what a witness will say, but the books, that's hard. Now I've made a stat copy of the indictment. Put your name on it and don't lose it. I'll take the interrogation home and read it and then we'll get together again and discuss the whole thing.' He put the papers in his bag and took off his glasses. 'Have you got the daily paper?'

'No, I haven't.'

'You must,' he said angrily. 'Zim, why hasn't he got the paper?'

'I'll order it straight away.'

'Have you got books?'

'I would like some on psychology.'

'No, impossible. I don't want you reading heavy stuff. Zim, get him some—who's that horse-racing writer?'

Zim smiled. 'You mean Dick Francis?'

'Yes, get him some Dick Francis.'

'But I can't stand horse-racing.'

'Doesn't matter. I'm not having you read philosophical things. You're not interested in such things. You've got to be as normal as possible. What about food?'

'Well a friend of mine mentioned salami.'

'You want salami? You get salami. Greek salami.'

He patted his case. 'I'll read this first, then give it to Zim to read. Meanwhile you study the indictment. I'm still very busy but Zim will see you next week and I'll drop by later. It's going to be a lot of work but we can do it.'

On the way back to my cell, the guard said, 'You needn't worry. You've got a very famous lawyer. I remember him before the war. Jesus, he was fast.'

CHAPTER FIFTEEN

Back in my cell, I held the indictment in my hands and thought, 'Not much point in doing exercise.' Seadom, Buki, Ian, Martin: I'll go to court if only to see them for the last time. It's a kind of relay race where they've handed in the batons and I'm left running. I'm sure the police chopped and changed my interrogation notes to look as much like the indictment as possible. I didn't convict myself. Far from it; they knew it all already. I couldn't deny the charges. What would have been the point of making them more angry? Now the question is, can they prove it? How can they prove an idea or how can I disprove an idea? The whole thing was so intangible. Those shots of the places we were supposed to be going to blow up, I don't think they've got a chance of getting away with them. If nothing else, I want to see those shots. I'll read this thing through, not because I want to but because I've been told to. Bizos seems different from Zim. He's realistic but he doesn't frighten me. No one frightened me, only myself and my inability to do solitary. I would rather do five years with others than a year of solitary. 'If you can't do the time, then don't do the crime.' It's impossible to imagine time in such chunks. I've always lived from one day to the next. The crimes, too, are unbelievable, which may be a good thing. Had they been smaller, it might have been worse. The time and trouble the police have gone to, just in the hope of proving we had an idea! That's why I see it very much as a game. If they'd wanted to, they could have deported us right at the beginning, but no, they had to prove more than they'd got. It's so exaggerated.

Bizos and Zim came again a few days later. Both of them had read the interrogation. It had terrified Zim.

'What if they bring up this piece here? Look, this piece. It's bloody well got it written that you wanted to hi-jack a dynamite truck from Modderfontein.'

Bizos slowly turned to him. 'Listen, how many times must

I tell you it means nothing. It's not a statement; none of it can be used.'

'But he's admitted to half the bloody things in the indictment.'

'Look, I know it can't be used, so stop worrying. There's no point in going backwards. We must concern ourselves with the future.' Then, turning to me. 'Have you got the papers yet?'

'Yes, I've got newspapers.'

'Now, over the next three or four days you will write a complete resumé of everything that has relevance to the indictment. I want to know when you had those talks, who was with you, how much you'd had to drink—or smoke. I want to know what you ate, what you were wearing, everything.'

'I've sent someone round to Wits to ask about Seadom. It seems he was a dealer in drugs,' Zim interrupted.

'It's ridiculous to put it like that,' I replied. 'He smoked a bit and he may even have got it for the others but he wasn't a dealer. He was a student.'

'And Ian Hill was a bit of a loud-mouth. He used to shout his head off pretending to be a Radical.'

'He is a Radical. There's nothing wrong with being a Radical.'

Bizos resumed, 'And when you're at it, I want you to do character studies of Seadom, Buki, Ian Hill, Martin, Dave and Henry because, when I walk into the court, I want to know every little thing about them, even how they will think. Not just the facts but how they will think.'

'How much shall I write on each?'

'At least two pages. It's got to be at least two pages.'

'And the story thing?'

'Twenty. And another thing, take the interrogation and correlate it with the indictment. This will save me time. I haven't read it properly, so I want you to help me by writing the section and the paragraph next to the piece of relevant interrogation. There's some paper. Don't let anybody read this. I shall just write on the cover "Notes in my defence, Quentin Jacobsen". Now nobody's entitled to read it. Do you understand? You take it to bed with you; you take it to the showers with you, everywhere. You understand?'

'Yes.'

'And here's your Dick Francis,' Bizos smiled. 'You will notice the title, *For Kicks*. Give that angle a thought. You know, why you brought the books in. We'll see you in three or four days. Oh, yes, he brought some food. The guard will give it to you later.'

My food parcel arrived: Greek salami.

When supper came it seemed almost unnecessary. I ate the veg and left the rest. Now to get down to my character sketches. Seadom was the youngest, doing biology at Wits, knew six African languages, quite well spoken, had many white friends, wanted to be a doctor, often slept at the studio overnight, worked hard, got on with Henry best but he was an easy guy to get on with. He sometimes did the floors and I paid him a couple of rand. We often went out to the Lyric cinema or to Wits to see films or plays. I remember once during a play called *Black and Blue* he and Buki stood up and called out, 'Tell it all, brother, tell it all.' In spite of his white friends he liked, I think, to see himself as a black militant. I then went on to Ian Hill. I liked thinking about them. After all, they were all my close friends; I was fond of them. Ian was a medical student. Sometimes I went with him to Stockfontein Mental Hospital. He would lend me a white coat and I would pretend to be a medical student, too. He came from a fairly poor background and his parents were divorced. Ian lived with his mother. He made a bit of extra money working in a betting shop on Wednesdays and Saturdays and often after work he would come up to the studio for a few beers. Henry and he used to stay out in Soweto together. He didn't have much use for the others, Martin and Dave that is, mainly because they were opposed to any sort of violent approach. Then Dave and Martin: I had come to think of them as rather apathetic young men, a kind of Rosencrantz and Guildenstern. Martin had a degree in mathematics, liked films, knew a lot about philosophy, was politely left-wing but not particularly radical. Dave was much the same, a bit more practical, had a degree in architecture. They had both worked hard but I had been trying to phase them out of the studio because I felt I was supporting too many people and it had become clear that their interests were elsewhere. I wrote a few more pages on them and finished. I did look forward to seeing them again. I would have gone out of my way to help any of them.

It was now almost night and I thought I'd read a bit of *For Kicks*. I can't think of anything less relevant. My life's at stake and they expect me to read a book on horse-racing. I can't stand gambling. But the book begins in Australia so it can't be that bad. It's accurate. I've spent four and a half years in Australia and he's got it right. I read about half the book and decided I must save the rest.

Next day I started on the 'story', everything relevant to the indictment. It took me a good two days. All the time I took it everywhere I went. Once I'd finished the damn thing, Zim and Bizos wouldn't come and collect it. For a whole weekend I had to drag it around with me. Eventually on the Monday I got the 'Visitor!' cry and thought it must be them, but the guard said something about a doctor or dentist and I was taken round to the hospital.

'What have you got wrapped up in that towel, Jacobsen?'

'It's my notes in defence.'

'Well, you can't take it to the dentist.'

'If I can't take it to the dentist, then I don't want to go to the dentist.'

'But we specially got him in to do your teeth.'

'I don't care. These are my notes and they're not leaving my sight.'

After a tug of war and a few tears shed, we both went up to the Commandant's office and I explained to him. In the end he insisted on running over every page and initialling each one at the bottom. After still more argument I was allowed to go to the dentist with my notes, only to find he couldn't fill holes, only do extractions. The whole thing began to look like a trick. I hoped Zim would come to-morrow, then I could pass the problem on to him.

He did, thank God, so I gave him my problem and he gave me another.

'These shots of the strategic targets the police have got, they weren't meant to be yours. They were shot by a police photographer under the direction of one of the witnesses who supposedly saw you take them. It makes it more difficult, you see, because it means we can't prove the shots are fake, only that the witness is lying.'

I thought about this. 'I tell you what, write to my mother and get her to send the three colour films. But make a point that it is only the colour film we want, not the black-and-white. Just the colour. Understand?'

Zim didn't look happy about it but he said that he would. There wasn't much more we could talk about until he had read my notes, so he left soon afterwards.

Bizos dropped in the next day. It was odd but, unlike Zim, he wasn't so concerned with facts as with attitudes. He wanted to know about the books the police had removed from the studio, in addition to the two in the indictment. I told him one was on philosophy and the other on existentialism.

'What in fact do you believe in?' he asked.

'Not much at the moment. My friends say I'm an existentialist. I think, myself, I'm more of a failed hedonist.' I looked at Bizos. 'What do I do if I break down in court?'

'Quentin, I am Greek. I don't believe in your Anglo-Saxon idea of reserve. If you want to cry in court, I don't mind.' We continued to look each other in the eye. Then he went on, 'Do you know much about communism? In its real sense, not the South African legal interpretation of it, but its real sense?'

'Is it the "greatest good for the greatest number"? Is that it?'

'No. Warm but not hot. "From each according to his ability, to each according to his need".'

'Yes, I've heard that before, probably in Hampstead somewhere.'

'And what's your attitude to this type of thinking?'

'I find it very boring. I've always thought nationalisation is just as bad as any other monopoly. I like individualism. I like competition.'

'Good, and do the others know this is your way of thinking?'

'Yes. Look, one thing you can be sure of is that no-one is going to say I'm a communist. Anarchist, in a light-hearted way, maybe, but not communist.'

'Do you know that in the final stage of Marxism the state is meant to wither away and you're left with a sort of anarchy?'

'No. I don't see it ever happening.' I paused. 'I think it would be safe to say I'm a progressive. Would it?'

'Yes, if you want.'

'I do have an odd philosophy of my own, based on accident. I do feel that accident has a kind of truth without bias. My whole life has been a series of accidents, starting with being born a twin and ending now with being busted. I didn't plan it that way. It just happened.'

'Well, nothing more is going to happen if I can help it. In this case we must plan. You know those character references you did?'

'Yes. What?'

'They're wrong, that's what. I'll give you an example. You say Seadom stood up at Wits University and shouted, "Tell it all, brother, tell it all". Now I tell you that in court Seadom is going to stand up and say you incited him into this conspiracy. What we have to prove is that he was an embittered, angry young man. He didn't need inciting. Do you see?'

'Yes, and in a way it's true.'

'I'm sure it's true. And the same for Hill, too. You say these people are your friends. Forget that. Forget it. These people are trying to save their own necks by hanging yours.'

'But they *are* my friends. And there are four of them and only one of me. If I could get them off, I wouldn't mind so much what happened to me.'

'If Zim had heard that, do you know what he would say? He would say, "Balls! Balls!" I would say, "Rubbish, absolute rubbish!" I'm not defending the others. I'm defending you.'

'But if it's going to be a mud-slinging match, I don't want to be in it. They've suffered enough already.'

'But, Quentin, it's you alone. You're on your own. They've abandoned you. They're trying to pile it all on you. If they were really friends, they wouldn't do it to you.'

'But they've been made to say it.'

'That's it. That's just what we've got to prove. I've got to know everything Seadom ever said, and Martin, and Ian Hill. Everything. I don't want to know how nice they are. I want to know what they said.'

'I do see there's little point in going to jail but I don't want the others to suffer, too.'

'But the others aren't being charged. If they've turned state witness, they'll go free. It's only you who are being charged. It's only you I'm defending. Forget them.'

'All right. I'll re-write the characters. But I think you're wrong.'

We parted, I to remember what rotten friends I had and he to remember what a good client he had. But he can always get more clients. I can't always get more friends.

My shots came from London a few days before the trial was due to start. It was as I said. They slipped into the indictment pretty well. On one side you had their black-and-white shots, stark, depressing, totally negative; on the other, mine, colourful, innocent and positive. Bizos beamed with delight. He had enough mud in one hand to incriminate an army and enough evidence in the other to make me look like Julie Andrews. All I needed was my stiff collars and they were arriving on Sunday with my mother, the day before the trial opened.

The plane was meant to arrive at ten and Zim had told me he would bring her to the Fort before lunch, but there was some misunderstanding about British Summer Time and the plane didn't get in till eleven, so I didn't see her till two. On the way down I saw François.

'Why are you in?' I shouted.

'Car theft.'

'How about that ten bucks?'

'Haven't got it.'

I was shown into a prison visiting-room with stout mesh on my side and bars on hers. My mother's nose was exactly at the height of one of the cross bars. We were separated by four feet of nothing. What does one say in the circumstances?

'Did you remember my collars?' I said through tears.

'Yes, my love.'

'It may look bad, but the worst is over. I'm afraid I wasn't very good at solitary.'

'I know, don't worry. At least that's over now.'

'How's Henry?'

'Hopeless. He wouldn't tell me anything and wanders round looking as though the world's coming to an end.'

We both laughed unsteadily.

'That's good. I'm so glad you came to-day. I'm not afraid, but I'm not exactly back to normal yet. Talking still seems odd. You've seen the indictment?'

'Yes, it's not—it's not too bad.'

We talked for an hour. It was both sad and almost exhilarating. It was an intense relief. I'm glad she knows everything. It's the moral support that I need. And there is this fact—that, if I'm found guilty, I won't see her again for at least five years. Mum told me about having lunch with Zim and said she'd brought me my old 'Twenties' wrist watch, and homemade fudge and marzipan for a belated birthday present. When the guard said, 'Time's up!' I wanted to say to her, 'I've never doubted your love,' but only managed to say 'I've always loved you,' as I left. I couldn't talk to anyone. The thing about solitary is that everything else becomes so concentrated.

Half an hour later Mum's parcel arrived. I ate the fudge till my teeth nearly dropped out. There was a new book, too, on the Pre-Raphaelites with all my old favourites, and some ties to choose from, and my stiff collars, shirts, my dark suit and a set of keys for the London flat which must have been a mistake. I've always seen keys as proof of ownership rather than a method of opening up, but in prison they seemed an odd thing to have in one's possession. I had thought of trying to escape but in solitary it's hard to get hold of anything. The two guys next door to me had managed to make keys but they had been caught and were now in chains from their ankles up to their waists. Another prisoner, who was originally in for six months, had escaped four times and been caught each time with the result that instead of doing six months he was now doing five years. I think he must have liked the place.

That night I took stock of myself. I wasn't in bad shape.

My spot had finally cleared up. Some chrome yellow paste from the doc had fixed it. He had also given me some anti-mosquito stuff: it was an unusually wet season and I was being eaten alive. Putting it on had become part of the ritual of going to bed.

I felt that I was at the beginning of the end of solitary and I went to bed and to sleep with confidence.

CHAPTER SIXTEEN

I went down for my one hundred and thirty-ninth plate of porridge, took my slab of butter and left the bread. I used a little butter to clean my shoes, had a walk in my cell and then got dressed. I used the lid of a biscuit-tin someone had given me for a mirror. There was no chance that my case would be forgotten; all the guards were as interested as I was. Finally Colonel Ferrara turned up and we went through to his car. We were far too early but he didn't have anything else to do. It was a new car, I saw, a VW and a bit more sensible than that clapped-out old black Dodge. The two policemen both wore flowery ties and brightly coloured shirts. How beautiful! It made me think of a joke one of the guards had told. 'I heard your black boy died.' 'Yes. It's funny, he never did that before.'

I climbed into the back of the yellow ochre lovebug. The stink of aftershave was overwhelming. My God, the police were putting on a show of force! I think for these political crimes they like to take a little trouble, look a little gay. The only thing was that the strain of Ferrara's fat neck was killing the flowers. He opened the conversation.

'Pity Dave's let you down. We sub-poenaed him but he skipped the country. Gone back to Australia.'

'He hasn't let me down. I didn't sub-poena him, you did.'

On arrival at the court I was put in a cell with a murderer. About the only thing we had in common was that we could both be hanged, though at the rate he was going through cigarettes he wasn't going to live that long. His jacket pocket was bulging with tobacco. He kept on offering me hand-rolled cigarettes and I kept on replying, 'I don't smoke.'

Presently I was put into another cell and Bizos arrived. It was the first time I'd seen him in full dress. He looked like a headmaster, black silk gown, set of books under his arm, very academic and wearing his funny-looking glasses.

'Now, when the judge comes in, stand up and when he

asks you how you plead, remember to say "Not guilty, my Lord."'

'Zim and I prefer, "I am innocent of these charges, my Lord."'

'All right, but whatever it is, say it loud. I'm off. Zim will probably drop in, so just keep calm. Don't ask questions. If you want to say anything, write a little note and pass it over.'

He left and I walked back and forth till Zim arrived. He looked just as usual, light grey suit and white shirt. As we were talking I caught a glimpse of Seadom in the cell opposite.

'Hey, Seadom, great to see you.'

I could barely see him through two lots of bars but it was him all right. He replied, 'Have faith, Quentin.'

I turned to Zim smiling.

'You see! He won't let me down.'

'Don't talk to him. You'll hear plenty from him in court.'

It was almost ten. Zim repeated what Bizos had said, and while we were talking the police came for Seadom and then for me.

I was escorted by two policemen and the court warder through a long corridor and across a big domed hall. I saw, in the crowd, friends I hadn't seen for six months. It was good to be able to smile at them and feel free, wearing my own clothes. The court itself was quite small and very crowded. I walked down past two rows of Africans and two rows of Whites and finally up a couple of steps into the dock. I looked round. Someone had done a wholesale job on the police. They looked like a row of outsize male models. Over on the far side I saw my mother with Mr Biggie. I looked up at the clock. It wasn't quite ten, so I walked over to give her a quick hug and assure her I hadn't lost my confidence. I shook hands with Biggie.

'Rather a small pitch,' he said. 'Do you want me to give you your crease?'

'I wouldn't worry. The State's batting first.'

I smiled and walked back. Zim was waiting for me. I asked, 'Where are the twelve angry men?'

'Oh, they went out years ago. But don't worry. You've got one of the best judges in the land, Mr Justice Marais. The press sit where the jury would have been and in a way do a similar job.'

He left me and I waited for the traditional 'Silence in court!', but before that happened, the prosecuting counsel came forward with an additional charge. Bizos explained that it was that I'd gone back to England to try to get funds from an illegal organisation with intent to use the money for sabotage. 'Innocent to the lot, remember.' The court usher shouted. 'Pas op!' and everybody stood up. The judge, dressed in scarlet, came in and sat down. I wanted to say hello but he didn't so much as glance at me. The whole thing was very confusing. He started off in Afrikaans and droned on for ages about, apparently, a Volkswagen and a Ford.

While all this was happening I looked at all the exhibits on the front bench. There was my enlarger, wound up to its greatest height; the three studio flashpacks which had had their side removed to reveal their sinister innards; Dave's surf board with a square hole cut out of the middle; a pressure-cooker; a tongue-press; the two books; a camera and five lenses. Why didn't they throw in the studio sink and a few chairs? What relevance half this stuff had with Terrorism, I just couldn't guess. The judge finished giving his verdict on the two cars, a few people left the court and it was our turn.

Mr Nothling, the Deputy Attorney General, started reading the indictment with great pride and confidence. Bizos and Zim sat back, not unnaturally looking bored to tears, but the members of the press scribbled furiously. I felt that Mr Nothling was letting a very mangy cat out of a very moth-eaten bag. We'd heard it all before. Even the judge had a copy and was calmly reading it for himself. Eventually Nothling sat down and I thought the police were going to applaud, but they contented themselves with rocking back and forth, grinning with delight.

'How do you plead?' the judge asked, and I answered, 'I am innocent of the charges, my Lord.'

Mr Nothling then proceeded to present the State's case at great length.

'Mr Jacobsen,' he said, 'arrived at Jan Smuts Airport from England with his twin brother, Henry, and two Australians,

Mr Martin Cohen and Mr David Smith on April 21st last year. Evidence will be led that Mr Jacobsen and others in his party came to South Africa on a twofold mission: they were to establish a photographic studio in Johannesburg and they were to investigate the political situation and, if necessary and if possible, would work for a change in the political situation. Mr Jacobsen had, in fact, told a witness, Mr Seadom Tilotsane, that they were in South Africa for the anti-apartheid movement. The accused met Mr Seadom Tilotsane and Mr Buki Monamudi and Mr Ian Hill in Johannesburg.

'Political discussion took place on a number of occasions between Jacobsen and his group and the others. They felt that the policy of the South African government was wrong and should be changed. There was, however, a difference of opinion as to the manner in which the change should be effected. The accused was one who expressed the opinion that this should be done by undermining the economy of South Africa by sabotage to bring about political change. The evidence would disclose that Mr Jacobsen propagated firstly a plan to put the Johannesburg telephone exchange out of order, and evidence would be given that he had said he could possibly obtain the original plan of the exchange from his father, a telephone engineer in England.' I looked at Bizos in amazement. 'The accused also propagated the sabotage of bridges on the highways to disrupt the free flow of traffic.'

Mr Nothling, a small, thin, dark man, spoke like a gentleman, almost afraid of what he was saying. He spoke slowly and carefully.

'Mr Jacobsen also mentioned a plan to destroy or damage the municipal bus sheds and the adjoining sub-power station and to disrupt the transport system. He made several suggestions to Mr Ian Hill about the placing of a time bomb in the luggage department of a bus...'

By then I was scarcely listening. His voice was not inspiring and it all sounded unreal. However, when he got on to the bit about going to see Dr Dadoo and went on to say that 'Jacobsen had said it would facilitate his task if he could get bombs and explosives from the Chinese and Russian embassies,' I laughed aloud. Nothling stopped and looked at me briefly and went on unshaken. The *Anarchist Cookbook* and the Army Manual came up next.

'The accused with the assistance of Seadom and Buki made enlarged prints from the negatives. He intended to publish the prints in booklet form and distribute the said publication in places where non-Europeans could get hold of them.'

Nothling dragged on. Finally he called the first State witness, Warrant Officer H. Herfor, a police photographer. He took the oath and proceeded to give evidence in Afrikaans. I looked round, waiting for something to happen. Eventually a small man materialised and translated in a whisper, but he only translated the answers Herfor gave, and since I had no idea what Nothling was asking him this wasn't much use. He said something to the effect on January 26th he took photographs of certain places indicated to him by Seadom Tilotsane. He identified thirteen photographs as those he had taken. These were then handed in as evidence. I was terrified that all the evidence was going to be in Afrikaans. I knew that Seadom spoke Afrikaans, and so did Ian Hill. It was a little upsetting.

Then Seadom was called. Mr Nothling informed the court that the State regarded this witness as an accomplice. Then the judge took over and calmly explained to Seadom that he must answer all questions, even those that might incriminate him, and that if he answered to the satisfaction of the court, he would be freed by the court of all liability to prosecution.

'What is your name and age?'

'My name is Seadom Tilotsane. I am twenty-three and I live in Soweto. I matriculated in March 1968.'

'And what happened during your conversation with the accused?'

'We talked about the political situation and the accused asked me how it was to be black in South Africa. I said it was pretty bad. I can't remember dates or details but we started talking about how to bring about changes in South Africa.'

'What sort of change?'

'A change in the political situation in South Africa.'

'Why had a change to be brought about?'

'It was necessary because of the oppression of the black people by the white people.'

'What was the general view of the government policy?'

'That the only method that would be effective in producing change would be violence. We talked of sabotage, that is crippling the economy of the country.'

'Who first talked of sabotage and crippling the economy?'

'The accused mentioned this, mainly because apartheid is based on the economy.'

'What else did he say?'

'He told me the studio was just a front and that there was something else very important he was doing. I also saw a map in the possession of the accused, of Modderfontein.'

'What was your attitude to the sabotaging of the factory?'

'I was interested when Mr Jacobsen told me it was one of the biggest dynamite factories in South Africa.'

'Where would the accused obtain explosives for the sabotage plans?'

'He said he would get them from London. They could be smuggled to Johannesburg through Lorenzo Marques and Swaziland.'

'Who would supply the explosives?'

'The accused said he would go to London and see Dr Dadoo, who would put him in touch with people. He also mentioned explosives that could be made in the studio.'

'Did he consider obtaining explosives in South Africa?'

'Yes, the accused said the thing was to hitch-hike...'

Nothling interrupted:

'Do you mean hi-jack?'

Seadom gave a little grin. 'Hi-jack ammunition trucks travelling outside the town to Lens. The driver would be shot on a deserted road.'

'Who else agreed with the accused's plans?'

'His brother Henry agreed one hundred per cent and I agreed, but Dave and Martin did not. Buki didn't take much interest. It was eating me up that so many of the people of my colour had resigned themselves to the political situation. But although I felt the need for political change I never thought of sabotage until I met the accused. The accused spoke to me and I was incited and I did agree.'

It sounded as though Seadom had got a dictionary like mine, only instead of 'hypothetical', he'd dog-eared 'incitement'.

'I agreed with him,' he went on, 'and I went to check places that were to be sabotaged. Mr Jacobsen suggested that I or Buki should get a job as night-watchman at the Johannesburg bus sheds so that we would be able to smuggle bombs into the yard, but I said it would be impossible to get such a job as I had no experience as a night-watchman.'

Well, I thought, Seadom doesn't forget much. He looks tired and frightened but his memory is all right.

'And bridges?' Mr Nothling asked.

'Yes, he said he wanted to sabotage bridges because this would draw people's attention, especially black people's attention, because they would see something actually happening at last.'

'What did the accused think of the Blacks?'

'He said the Blacks would not seek political change through violence unless they were pushed into it.'

Mr Nothling returned to the subject of bridges and Seadom said: 'The accused said the bridges to be blown up were those on the Ben Schoeman Highway and the De Villiers Graff Motorway. Another plan involved blowing up radio masts and army vehicles and the Durban-Johannesburg oil pipeline at Croesus.'

'Yes, go on.'

'He said the Voortrekker Monument should be blown up because Blacks regard it as symbolic of white oppression. The Pass Office too, because that was where cheap labour was controlled. I agreed with the accused that it would be a great thing if it was blown up.'

'What did the accused tell you about the books?'

'The accused told me he wanted to print a lot of the books in order to distribute them in the big cities, because the books would agitate the Blacks, sympathetic Whites and intellectuals in the manufacture of explosives. The accused had said it would be very expensive to produce many booklets by photographic printing and that they would have to start a printing-press.'

'Were any reproductions made?'

'No, I know of none.'

At this point there was a long digression about the dagga found in the studio. Seadom said rather pathetically: 'I may be a bad man, my Lord, but at least I sell good dagga.'

The judge, who had scarcely raised his eyes all day, commented drily, 'Yes, export quality.'

Eventually they went back to the meat of the matter.

'Did you ever receive money from the accused?'

'Yes, he was my friend and I helped him in the studio.'

'Regularly?'

'We were much more like brothers. He gave me money any time.'

'And Buki?'

'He received some money too. If he asked for it, he would be given it.'

'Did he get more or less than you?'

'Whatever he asked for. The accused wanted to buy a farm in Swaziland near the Mozambique border and another outside Johannesburg to store ammunition. He said that arms and explosives could be smuggled into the country in the buoyancy tanks of glass-fibre boats, coming from the sea through Lorenco Marques.'

'Who would have committed the acts of sabotage?'

'Myself, the accused, Henry, and people I was going to recruit. I'm not sure of Buki.'

'Who would have trained you in the use of explosives?'

'The accused said he would arrange training in Swaziland. He would train me.'

Mr Nothling then asked him about the photographs and he said he'd done the best he could to point out the spots where the accused had taken photographs.

Finally Mr Nothling said: 'Were you detained on November 7th last year?'

'Yes, at seven-thirty on a Sunday morning.'

When we broke for lunch, I went over to Zim, who said: 'Don't worry. It's going all right.'

'Well, I hope so. Is it all right if Mum has lunch with me?'

He said he had already arranged it. 'Yes, I'll order in two steaks. Is that all right?'

I put my arm round Mum's shoulder and we walked like

that surrounded by policemen back through the long corridor to a distant cell. A second chair was fetched and put in and the door was locked on us.

'Not a good beginning,' I said. 'Does he sound convincing to you?'

'I think he sounds all too convincing. I think he's making out an excellent case for the Blacks but I don't see that it's going to do you much good.'

'I know.' I paused. 'I didn't think he would do it. Zim's right, but it doesn't matter. Anyway we might as well talk of other things. How do you like the place? You know our studio used to be just down the road. I used to pass the court practically every day.'

After a lot of talk and quite a lot of laughing, the steaks arrived. Half an hour later we were interrupted by the rattle of the key in the door. Back to business.

The court was full and overflowing. I had to go through a milling crowd of Africans waiting to get in. It was obvious that they found the trial exciting, but I couldn't help wondering if any of them would have done anything more than that. This time Bizos was cross-examining. He started with a characteristic gesture. He lifted his arms so that his white starched cuffs were displayed. Seadom, in the box, was wilting slightly.

'Is it true that your father was a Sharpeville victim?'

He hesitated and stammered, 'No, it isn't.'

'Then why did you tell the accused that?'

'I didn't.'

Bizos folded his arms and stared triumphantly round the court.

'Why do you pretend to have passed your matriculation and to be a student at Wits?'

'I don't.'

'Well, we'll have more to say on that subject later. Isn't it a shame we can't get back those photographs the Chinese and Russian embassies are supposed to have?'

Seadom rubbed his head and agreed that it was unfortunate. Then Bizos said with heavy sarcasm, 'Would it surprise you to learn that the Chinese and Russian embassies have obligingly returned these photographs?' He held up a number of colour transparencies and said, 'I may say these photographs were in the possession of the accused's mother, who is in court. These are the sort of photographs that a good photographer would take of places visited by tourists, are they not? Look, I ask you, look at this picture and recognise yourself in happier days.'

Seadom took the photographs and looked at them.

'Why didn't you run for cover if you were on such a dangerous mission as you say you were? These, I submit, my Lord, are not the sort of pictures taken with sabotage in mind. Neither would they be the kind of pictures that a communist would want to receive—shots of happy, fat, smiling Africans getting married!'

He passed another picture over to the court usher who, in turn, passed it to Seadom, who then passed it on, via the usher to the judge.

'My Lord, may I ask you to compare the police picture of the Voortrekker Monument taken from a position pointed out by Mr Tilotsane with the photograph which was taken by the accused. The police picture is of the back of the monument, with bushes in the foreground, whereas Mr Jacobsen's photograph was taken from the front and shows people happily climbing the steps ... a touristic photograph.' Then, turning to Seadom, 'I put it to you that your allegation that Mr Jacobsen had taken pictures of motorways for sabotage purposes was a figment of your imagination. You have made a deliberate attempt to mislead the police, did you not?'

'Well, I wouldn't say the police took the picture in exactly the same position.'

Justice Marais intervened to ask Seadom, 'Are you convinced that the accused acted as an ordinary tourist would and you were merely a hanger-on?'

'We always acted very coolly because we didn't want to attract suspicion.'

'So the accused is more than your friend, he is your partner in crime,' continued Bizos. 'If your evidence is correct, you say, "I was incited, and yes, I agreed". Is this so?'

'Yes, I was incited and I agreed.'

'You know that the accused was a busy professional photographer who earned 12,000 rand in five months?'

'I knew he worked hard but I didn't know how much he earned.'

'And the accused was surrounded by a lot of spongers, like you?'

'I don't understand. "Spongers"?'

Bizos hotted up. 'The accused treated you like a brother, gave you money, and you were loyal to him. Why, then, did you tell the court all that you have?'

'Because he was detained by the police, and then I was. I had to tell the truth.'

Bizos folded his arms. 'Why?'

'I thought when the police arrested the accused he would have talked. The police already had information that I was his friend and they found my jacket and some books in the studio.'

'Then why did you tell the police of your plans for sabotage and murder?'

'When I was arrested, they already knew everything. Quentin, Mr Jacobsen, had told them. And Buki was also arrested, so I knew I stood no chance.'

'Did the police tell you you would get out of trouble if you talked?'

'Major van Rensburg, Warrant Officer van Zyl and Sergeant Grobbelaar said I must talk. They didn't say I would get out of trouble if I did.'

'But the police didn't have photographs of the bus sheds and the bridges, did they?'

'No.'

'Then, why did you tell them of your secret talks?'

'I had to tell the truth.'

Bizos changed his ground again. 'At a public function at Wits, when a protest poem was read out, did you stand up and give the Black Power salute and call, "Tell it all brother, tell it all"?'

'I don't remember saying that.'

'So it's possible, is it?'

'I don't remember.'

'But it is possible?'

'I don't know.'

'All right. I'll ask you another question. Did you find the accused a generous man?'

'Yes, he is quite generous.'

'How many times did you go to Pretoria with the accused to take photographs?'

'On two occasions.'

'Did you go to take photographs or to listen to Philip Tabané's band?'

'I wanted to hear the band and Mr Jacobsen came along to take photographs of places to be sabotaged.'

'Did he take photographs of the bridges secretly?'

'No, openly.'

This went on for another two hours. Finally the judge said, 'The court will adjourn till tomorrow at 9.30.'

He walked out and the court rose. I went over to Zim.

'How's it going?'

'Fine, don't worry. Now I want you to cast your mind back over everything Seadom has ever said. Write it down and bring it in with you to-morrow and we'll run through it before court.'

'Fine.'

I said good-bye to my mother, and Colonel Ferrara and I, under escort, were driven back to the Fort. On the way he said, 'Quentin, how long do you think your counsel will take?'

'I don't know. Why?'

'Well we've got other cases coming up. I hope this finishes in a few days.'

'You really think I haven't a chance, don't you?'

'Look, man, you heard the evidence yourself.'

'You've made him say all that. The guy's beginning to break. Anyone can see that.'

'No, you're wrong, Quentin. We've still got Hill and Martin.'

We arrived, and I went through the damp dark tunnel to an office where Ferrara had his receipt for me stamped. Being handed over specially by the police meant I had to be searched in depth—shoes, socks, the lot. I found my cell had also been gone over. I think they were looking for a confession or something. My food was cold and someone had pinched half of my personal store. My newspaper hadn't arrived so I had to walk. Seadom had upset me. The guy must have been pushed to the limit. I didn't hold it against him; it was just very sad to lose a friend.

CHAPTER SEVENTEEN

In court the next morning Bizos resumed the attack on Seadom, who was looking far from well.

'You will have been aware that since the court rose there has been some unfortunate publicity in the newspapers about the fact that you were giving evidence and, as a result, a number of people have come forward with information about the stories you have told. Do you remember meeting a woman who had a French background? Do you see a French person in court?'

'I don't know the difference between French, English and Italian.'

Bizos pointed to a woman in court. 'This is Christine Duval. Let me refresh your memory. You have been to her house.'

'I might have gone to her home. I don't remember.'

'Do you remember her having a job as librarian in a newspaper office?'

'I have been to the *Rand Daily Mail* offices but I don't remember the library.'

'Wasn't there a coloured girl there that you tried to be friendly with?'

'I know a coloured girl called Linda.'

'I think you may be trying to mislead the court. Her name is Rosemary Arnold.'

'I know Rosemary Arnold.'

'Were you playing the role of a tough and embittered African at this time?'

'I was embittered over the situation.'

'Were you playing the role of a tough Africanist?'

'I don't know. I did talk about the situation.'

'And did you try to shock people?'

'I don't know.'

'Would you please look at this long-playing gramophone record by the New York Art Quartette. Whose is it?'

'It's mine, but I don't understand the music. I've played it

often but I don't understand the jazz, it's too complicated.'
'You don't know the words?'
'I don't understand the words.'
'Did you know it was banned?'
'No, I didn't.'
'I am told the music is interrupted by pronouncements of Black Power philosophy.'
'I agree it is about Black Power but I don't know what the principles of Black Power are.'
'I am told that the statements in the music run like this: "The day of the Black is coming, the day to kill the White is near, rape their daughters, rape their mothers, kill their fathers, use anything to do it, razor or knife. The day of the Black Dada Nihilismus will come." Do you agree that those words are on the record?'
'I don't remember the words. I don't like the record.'
'You have tried to persuade the court that you are a peace-loving man.'
'Yes, I am.'
'Would you like to correct yourself. That you were a peace-loving man until you met this revolutionary in the dock?'
'The accused incited me. He hammered things into my head.'
'Which is more penetrating, the shocking words you heard often on this record accompanied by the drumbeat of alleged spiritual music, or the soft words of the accused?'
'I don't understand. I never liked the raping of white women or the killing of white men. That's why I didn't like the record.'
'The sentiments expressed in the record are those of the mentally sick.'
'I actually did not like it. The record did not impress me at all.'
'You took a lot of people for a ride, didn't you? Including the interrogation officers on this case?'
'I just told the truth.'
'Did you go about at night wearing dark glasses?'
'Sometimes at night.'
'Why?'
'Well, when I went to a party, I put on glasses.'

'Is it because one of the leaders of the Black Power movement is frequently seen wearing dark glasses?'

'I don't know that. I know Stokely Carmichael, Eldridge Cleaver, who left the Black Power movement and went to the Black Panthers, and Malcolm X. I have pictures of these people wearing dark glasses. But what's wrong with that?'

'No, you have done worse things than that. Is it also true that you have banned books?'

'Yes, I have read a book by Carmichael.'

'Did you express your pleasure in having blood-curdling records and books describing dangerous things?'

'I don't remember.'

'Now, is it true that you are a habitual dagga smoker and you have been on at least eight LSD trips?'

'Yes, I have.'

'And you have told some people that you are a Sharpeville orphan and others that your father was a rich man who ran a bus service in the eastern Transvaal.'

'This is not true.'

'I am going to put it to you that you have told so many lies, depending on the circumstances in which you found yourself, that you cannot tell falsehood from reality any more.'

'I can.'

'Did you tell the accused your father was killed at Sharpeville?'

'I deny that.'

'Oh, to-day you say "I deny", not "I don't remember" as you did yesterday. Has anyone suggested to you that you should be more emphatic and say this?'

'Nobody told me.'

'When you agreed with the accused about blowing up a railway train leaving the Modderfontein Dynamite Factory, did you not consider that your friend Gareth and his parents to whose party you went might be amongst the victims?'

'Yes, it is possible. He might have been killed, but it was the accused who suggested the plan to me. I didn't say anything.'

'Are you just a piece of putty?'

Poor Seadom was looking more and more just like that.

'No. I agreed with him on changing South Africa by destroying the economy.'

'And your black brothers on the nearby location, did you not think they might be killed in the explosion?'

'I didn't think of it. I just agreed to the plan.'

'Did you agree to the plan after you had had your daily dose of dagga?'

'I don't remember if I smoked dagga that day.'

'You listened to records and read books about nihilism. Is it not strange that you never thought of sabotage before you talked to the accused?'

'No, because I never thought that sabotage would achieve change. I only thought of it after I was incited by the accused.'

'I am suggesting to you that you did not need to be incited, but played the part of a Black who had suffered at the hands of the Whites?'

'I only thought of sabotage after I was incited by the accused.'

'If you were dedicated to the liberation of the black people in South Africa, why did you not get a copy of the prints you helped to make—to see how to make TNT, for example?'

'Well, we were told not to take one, and I was scared.'

'Didn't you think it was terribly dangerous to agree with the accused on these country-wide sabotage plans?'

'I knew it was dangerous.'

'And yet you were too scared to take one sheet of the *Anarchist Cookbook* to study at home?'

'The accused said I should not, in case I was stopped by a policeman and searched. It happens all the time.'

'Did you ever buy a hammer or a battery or some chemicals or anything of the sort? The slightest bit of material, in fact, to make bombs and start your sabotage?'

'No, we never had anything in the studio.'

'And how long had the conspiracy been going on for?'

'I cannot say. We did not agree on any specific day. It was a continuous process.'

'Was it decided by the beginning of June?'

'Yes, I was incited by then and I agreed.'

'Then can you explain why during a period of five months not a single step was taken towards putting your plan of sabotage into effect?'

'Because it was still being planned. It is not a thing that can be done in a month.'

'Let me read you some sections from the introduction to the *Anarchist Cookbook*, my Lord, to sum up some of the attitude of this witness.' Bizos spread himself, hitched his cuffs into position and read. The first page finished with, ' "Anarchism as an idea is non-violent. Its philosophy is Spinozean, ethical and nature-loving." Do you like that?'

'I don't understand it.'

Mr Justice Marais showed signs of getting restive and Bizos reluctantly put the book aside and went on to another point. 'About the Marxist names suggested for your party, the People's Democratic Party, the People's Communist Party, and the People's Liberation Party, what I don't understand is that the *Cookbook* is just as critical of Russia as of any other state. It also says advertising is not a worthwhile occupation. Wasn't the accused, among his friends, accused of being terribly English middle-class with all his travelling and making and spending money and so on? Didn't you label him "bourgeois"?'

'No, I didn't.'

'I find it difficult to believe that the accused, a successful advertising photographer, could be associated with a party whose name had Marxist connotations.' Bizos was clearly drawing, not exactly to a climax, but at least to a close. 'I put it to you that there was no agreement between you to commit acts of sabotage and that you never were incited to commit acts of sabotage.'

'We did agree. That's why the photographs were taken.'

'You, for reasons of your own, decided to build up this conspiracy in your mind and give evidence of it to His Lordship.' He paused for effect. 'Many a witness will give evidence if need be of the false and lying life you have led.'

'I don't agree. The *Anarchist Cookbook* was found in the studio and the accused did take photographs to London.'

Bizos sat down and Seadom cradled his head in his arms, which he had been doing more and more as time went on.

When Mr Nothling followed Bizos with his re-examination, almost at once Seadom interrupted him. 'Excuse me, can I have some of my tabs?'

'Do you mean some aspirin?' asked Nothling.

'Anything that will get me right, so long as it's not LSD.'

'What is your complaint? Do you have a headache?'

'Yes, I've got a headache and when I was in jail I had some teeth out.' (This surprised me. He had always had good teeth.) Colonel Ferrara was just about to run over to give him some tablets when he remembered apartheid, and a black policeman had to be summoned to do so. It was obvious to me that Seadom was smashed. It seemed pointless of Nothling to try to salvage any of his evidence. It only made it more like a put-up job. Quite unintentionally he seemed to be proving I wasn't a communist.

'What kind of person is the accused?' Seadom was finally asked. 'Is he able to influence people easily?'

'Yes, he is very influential.'

Seadom said that he had given his evidence freely and voluntarily and added that after the trial he would like to travel round Europe. His last remark was about as realistic as the rest of his evidence. His chance of getting a passport was about as good as his chance of me lending him money for the ticket.

Mr Nothling called the next witness. It was the photographer, Warrant Officer Herfor again. As soon as I saw him, I knew that something fishy was happening. My interpreter arrived and I took down every word he said, though again I was given only the answers, not the questions. But it was clear that he was running over the photographs. He said that he had gone out with Seadom on January 26th and because of the slow film he was using it had been necessary to take out a flash-gun. They had taken half an hour on each shot, and had taken them from exactly the position that Seadom had indicated that the accused had used.

When Mr Nothling had finished Bizos stood up.

'My Lord, as you know, my client is a photographer. I wonder, since it is a half-day and it is already late, if it might be possible to adjourn so that my client can study the photographs himself.'

Mr Justice Marais asked if Mr Nothling had any objections. He had none, so permission was granted. Bizos gave me a set of prints of the police photographs, said 'Good luck' and I was led out with my guards.

That evening I studied the shots. All were standard perspective, all were in a horizontal format, all were ten by eight, staple-mounted on to sheets of plain foolscap, the number of the shot written on the foolscap mount. Now for the lighting. Some had been taken in soft daylight, some in flash-light, some in hard sunlight. They could all have been done on the same day but ... but it didn't seem likely. There was something fishy. There would be two shots of the same thing, but with different lighting, one soft and overcast, and the other hard, direct sunlight. Why?

Now the numbers. Some of the numbers had been crossed out. Again, why? There must be a reason. I laid them out in the original number pattern and got long shot, medium shot, close up, long shot, medium shot, close up, of a big fat bridge, bus sheds, transformer, vehicle park, communication masts, oil refinery. Now, if I were a picture editor or an art director, I would lay them out in order of picture value as, in fact, they were in the present system. They started off comparatively harmless and got more and more destructive as they went on. So that's the first order. The second order, then, would be as they had been renumbered. Laid out like that the story was lost. It was all over the place. There was no sense of progression. Those numbers had been crossed out for a reason. But why? Why alter the numbers?

Pretoria, Pretoria, Pretoria, Jo'burg, Jo'burg Jo'burg. No, that's not it, but something stinks here. But I'll get it, I'll get it.

The last shot of the Paul Kruger statue had been withdrawn and they had substituted the Voortrekker Monument. There must be a reason. I leant over to pick it up. It had been put in late. Why? It wasn't mounted like the others. I turned it over quite casually and my hair rose on my head. It had a date and negative-number. The date was January 24th and the number 126. I went back to look at the others, which meant opening up the mounts and looking inside. I found January 18th, Negative Number 67. Then the next was January 25th, Negative Number 88; next January 25th, Negative Number 95. The bastards were lying! How can you print something on the 18th if it wasn't shot till the 26th? The negative numbers were all over the place. I opened up each print and on the front wrote the date when it had been printed and the negative number, then looked at the system again. Straightaway, it was as clear as daylight. Each negative had been stamped in Johannesburg by the same person; they all had the same signature. All the shots done on the first day were the passive, non-committal, long shots. They could have been tourist shots. Then the police Art Director had clearly come along and said, 'Not good enough, no drama. Get in there, use a flash, shoot the guts of it.' So next day they go all the way to Pretoria and shoot series B, but the police decide that though they're good they still lack value. What about a nice fat bridge? So the photographer does that and then the police go wild: vehicle car park, bus shed, oil refinery, end of story.

So to re-cap: how can you print something before it's shot? Second, why go back to the same location a day later to do close-ups? And third, why were they shot on different days? If Seadom actually knew what I shot, they could have done them all on one day. And why take half an hour on each? It was obvious that Seadom never went out with them at all. He may have told them, but they took the lead and glamourised it. For a start I don't have a portable flash-gun and secondly the chances are that my colour film is slower than his black-and-white. Again, why use a standard lens? A telephoto would be more logical.

It was very exciting. I mean, sure enough, I had shot the places, but the fact was that their evidence was wrong. I had told them in interrogation that Henry had done a few shots on town-planning around Jo'burg. All right. They can't get Henry, so they try Seadom: pull his teeth out, stick him in solitary for three months and then ask him, 'Now do you remember?' If there's one thing I'd learnt it was, 'Don't say anything; they'll only use it on the next bloke and then bang it back on you.'

Next day when Colonel Ferrara collected me, I tried to

appear as normal as possible. I hoped to God they hadn't looked at the back of the photographs.

Bizos had a story about pins which he used to emphasise the importance of small details. He told how he had worked on a divorce case where a husband was accused of beating his wife. In evidence the wife said that he used to hang up the blood-stained towel that she had used after his beatings as a warning. He denied this, but when her counsel held out his hand in which there were three pins which he said had been used to pin up the towel, the husband casually said, 'I thought there were four!' Ever since then Bizos had been counting pins. So the next morning when I told him I thought I'd found some pins, I added, 'Don't worry; they're not mine.'

The police photographer went back into the box and Bizos began his cross-examination.

'Warrant Officer Herfor, you said earlier that you went out with Seadom to take photographs on only one occasion. That was January 26th, was it not?'

'Yes, that is correct.'

'Well, would you kindly tear off the back of photograph Number 1 and tell the court what it says on the back?'

He tore it off and looked at it.

'South African Department of Police Photo. Date 18th; negative-number 67.'

'Can you tell the court how it came to be printed almost a week before it was presumed to be shot? And the next shot, Number 2 of the same bridge, is printed a day later with a totally different negative number. Why?'

By this time both the counsels and the judge, all of whom had copies of the photographs, were ripping them out of the mounts. It was an oddly shocking noise in the normally hushed court room.

'My Lord,' Bizos continued, 'if you look at the series of photographs, it is obvious that the police have tried to make a story. The fact that the negative-numbers and the print-dates progress in parallel with an ever higher degree of drama in the pictures is a clear indication of a fabrication.'

The judge, who was still turning over the prints, indicated that there would be a short break, and when we resumed Mr Nothling re-examined the police photographer.

'Tell me, Warrant Officer, is the negative-number any proof of when the photograph was taken?'

'No. It has no reference at all.'

'And please, the print-date, what does that signify?'

'It means nothing. It is just a code for filing.'

The covering up only made it worse. Why couldn't they admit they were wrong.

The next State witness was Major van Rensburg who had been Seadom's chief investigator. He refused to admit that witnesses were 'interrogated'. He insisted that they were 'investigated'. He was a big, coarsely handsome man with blond, wavy hair and a very flowery shirt. Nothling took him through the police photographs and he agreed that they were taken at the places indicated by Seadom.

Then Bizos went into action.

'As a senior police officer, did it not occur to you that a person addicted to drugs is dangerous to rely on?'

'That is a difficult question to answer. During most of my career I have been concerned with security matters.'

'While in the witness box Seadom has on various occasions asked for "tabs". Did he ask for tabs on the course of your questioning?'

'Yes, he asked me for them on two occasions. Once he had a severe headache and on the other occasion I think he had had two of his teeth extracted.'

'The purpose of detention under Section 6 is to get information which would enable you to safeguard the security of the State, is it not?'

'That is correct.'

'Shortly before Seadom's detention there was a considerable amount of disquiet about the treatment of persons detained under Section 6 of the Terrorism Act?'

'Do you want me to comment on that?'

'Well, there was disquiet by the public. You know the newspapers were making a lot of noise. I merely want to establish the fact that there was general disquiet.'

'Yes.'

'There had been the death of a person who died as the result of a fall out of a window in the police station, and that received wide publicity shortly before Seadom was detained.'

'The only disquiet then was about the death of that person.'

'And also about the finding in hospital in Pretoria of another person who had also been detained under Section 6 of the Terrorism Act.'

'That is correct.'

'And Seadom had lots to fear?'

'I can assure the court that Seadom had no knowledge of these two incidents.'

'Don't be so quick to give that assurance. When was Seadom detained?'

The judge intervened firmly. 'The two cases being referred to are the Timol case and the Essop case.'

Van Rensburg replied, 'He did not know about the propaganda in the newspapers. Ah, it has just occurred to me that he may have known about Timol's fall.'

'So you were wrong when you gave His Lordship these assurances?'

'Yes, I was wrong.'

'The Essop case was given wide publicity on October 29th and Seadom was arrested on November 7th.'

'Seadom must have read about the Timol case and the Essop case in the newspapers before his arrest,' the judge said.

'Yes, it seems so,' Van Rensburg reluctantly admitted.

Bizos took over again. 'Did you indicate to him that you needed the information, and that unless he gave information that you thought was correct, he would not be released?'

'That is more or less a threat and that is not the way we work. Detainees are told that as soon as they tell the truth they will be released. That is not a threat.'

'But Section 6 obliges a person to make a statement, and unless the statement is to the satisfaction of the Commissioner he will be detained indefinitely. So he is compelled to make a statement.'

'That is right and it is correct that persons detained would quite naturally want to bring their detention to an end as soon as possible.'

'Has it occurred to you that a weak, timid or dishonest person might want to satisfy you by telling a half-truth to avoid further detention?'

'I would only be satisfied when he told the truth.'

'And do you not even sometimes make an intelligent guess?'

'Yes, it is part of our job to make intelligent guesses and part of our work to assume the worst, that a conspiracy had been laid to overthrow the State. It is surprising how many people, I would not say confess, but take us into their confidence and explain the whole story.'

Bizos sat down.

I thought to myself, it's also surprising how many people detained under Section 6 have fallen to their death out of windows or done themselves fatal injury by slipping on a bar of soap. There have been something like nineteen dead so far. And as for intelligent guesses, I felt they were in the same class as their inspired questions, like, 'Why were you arrested?'

Mr Nothling now called Ian Hill. Ian came in looking very respectable, his hair cut, and wearing a dark suit.

'Mr Hill, how old are you?'

'Twenty-three.'

'And you are a medical student at Witwatersrand University in your fifth year of study?'

'That is correct.'

He was taken through the usual personal details, and he told how he came to know the studio.

'Now, in the studio, were politics ever discussed?'

'Yes, they were.'

'Will you kindly tell the court about these political discussions?'

'The general view amongst those people present at the studio was that the present set-up in South Africa was a bad one and that apartheid was shocking and it would be far better if the situation was changed.'

'Was the possibility considered that it could be done in a constitutional way?'

'It was considered, but I think it was generally felt that there wasn't much chance of this happening.'

'Were alternatives considered?'

'Yes, the chances of outside intervention were discussed.'

'Tell us about that.'

'It was felt that the country was aware of this and very much on the alert and, with its armed forces, this was not considered to be a feasible possibility. And then discussion came round to changing the system from within.'

'Yes, go on.'

'We then talked about how undermining the economy would be a beginning to this change.'

'Do you remember who raised it?'

'The accused first raised the possibility.'

'Yes. Tell us what was said by the accused.'

'The first idea was to knock out the Johannesburg telephone exchange, because it was felt it would have a profound effect on the economy within the city, at any rate.'

'Do you remember what he said in that regard?'

'In that regard the accused said he would, or would attempt to, get the plan of the exchange from his father in England.'

'Now, when this was discussed, who was present?'

'The accused, his brother Henry, Martin, Dave, myself, Buki and Seadom.'

'What was the view of Henry Jacobsen in regard to this suggestion?'

'I think he went along with the accused.'

'And Martin and Dave Smith?'

'They were opposed to this and indeed any violent form of changing the government.'

'And the Africans, that is Seadom and Buki?'

'I think they agreed with the accused's suggestions.'

'What was your view?'

'My own view at this stage was somewhat mixed. I didn't think that these discussions would ever actually be carried out.'

'It was all rather academic as far as you were concerned?' interrupted the judge.

'At this stage, yes.'

Nothling continued, 'Were you prepared to assist in any such activity?'

'No. At this stage, I don't think there was any thought of my assisting, but if there had been I would not have been prepared to do so.'

'Yes, please continue.'

'Well, the accused also suggested blowing up the bus sheds.'

'Did he explain how this would be done?'

'Not on the first occasion, no.'

'Did he explain why this should be done?'

'Yes, he said the Whites in this country were upsetting the Blacks and that they didn't treat them as human beings. It would be an easy way of making the Whites aware that somebody was working against them, and a reminder that the Black people were human beings as well.'

'Was the effect on the economy specifically mentioned?'

'Not really. I don't think so. If people didn't get to work on time it would have some minor effect, but it was intended more as a harassment, I think.'

'When did this discussion take place?'

'I think it must have taken place in July, 1971. Then in August, before the accused went overseas, he asked me if I would go out and help him construct petrol bombs.'

'For what purpose?'

'I think he wanted to experiment with the making of petrol bombs with a view to using the experience at a later stage.'

'Did he tell you for what purpose he wanted to use the petrol bombs?'

'To blow up the bus sheds.'

'He wanted you to assist in the experimenting?'

'That's correct.'

Nothling again went through the list of the attitudes of each of the others, and Hill said that the attitude of the others had changed. The accused, he said, didn't want to talk about things in front of Martin and Dave because they were opposed to violence and might be a security risk.

'And what was your own attitude to the accused after he had asked you to assist in making petrol bombs?'

'This was a progressive thing. To begin with I thought it was, as it were, academic but when he began wanting to exclude David and Martin and not talk about these things in front of them, I began to get wary, and by the time he actually asked me to help him in the construction of petrol bombs, I began to think he was serious. Then the accused left for England in August and I didn't see him for some time. I decided then that I wouldn't return to the studio and that I would break off my association with the accused and the others, giving as my reason that I did not want to endanger my medical career.'

Question and answer went on and the story unfolded. When he got to the bit about having the books at his place, he said, 'I got a phone call from the accused telling me that if I went to the garage I would find a packet in a box the contents of which I should find very interesting. I brought the box into my room and opened it and inside were the photographic prints. I told him he must take the book away. He told me he wanted to make prints of the *Anarchist Cookbook* and leave them lying around strategic parts of the city, such as the African railroad stations where they could be picked up, and possibly people would then take the initiative and make their own explosives. He went on to say that he had given up the idea of blowing up the bus sheds and had a more important plan, which was to blow up the Modderfontein Dynamite Factory which supplied all the explosives for the mining industry, which would come to a stand still. I told him again that I thought this was ridiculous, but he said he had been up there and there weren't very good security measures, and if you could blow up a train as it came out of the factory you could in this way blow up the whole factory. He said a bazooka wouldn't be too difficult to construct but he would have to get the explosives in from outside the country. These could be picked up and fibreglassed into a boat and then the boat could be smuggled in.'

'Did you tell him that you wanted nothing to do with this plan in regard to Modderfontein?'

'Yes, I said I wasn't prepared to get involved in these hare-brained schemes of his.'

'And what was his reaction?'

'He said that Henry and he would be responsible. Possibly he might use Buki and Seadom as well.'

Eventually, Mr Nothling asked, 'Was anything said about bridges?'

'Not on that occasion. At an earlier stage he said he had been round photographing bridges with a view to sabotage. He asked if I would accompany him. I didn't go with him.'

The court was adjourned.

When it resumed, Mr Nothling went back to the subject of the party Hill had gone to with the Jacobsen brothers.

'Do you remember if a man called Winston Tsaole was at the Du Plessis party?'

'Yes.'

'Was there an argument?'

'Yes.'

'What was the argument about and what was said by the accused?'

'He said that Mr Tsaole was just running away from the problems of this country, and an argument ensued.'

'Can you remember anything being said about a truck?'

'Yes, the accused said the problem with the urban African was that he wasn't prepared to work for his own freedom and he quoted, as an example, that every day a truck laden with explosives drives past Soweto, yet no attempt had been made by the Africans to seize the truck.'

'Did he speak with enthusiasm, the accused?'

'I think he spoke with a great deal of enthusiasm.'

'And was he an unimpressive personality or was he able to influence people?'

'I think he was an impressive sort of person, not one you could easily forget.'

'Would you say it would have been possible for the accused to influence the Africans, Seadom and Buki?'

'I think so, yes. Insofar as he took an interest in them. He treated them as equals and this had an influence on them.'

'Now, were you detained by the police in connection with this case?'

'Yes, I was detained by the security police on November 12th 1971.'

'And when were you released?'

'I was released on December 15th 1971.'

'No more questions.'

Mr Bizos rose to start his cross-examination. 'Mr Hill, please accept that nothing I am going to say is intended to embarrass you, and, you know, I am hoping one day to address you as Dr Hill. But the picture you painted of yourself, say, in October 1971 isn't the picture of yourself that you want His Lordship to believe now. Did you have a special hair-cut for this occasion?'

'Yes, I did cut off a fair amount.

'You have said in your evidence in chief that by October 1971 you were attempting to disaffiliate from the accused and his group. But you had dinner with him late in October?'

'Yes.'

'If I was going to disassociate myself from somebody the last thing in the world I would do would be to ask him over for dinner.'

'I invited him to dinner to ask him to take the stuff away.'

'Mr Hill, do you think you owe any sort of loyalty to society—never mind government—to the society in which we live?'

'Yes, I would say I have a civic responsibility.'

'Civic responsibility? Well, civic responsibility goes a bit further than loyalty, because civic responsibility really means that you are prepared to do something concrete to help society.'

'Yes, I am a medical student.'

'All right, now, can you tell the court which came first, the talk about the petrol bombs or the talk about the bridges?'

'I can't recall exactly.'

'Well, I put it to you: to anybody, or at least to any fourth-year medical student or anyone with any commonsense, to have entered into a conspiracy would be a very vivid event, one that could hardly be forgotten.'

Hill took some time. 'I have no comment.'

'No comment. Well, let me put this in perspective as well. Did Seadom tell you he was a Sharpeville orphan?'

'Yes. It was at the Du Plessis party.'

'And you believed him?'

'I believed him.'

'Did he also tell you he was a student?'

'Yes, I lent him a white coat for a practical exam.'

'By the way, did you ever get your coat back?'

'No, I didn't.'

'Having heard Seadom, it doesn't surprise me. Now, if you called yourself a radical, what would you mean by this?'

'I don't ever recall calling myself a radical.'

'But didn't you hold yourself out as a radical on the campus?'

'As I explained, I didn't frequent the campus very often.'

'Now, before your detention, you knew that the accused had been taken in?'

'Yes, ten days earlier.'

'You knew of something that the State was going to be interested in and you didn't intend to hold out?'

'Let me explain. These ten days prior to my arrest were very difficult.'

'Why?'

'Well, I didn't know whether I was going to be arrested or not. It was obvious to me that someone had spoken during interrogation. Then I was arrested on the Friday night after having written an examination. My place was searched completely and they also searched my room in Hillbrow. Then I was taken to John Vorster Square police station and told I had the weekend to think about it and that I was being held as a political prisoner. Come Monday morning I was told that I was in serious trouble and that, unless I helped the police, I would find myself, you know, in very serious trouble. Bearing that in mind and that I am, or was at that stage, a fourth-year medical student hoping to qualify as a doctor and not to rot in some prison, I told the police what I knew.'

'Tell us about the interrogation.'

'Well, it is a very frightening experience suddenly to be taken and arrested under the Terrorism Act and told that you are in trouble. And I knew that I knew certain things that the accused had told me. I reasoned that I wasn't in favour of all his ideas and that I should tell the authorities.'

'You see, the portion that interests me is this. You had committed no crime, had you?'

'I didn't know. Subversive stuff had been found on my property.'

'But didn't you make it clear that you were really bluffed by the accused? I mean he told you that he would leave a surfboard and then he left subversive stuff.'

'That's true.'

'Did they believe you?'

'I don't know to what extent they believed me or not. I think they thought I might be withholding a further part of which I knew nothing.'

'Did you read about one of your fellow medical students, Essop, who was found in hospital somewhere in Pretoria?'

'Yes, I did read about it.'

'And this was the state of mind in which you entered interrogation?'

'Yes, I was terrified.'

'You were terrified. Now, the literature of detention speaks of a dependency that develops between the prisoners and the person who has the power to let him go, or to leave him in solitary confinement. Did you find yourself wanting to see the person who interrogated you?'

'Yes, it got to the stage where I wanted anything to happen rather than just to go on sitting there on my own.'

'In absolute solitary confinement?'

'Yes.'

'Was your statement brushed up after it was made?'

'Yes, two weeks later.'

'And after your mind was receptive?'

'It was rewritten just before I left prison. I used my first statement as a basis for my second.'

'Why was it necessary to make a second statement?'

'I am not the person to ask that.'

'Now, having made this statement and been released, were you told you had to keep to it?'

'Yes.'

'And did you have to keep to it?'

'I was phoned and asked to go and see the Security Police after that, and my statement was gone through and I had to verify that it was so.'

'When did that happen?'

'I think the first time was in January, and then again in February.'

Mr Justice Marais intervened. 'I think it would be best to adjourn at this stage. We will recommence on Monday morning at half past nine.'

CHAPTER EIGHTEEN

As the court rose, I went over to Zim and Bizos. All three of us were looking a little despondent.

'We've done a good job on Seadom and the police,' I said, 'but Hill's a bugger! This disassociation thing is pure crap. And as for him pretending not to be a radical!'

Zim in his usual way said, 'Don't worry. It's going fine, but we'll be up at the Fort to-morrow to discuss things. All right? And I've also arranged a visit from your mother on Sunday so you just hold tight till then.'

I didn't think things were going fine but I followed the police out to the car and so back to the Fort. After every day they would search both me and my cell. It wasn't easy. Still in solitary, feeling attacked from all sides. Hill was obviously trying to help the police from every angle but he was over-doing it, trying to look too innocent.

Next day Zim and Bizos came in and told me that, as had happened after Seadom's evidence had been published in the newspapers, the publicity given to Hill's evidence had produced a crop of telephone calls at all hours to say that he was lying. The thing is, you may not have a jury but as soon as evidence is released, members of the public come forward and contest it. It's just as good.

'About this Last Supper you had with Hill,' Bizos said, 'I want fifteen pages on it. Do you hear, fifteen pages, no less.'

There was a lot I could write on it but fifteen pages seemed a bit much. However, solitary helps you to concentrate and I managed to remember details which I'm sure Ian Hill had forgotten.

My mother had brought me a book on Pre-Raphaelites which she knew I would like and I had just got round to reading it, and was looking forward to discussing it with her when she came on Sunday. The only trouble was that I saw her with about four other prisoners on my side of the bars and rather more of their wives, girl-friends and mothers on hers. And they didn't want to talk about the Pre-Raphaelites.

It was both sad and slightly hysterical. The other prisoners were having their first and last visits before going to the Central Jail in Pretoria and their conversation was a good deal more dramatic than ours and certainly louder. 'The money's under ... you know, where we used to go. No not there. Under the....' Whereas I was trying to shout, 'I don't like Burne-Jones as much as I used to do. I prefer Millais, especially the early work.' We both had to laugh. One could have made a fortune if only one could have unravelled the conversations but it was more than we could take, so we gave up and waved goodbye till the following day in court.

On Monday morning when Bizos rose to continue his cross-examination, he started by saying he wanted to put on record that he had received a telex message from Geneva from Mr Jacobsen's father 'who is a distinguished scientist, My Lord' that he emphatically affirmed that he had at no time given information about the Johannesburg telephone exchange to his son and that no plans of the exchange had been in his possession or known to him.

Then he turned to Hill.

'Were you at the protest meeting against the detentions that took place from October 22nd onwards?'

'I attended a protest meeting at the medical school, yes.'

'If, at this stage, that is on October 22nd, you felt yourself vulnerable as a result of what you knew about the plans of the accused, the very natural thing would have been to keep away from it, away from protest, to keep away from a place where your presence might attract the attention of the Security Police.'

'I believe in an entity called social conscience.'

'I beg your pardon?'

'I believe in an entity called social conscience.'

'But now, please do not misunderstand me. My criticism of you is not that you went to the protest meeting. What I am putting to you is that if you were terrified as a result of the knowledge of the accused's plans that you had, the most natural precaution, even for a person with a social conscience, would have been to keep away from the protest meeting.'

Hill made no reply.

'Did you know Ahmed Timol?'

'No.'

'He meant nothing in your life? You had never heard the name before he died?'

'No.'

'He was buried on October 22nd, a Friday. Do you remember?'

'Yes.'

'And you went to the funeral?'

'Yes.'

'He was a Moslem?'

'Yes.'

'And I understand that there were thousands of people there.'

'There were a lot of people at the funeral.'

'The Whites at the funeral must have stuck out like a sore thumb to the Security Police?'

Again, Hill made no reply.

'Well, let's take it like this. Because of the public disquiet, the funeral was not an ordinary funeral. Mr Timol had become the symbol of what was believed, albeit by only a section of the public, to be the excesses of the Security Police. Is this so?'

'Yes, I would say this is true.'

'Don't you agree that a White there, in these circumstances, would have stuck out like a sore thumb?'

'Yes, that is true.'

Bizos then asked about a protest meeting at the medical school. 'Why did you go to the protest meeting and why did you go to the funeral when you might have attracted the attention of the police?'

'I went to the protest meeting because a colleague of mine had been detained.'

'That is Mr Essop?'

'That is correct.'

'It is the last time I am asking the question, so please try to give an answer. Why did you go?'

There was a long silence. Then, reluctantly, Hill said, 'I went there despite the danger.'

'Is that your answer?'

'Yes.'

209

'Now, you had never been to an Islamic funeral before, had you?'

'No.'

'And do you, like all of us, when you find yourself in a strange situation, want to sort of hang back and do as little as possible? You know, like if you go to a funeral of your own section, you know what's happening and you can participate but, if you go to a strange funeral don't you feel somewhat embarrassed?'

'Yes, I will say that is true.'

'Now, there were two parts to this funeral, one part which was in the presence of thousands and the other in an inner sanctum where members of the family and close friends gathered at the cemetery. Is that right?'

'Yes.'

'I am told that for all practical purposes you were the only White in that inner sanctum.'

'I saw at least fifteen or twenty other Whites.'

'Fifteen or twenty as opposed to thousands of Indians. Did it occur to you that by going there you might be giving the Security Police a very important lead to yourself, and through you, to the accused?'

'Well, I don't think so.'

Bizos made his characteristic movement of the arms. 'You see, isn't the explanation that you felt you were quite right and entitled to take part in that protest meeting and attend that funeral because you were not in possession of any information about terrorism and, in fact, you had nothing to fear?'

'No, I don't think that's true.'

'Did you march to the John Vorster Square from the University in May 1970?'

'I did. I was there.'

'Again the victim of circumstances, or did you deliberately defy the ban that the procession was not to take place?'

'I joined the protest march. I was one of the people.'

'And did you attend a lecture given by Miss Joan Lestor?'

'Yes.'

'Is it correct that one of the things she was asked about was her attitude to the Springbok tours?'

'I don't remember.'

'No, but you should remember, because you were one of the few people in the audience who gave her a standing ovation when she said that she was against it.'

'It is possible.'

'You were the person hollering about everything. Do you remember walking with the accused at Zoo Lake and when you saw a man wearing a Springbok blazer, you said you wanted to stop and wring his neck?'

'I don't think I would have used that sort of language.'

'Well, do you remember the incident?'

'I remember seeing a man and saying I didn't know how he could be proud of representing a uni-racial team.'

'Yes, but this was the simple stimulus that led to a violent reaction from you?'

'I don't know about violent reaction.'

'Well, you know I want to tell you that most people, when they see somebody with a Springbok blazer, will say, "This man must have been a good sportsman; he's really reached the top". That would be most people's reaction even if they did not agree with the policy of the government. I don't know what you would have done if my instructing attorney put on his blazer.' Zim grinned hugely and Hill looked, if anything, more uncomfortable than ever. 'Haven't I produced enough evidence to convince even you that you were a loud-mouthed protester?'

'Yes, I did protest.'

'Yes, and you were a radical of sorts?'

'I never claimed to be a radical. I thought of myself as a liberal.'

'Some people think that is quite radical enough in South Africa. Is that not so?'

'Yes I agree.'

'Now, tell me, did you ever doubt the accused's sanity?' Bizos looked at the judge almost conspiratorially. 'There's no danger of a change of plea, My Lord, I may say.' Then back to Ian Hill. 'Is the expression a "Walter Mitty" known to you?'

'A "Walter Mitty"? I have heard of it.'

'You have. Does the description suit him?'

'At no stage did I doubt his sanity.'

'I beg your pardon. Did you consider him a bit of a Walter Mitty?'

'No, I don't think so.'

'Wasn't he a man with grandiose ideas?'

'Yes, in some ways.'

'Now, the last supper. At this supper, you say you wanted to disaffiliate yourself, but, in point of fact, you went on to show him a very intimate letter from an American girl-friend of yours that you met in Paris.'

'Yes.'

'Are you in the habit of showing very intimate letters to people you want to disaffiliate yourself from? Wouldn't she be very perturbed if she knew you had shown the letter to the accused?'

'No, she's not that kind of girl; she's a Woman's Liberationist.'

'I will spare your Lordship the details of what the dinner consisted, but do you remember lending the accused one of your favourite records? A Cat Stevens record?'

'Yes.'

'When you lend a man a record you like, you expect, sooner or later, to see that man again to get it back? The point I'm trying to make is, that if you lend someone one of your favourite records, it is not a step clearly indicating an intention to disaffiliate.'

'It is a minor detail on which to base this assumption.'

'Do you remember that there was talk about making films in South Africa?'

'Yes.'

'And wasn't Modderfontein Dynamite Factory discussed along the lines, "What a wonderful film it would make if embittered Blacks blew it up"?'

'Not at all.'

'What sort of film was it thought to make?'

'It wasn't discussed in terms of a film at all. When Modderfontein was first mentioned to me by the accused, he told me he had decided to discard the plan to blow up the bus sheds but was aiming for bigger things, and that he wanted to hit Modderfontein and cripple the mining industry.'

'Not in relation to a film?'

'Not in relation to a film.'

'Why didn't you tell him to get out of your house?'

'I told the accused that I thought it was a ridiculous idea.'

'Did you really believe that he was involved in a plan to blow up the dynamite factory?'

'Judging by my experience of the accused in this sort of field, and the fact that he had asked me to go and help construct petrol bombs, I didn't put it past him. He told me he had been out there and that you could see the factory from the road.'

'You are not trying to allude to a sort of Last Supper, are you, Mr Hill? I want to put it to you that you wouldn't have invited him to dinner, you wouldn't have shown him that intimate letter of your erstwhile girl, you wouldn't have lent him a record and you wouldn't have spent hours with him talking, if you only intended to tell him to move the stuff from the garage. Why didn't you say, "Look, never mind the surfboard, but please take this highly incriminating stuff that I have wiped my fingerprints off"? He could have taken them on the bus, couldn't he? You see, the accused seems to recollect that he did take the prints back with him.'

'No, he didn't take any part of it. In fact, he wouldn't, till he knew that Henry was safely back in England.'

'Oh, I see. You realise, of course, that you have made the story a little worse for yourself. You were prepared to continue being his accomplice of sorts?'

'The stuff remained at my house.'

'But if, in fact, you wanted to dissociate, the obvious thing to do was to say, "Take the stuff and get out and don't let me see you again." As it is, you were helping him by keeping it there, hiding it?'

'What can I say?' He shrugged his shoulders.

'What, indeed, can you say? Now, at what stage did the accused tell you on the evening in question that he intended distributing the *Anarchist Cookbook*? Before you showed him the letter from the American girl-friend or later?'

'I can't remember.'

'Did he mention the Modderfontein Dynamite Factory before he mentioned the book or after?'

'I can't remember the sequence in which he mentioned each of these.'

'Before or after you had drinks?'

'We didn't have a drink that night.'

'Well, you must have drunk something?'

'In fact we drank Golden Flo orange juice. We didn't drink any alcohol at all.'

'You have no difficulty in remembering that sort of thing, have you, Mr Hill?'

'No, but I can't remember the sequence of things.'

'Wasn't it true that, in your better moments, you would say that you were going to devote your life as a medical practitioner to the Homelands?'

'Yes.'

'And sometimes you would say you couldn't bear oppression any more and that you were going to leave the country?'

'That is also right.'

'The lament of an unhappy youth who couldn't make up his mind.'

'Well, it is a difficult decision to make.'

'Who has got your passport?'

'It was taken when I was arrested.'

'Who has got it?'

'The Security Police.'

'My Lord, I have no further questions.'

Mr Bizos sat down. Hill was looking tired but was standing up to things pretty well. He had been very slow to make his answers and when they came they were sometimes slightly defiant. At other times he would shrug his shoulders and make a rather helpless gesture with his hands, which he seemed to feel was answer enough.

Mr Nothling began his re-examination, in his usual thin, anxious, rather diffident way, very different from plump Bizos who showed confidence even when he must have been very far from feeling it.

'Mr Hill, I do not measure a man's character by the length of his hair, but seeing that my Learned Friend seems to want to make a point about the fact that your hair was at one stage longer than it is now, I want to ask you a question. Who is the man in this photograph?'

The court usher took a five-by-four print over to the witness box. Hill took it into his own hands and studied it for a moment. It was not long but it was more than a casual glance.

'It's Henry Jacobsen.'

At that moment both Zim and I burst out laughing, and in a dignified way there was consternation on the police bench, but Nothling continued, 'Now, I see his hair is quite long, semi-long. How did the hair of the accused compare to the hair of Henry and to your own hair.'

'It was shorter.'

'A little shorter or much shorter?'

'Quite a lot shorter.'

'My Lord, no further questions, but I would like to hand in the correct photograph. This apparently is not the...' He paused and there was a great turning of papers. Two other photographs were produced, both of Henry. They were handed back to my mother, but it was no good, they were both of Henry. Mr Bizos conceded the point that they had one of me somewhere and the judge let the witness stand down and adjourned the court till after lunch. Nothling didn't seem to have done his own case much good.

The next witness was Martin Ivor Cohen, wearing jeans and a thick red, rawhide jacket, with his long dark hair and a long dark beard. He looked like an anarchist lumberjack.

Mr Nothling began, 'Mr Cohen, were you born in Australia on September 4th 1945?'

'Yes, I was.'

'It has been suggested by the counsel for the accused that you yourself did not do your duty in the studio and that the accused did all the work and the rest of you were just sponging on him. Is this correct?'

'No, this is not correct. The accused has never said this of me. He was certainly responsible for bringing in and shooting most of the work but I did do a very goodly share of the processing and printing. I think it is fair to say that all of us more or less pulled our weight, certainly unequally because Quentin was the principal in experience and in talent, I suppose.'

'Now, we know that you came to South Africa together. Whose idea was it to come out to South Africa?'

'Well, it was Quentin's idea.'

'When did he tell you of his idea?'

'Late November or early December 1970.'

'Did he tell you what he intended doing in South Africa?'

'Yes, he said he intended to set up a photographic studio, and while he was in South Africa he wanted to have a look at the general situation and, in particular, the political situation, and that he was interested in making a film if possible, or investigating the situation.'

'Did he tell you why he wanted to do this?'

'Yes, he said that there were various unfavourable news reports which he wanted to investigate and see if they were true, and perhaps, if they were true, to do something about it.'

'What would he have done?'

'I must emphasise, if he found that these reports were true, he was first interested in giving an honest and accurate account of the situation in terms of, perhaps, propaganda film. He mentioned in passing that he was prepared to consider acts of a less ... well, of a violent kind if he found it necessary, and if he found that a propaganda approach wouldn't be successful.'

'Did he say what violent means he would consider?'

'No, he didn't specify anything at all.'

'Did you tell him what actual acts of violence you would be prepared to support?'

'No. But I did make one stipulation, that any acts of violence should be injurious only to property and certainly not to human life.'

'Was any decision taken by the four of you in regard to the conduct of the business and in regard to any political activities?'

'Yes, there was a general understanding amongst us that any decisions we might make would be on a democratic basis; there would have to be a three to one majority.'

'That is in political action?'

'Well, any action. I must add that everybody acknowledged Quentin as the captain of the ship when it came to business, because he was more experienced; so we automatically ratified any decisions he made.'

'But in regard to political actions, was that the agreement, that it should be decided on a majority vote?'

'Correct.'

'Is it true that you met the Bantu males, Buki and Seadom, during the early part of your stay in South Africa?'

'Yes.'

'Who invited them?'

'All of us.'

'And for what reason?'

'So that Quentin and all of us could pursue our policy of meeting as many South Africans as possible, and in particular meeting black Africans.'

Nothling started taking Martin through each of the potential targets.

'What did the accused say in regard to the bridges?'

'He asked Dave if he would know where the best place would be to put explosives and Dave said, that being an architect, he would know.'

'And the Pass Office?'

'I remember a large discussion where we all more or less agreed that, if we ever seriously decided to attack anything, this would be high on the list of priorities.'

'And was it, on that occasion, said when or under what circumstances sabotage would be committed?'

Mr Bizos rose. 'With respect, My Lord, I have refrained from objecting in the past, but the witness has, on several occasions, put it on a purely conditional basis and, loath as I am, My Lord, to object, I submit that my learned friend by now must take cognizance of the witness's statement that it was completely conditional. The words he uttered were, "If ever we decided".'

Mr Justice Marais lifted his eyes briefly from his notes and said, 'Right.'

Nothling took over again. 'When were the symbolic targets discussed—that is, the monuments and the Union Buildings?'

'It was round the time that we discussed the Pass Office.'

'What did you intend to achieve by this?'

'I think it would come under the single word "awareness".
It would have very great propaganda repercussions both
within and without South Africa.'

'Why did the accused go to London on August 18th?'

'He said he wanted to collect money owed to him in Paris
and he wanted to approach various anti-apartheid and anti-
the-present government organisations, to make himself
known to them and to listen to their suggestions and to offer
our possible assistance to them.'

'Was the name of any organisation mentioned?'

'I think it's the Anti-Apartheid Movement. Oh, and there's
another one, the ANC.'

'Who mentioned these organisations?'

'It's quite hard to remember. Actually these two organisations may have been planted in my mind by the police. They
mentioned them on many occasions.'

After some discussion on this point Nothling moved on.
'It was put to an earlier witness by the defence counsel that
the accused had made 12,000 rand during his five months'
stay in South Africa.'

'That's very possible.'

'Were you all earning the money or was one man earning
the money and the others spending it on travelling and other
things?'

'I think it's fair to say the money was almost equally di-
vided. We nearly always travelled together and we lived to
the same standard. It may be that Henry spent a little more
money than the rest of us, but with our approval. He used
to spend money on his African friends, on food etc.'

'Now did the accused return from England on September
18th?'

'Yes, he did.'

'Who met him at the airport?'

'Dave Smith and myself.'

'Tell me, were you all neglecting the photographic business in the accused's absence?'

'Well, we more or less let things run down so that we
could have this holiday in Swaziland.'

'Very well. What happened after the accused's return
from England?'

'As I said, Dave Smith and myself collected him from the airport and drove back to the studio and he told us briefly that London was just as he'd left it and that he'd been to see several organisations—he didn't specify them—and said that none of them were at all interested in anything we might be able to provide by way of propaganda, and they weren't interested in supporting us with the money that we would definitely require to make a film. He also said that he'd brought some things back from London with him.'

'You say he said that he had brought some things back from England?'

'Yes, he opened up his photographic folio, which is largely on ten-by-eight transparencies, and...'

'Is that now a sort of...?'

'It's a sheet of film, ten inches by eight inches, colour film which has a photograph on it, generally commercial. It's mounted in a black cardboard mount. Well, when he came back, he produced one of these folio shots and stripped off the plastic casing and peeled the mount apart and hidden inside was a small thin paper bag containing several strips of 35mm black and white film.'

'How many strips were there?'

'My experience tells me that there were perhaps half a dozen in the paper negative-bag I saw, and he opened several other folio shots to reveal similar bags. I must have seen about six bags altogether.'

'Would you kindly look at these strips? I am now showing you exhibit R33.'

Bizos rose. 'My Lord, there is a formal admission that these strips were introduced by the accused into...'

The Judge: 'Yes.'

Nothling: 'May we remind the witness to refresh his memory?'

'Yes.'

'Thank you. What happened then?'

'He told us that when he was in London he photographed two books in a bookshop; one of the books is the *Anarchist Cookbook* and the other was, I think, the *US Army Manual of Guerrilla Warfare*, and he said that this film was in fact the film he used to photograph the books.'

'Yes?'

'Well, at that point we had a bit of an argument.'

'Yes, what was the argument about?'

'The main argument was that Quentin said he wasn't *au fait* enough with the contents to be able to make any decisions about the material, whereas Dave and I insisted that it was clear enough from the titles of the books. So Dave eventually stormed out. At that point Quentin then proceeded to do exactly what he had argued that he wanted to do, that was to print the negatives.'

'How long did this printing continue?'

'Well, it continued all that evening until at least one o'clock, and then most of the next day. I think that, at this point, both Buki and Seadom were assisting Quentin.'

'Tell, me, was it a cheap way of reproducing?'

'Oh, I think it is probably one of the cheapest.'

'Why was it necessary for the accused to go to a lot of trouble to produce clear prints of the negatives?'

'I really don't know. He told me that at some future stage he might reproduce them in some way and he didn't want to do a double printing job. He also mentioned, *en passant*, that he might invest in a printing-press. He didn't say what for.'

'Was there at any time any dissension among your group?'

'Yes, at this stage Quentin said he wanted to include Buki, Seadom and Ian Hill in the studio circle, but David and I were violently against it. However, Quentin felt that he should be able to reserve the right to expand the community if he liked.'

'Did he say this with regard to your business or your political association?'

'We understood it to be political. Eventually he said, "If I am up to anything, then you are not really involved in it, are you?" and I said, "No".'

'Now, before the four of you came to South Africa, was anything said by the accused about films he had seen?'

'Yes, after I had accepted his offer to come, I was naturally interested in what had motivated him, and he told me that —this is a little bit difficult to describe—he had had—I think the best term for it would be an odd psychological experience.

I think they call it an "Aha" experience. Probably the most famous example is Archimedes in his bath, when a lot of factors come together in your mind at once and you realise that a certain course of action is highly desirable, that it is the right thing. He told me, in his case, how, when he was in Paris, he had gone with a South African girl to see a film, *Wild River* by Elia Kazan, and he had had this extraordinarily strong "Aha" experience that South Africa was the place he must go to.'

'For what purpose?'

'Well, lots of purposes, financial, political—a whole complex of factors.'

'Now, in what manner did the accused express his views in regard to the solution of the political situation? Was he convincing and persuasive, or colourless and speculative?'

'I didn't find him very persuasive.'

'Did he try to persuade people of the correctness of his views or was his approach a neutral one?'

'Neutral doesn't describe it exactly, but he doesn't go out of his way to persuade people to fall into line with his viewpoints.'

Nothling finished and sat down. The court adjourned and Zim came over to me.

'Well, he's telling the truth,' I said, 'but is it any use?'

'Quentin, I tell you not one word of his evidence can incriminate you. The way it stands now, it's Hill against Martin and I am hopeful that the judge will accept Martin's evidence and not Hill's. It's going well; we may not even have to call you as a witness.'

Certainly Martin's evidence was more believable than Ian's and it was all hypothetical. But still, a lot of it corroborated Seadom and Hill.

Bizos cross-examined Martin. 'I am not going to keep you very long but I think you are probably in the best position of all the witnesses we have had up till now. Is it the vogue for young people such as yourself to seek some sort of moral context in your actions?'

'Of a minority of young people this is certainly the case.'

'Would you put yourself in this minority?'

'Yes, I would.'

'And David Smith?'
'Yes.'
'And the accused and Henry?'
'Yes.'
'This, then, is a group of people who challenge the correctness of established authority?'
'Yes.'
'Didn't you perhaps over-emphasise the idealist motives in your discussions?'
'Well, not really, because discussions didn't take place very often.'
'And throughout there was never a pre-arranged meeting, so to speak?'
'No, they were entirely spontaneous.'
'And all the targets—they were merely given as examples of theoretically possible targets?'
'Yes.'
'Should violence ever be decided on?'
'Yes.'
'Did Seadom Tilotsane give you the impression that he was an embittered man?'
'He did give a general impression of being embittered.'
'Did he make any contribution to the group discussions?'
'He wasn't really able to make much contribution.'
'Was he a sort of Exhibit 1. of the result of apartheid?'
'He was certainly an exhibit of apartheid.'
'Did he hold himself out to be a student?'
'Yes.'
'Did he tell you that his father had been killed in Sharpeville?'
'Yes.'
'He certainly took you in.'
'Yes.'
'Now, Tilotsane told his Lordship that the trip down to Pretoria was in order to take photographs of strategic targets. You are smiling—?'
'I think that was a fantasy on his part. Quentin took photographs. He made it a habit wherever he travels. He sells them to magazines.'
'Now, have you had a university education?'

'Yes.'

'You have; Smith had. You know the accused had little formal education; he left school at sixteen. He was not as articulate a man as you are?'

'He communicates very adequately.' Martin smiled.

'Yes, but in a graphic way. Isn't he—not a man of abstractions, but communicating rather in a graphic way, by giving examples?'

'Yes, very much so.'

'Did Quentin have a strong need to do things, concrete things, give concrete examples?'

'Yes, I think he prefers to work rather than to think.'

'Did the police try to make you say that the accused had a vision that he was to liberate South Africa and that is why he came?'

'Well, I described this experience which I called an "Aha" experience. This is a bit comical. You don't really say this to a policeman. They don't really understand philosophical jargon that much. I described it as a sort of visionary experience.'

'Before going to John Vorster Square, you went to a good friend of yours, I believe?'

'Yes.'

'You wanted advice as to whether to go to John Vorster Square or not?'

'Yes.'

'And I'm told that the way you put it was, "There was a lot of talk and Quentin brought in a couple of banned books", and that was the sum total of your knowledge of the accused's allegedly wrongful acts?'

'That was the gist of it.'

'No further questions.'

Mr Bizos sat down, looking for the first time almost happy, and Mr Nothling began his re-examination.

'Mr Cohen, you were asked in cross-examination whether the police made any suggestions to you?'

'I was asked to clear up all sorts of points about which I had no real knowledge at all. I was asked to comment on all sort of situations and people whom I have never met.'

'Now with regard to Seadom, you say that you saw him

223

under the influence of dagga on several occasions?'

'Yes.'

'Now, to what extent was he under the influence of dagga?'

'I think the technical term in young people's jargon is—"stoned".'

'Oh, I see. No further questions. Thank you.'

After the re-examination the State closed its case, which produced a feeling both of slight shock and of anti-climax in the court. The judge said that Martin should be released forthwith. Colonel Ferrara left the court-room with another policeman only to return a few minutes later, rather red in the face, to say he had already left for Pretoria. The judge said crisply that he must be brought back and released at once. Meanwhile Bizos had risen and asked for the case against the accused to be dismissed. I was told later that this was more or less routine but I wasn't the only one in the court to feel a change of atmosphere, an unexpected flicker of hope. Bizos by now had an immense pile of law books round him, with white tabs marking places, and seemed quite prepared to read the lot.

'My Lord, I refer to the case of the State versus Naidoo (1966). The question is, is the evidence of such a nature that a reasonable man might convict the accused? I submit that under the Terrorism Act it was still necessary to show that an act had been committed by the accused. Even if one thinks of blowing up bridges, that in itself is not an act of terrorism: the argument is, My Lord, that if there is not an act, there is no evidence of conspiracy or of incitement, and because the State has not established an act, so it cannot be said that there is any onus on the accused to prove his innocence. Mere intention was not sufficient; there has to be actual agreement. An act connotes some physical movement. I submit that in the Dean's trial, Mr Justice Cillie had held that the possession of leaflets with the intention of distribution did not constitute an act under the Terrorism Act.

'Now, let us assume that you cannot reject the evidence of Mr Hill. Let us take as an example, the request, "Come with me to assist me to make a petrol bomb". This is not incitement to do an act, and even if Mr Hill was asked to have a look at a bridge and it was said that it would be a good thing if it was blown up, this still would not be incitement.

'The main evidence in point of time was taken up with the conspiracy said to have been entered into. That was the evidence of Mr Tilotsane. The submission made in this connection is that the State has chosen to charge the accused with a conspiracy, and in the first of the act, the conspiracy is said to have consisted of the accused, his brother Henry, Seadom Tilotsane and Buki Monamudi. The court has not heard the evidence of Henry. He is in England, and Buki was not called to give evidence because the prosecutor said he had been inconsistent. So the court was left with the evidence of Seadom, and it is patently clear from his evidence taken on its own, contradiction for contradiction, that no reasonable man can rely on it. He is to a greater or lesser extent addicted to drugs. He is living a lie by holding out to gullible young people that 1. his father had been killed at Sharpeville; 2. he was a student; and 3. he was supported by the church.

'His persistent use of the phrase, "I was incited and, yes, I did agree", with such monotonous regularity, clearly indicates that he had in one way or the other been made aware of the legal requirements of the charge, and his sudden change from "I do not remember" to "I deny that" after a night's adjournment clearly indicates his susceptibility to suggestion. The fact that he possessed blood-thirsty literature and records clearly shows that a comparative stranger was not needed to incite him.

'Now the reasons why Hill cannot be believed are these, that under cross-examination he had to admit that the picture that he tried to paint of himself was not the correct one. Hill also thought that he had a simple way of avoiding the difficulties of cross-examination; he thought that if he failed to answer, the cross-examiner would go on to the next question. On several occasions, he said that he had no reply; he also admitted that this statement was "brushed up"! '

Mr Bizos went on for some time and then the State put forward its argument. Mr Nothling said that the State was prepared to reject Seadom's evidence. 'It has been found that there is no evidence of his matriculation or that, in fact, he went to university. But I submit that there is no reason why the judge should reject the evidence of Hill, and Mr Jacobsen has given no explanations as to his possession of the two books.'

He sat down and the judge said he would give his decision at nine-thirty the next morning as to whether the case would be dismissed.

The feeling in the court changed fundamentally while Bizos was talking, but I was not so optimistic.

CHAPTER NINETEEN

One never knows with things like the law. Zim and Bizos were trying to look hopeful but I felt they were doing it more as a matter of procedure than conviction, and really to give me confidence, keep my spirits up. It was like the earlier time when we asked for bail. I knew we wouldn't get it, though Zim insisted on trying.

Every time I went back to the Fort the others would ask, 'How's it going?' and I would answer, 'Fine, fine, no problem at all.'

Well, the next day we waited for the judge's decision. The court was absolutely full and more than usually expectant. He came in and sat down and to all intents and purposes said 'No.'

So, I thought, he wants to hear my version. Bizos rose and asked for an adjournment, because 'It is necessary to consult with Mr Jacobsen at some length and to interview a number of witnesses.'

Mr Nothling opposed the adjournment, rather tersely for him, on the grounds that the defence should have anticipated that the application for discharge might be refused, but the judge stood his ground and postponed the trial till after the Easter recess. It was then March 30th and we were to resume on April 10th.

I followed the police out to the cell at the back of the court where I had had lunch with my mother every day when the court was sitting. She was allowed to join me there for half an hour. She had come over on a cheap two-week, all-in, 'Come and see South Africa' ticket and the case had already cleaned us out of £4,000, which I didn't think we had anyway. I knew my mother always kept a few notes tucked into a book called *Enemies of Promise*, which were meant to cope with rainy-day problems, but were clearly inadequate for absolute floods like the present one. I gathered that my father had managed to raise money in Denmark.

So my mother was leaving on Easter Sunday and Zim had

managed to arrange that I would see her that morning at the Fort, with four feet of bars in between us. The main thing to discuss was what I should do if I was found guilty. We had skirted round it before but now it was for real. One of the advantages of leaving school at sixteen is that I have plenty to catch up on and, as I had an interest both in advertising and propaganda, we settled for a course in psychology. I thought it would be possible to learn a lot in jail, the Pretoria political jail that is. I was told by Mum that it was reputed to be one of the most exclusive clubs in the world, all male and all white, with a total membership of eight, of whom several were life members. It's the only club, too, where communism is acceptable. True, eight is not many but it's an awful lot better than none. The only annoying thing was there's a total news ban in a political jail—no radios or newspapers—and apparently one could only write three times a month and then only five hundred words at a time. If you go over, they snip it off. The same applies to incoming mail, and all news is cut out. Mum and I agreed that all mail should come through her.

Then there was the question of visits. So far, apart from legal and consular visits, I had only seen my mother. Not that I didn't appreciate these consular visits; both Mr Biggie and Angela had become friends as good as any I had made in South Africa. If I went to prison, I should be allowed other visitors, but the question was, first, who would have the courage and secondly, who could do it without attracting too much unwelcome attention from the police. I would dearly have liked to see Henry but that was totally impossible unless he wanted to join me inside. I wouldn't put it past him. It might even be worth it if we could have halved the time between us.

But it was not certain yet that all was lost. Mum reported that the Judge had the reputation of being an all-or-nothing man. I gave my mother a great hug. 'Get Henry to write, too.'

Ferrara said, 'Time up!' and I went back with him to jail and she to lay in a basic stock of instant coffee, condensed milk, fruit, nuts, chocolate and books for my Easter recess.

That was the Thursday before Easter and I knew that Zim

and Bizos had been staying up till all hours planning our defence strategy. They needed a couple of days off. Come Sunday, I did feel very much alone. Mum came for her last visit, and we talked for, I should think, half an hour. I told her that Henry must do all that I couldn't do; that I pinned my hope on him and, as long as he was happy, then I was, but he must use his freedom. One cannot feel happiness without knowing pain. And as the police kept telling me, 'We've known people come out the better for it.' When the guard came for me I said, 'You know how much I love you,' and we both turned away trying, not very successfully, not to cry.

The next week was hell. We had to go through every scrap of evidence; we had to remember everything I wanted to forget. It would have been so easy just to give in and say, 'Bugger it, am I really worth all the trouble?' But when I photograph a soap-pack it's much the same. I don't say to it, 'You're not worth the trouble. Forget it!' One has one's professional pride. I say to myself, 'I love that pack more than any other,' and get on with it. 'You know,' Zim used to say, 'you'll be sick of the sight of us by the time we've finished with you.' But I think what he really meant was the opposite. I've always thought that, when things go wrong, there's some purpose in it, like those ten days. They were hard, but without them we might have been sunk. My script was forty pages long and, according to Bizos, it should sound like music. Over the last few days I learnt my script and re-wrote my lines.

By the time we got to court on the 10th, I had it off pat but felt that it was a little pretentious and certainly lacking spontaneity. I went into the dock as usual and then was called over to the witness-box at the other side of the court.

Bizos started his examination. 'Mr Jacobsen, you are the accused in this matter. What is your age?'

'I am twenty-six.'

'And what formal or other education did you have?'

'I went to school up to the age of sixteen.'

'You have a twin brother called Henry?'

'Yes. I do. An identical twin.'

'Now after your schooling, you went to Australia?'

'Yes, I spent three years there. I worked in many different

fields and then I started to do photography.'

'Did you return to England?'

'Yes, I returned and went to Guildford School of Art. After the first year there I won the *Sunday Times* photographic competition which gave me 500 rand and led to other work.'

'And did you go to India?'

'Yes, I knew the son of a High Court Judge whose daughter was getting married and I was invited out there to the wedding.'

The Judge interrupted: 'Mr Jacobsen, you must speak a little more slowly if possible.'

'That I will.'

'You are apparently inclined to slur your words a bit.'

'Yes, I will try not to.'

Mr Bizos continued, 'And you spent three months there?'

'That's correct. I bought a motor-bike and went overland.'

'And then a year later you went out to Australia again?'

'That is correct. I was offered a job with an advertising firm, J.W.T., and after a year with them I returned to England.'

There followed a great deal more about my various travels and photographic work.

'Now, in April last year,' Bizos went on, 'did you come to South Africa with Martin Cohen, David Smith and your brother Henry?'

'Yes, on April 21st.'

'And did you start getting work immediately?'

'Yes, we were quite lucky. I got work straight away and we were able to rent a studio after a few days.'

'How much work have you done in the five months you were working here?'

'I have done about 12,000 rands' worth.'

'Now, at the studio after work, did you ever discuss politics?'

'Yes, inevitably. This country seems to be obsessed by it.'

'What were the types of political discussion in the studio?'

'Well, quite a few of the Africans I met, Seadom for instance, used to say that violence was inevitable in this country and I said I could see no indication of this and that the African is very well-off compared with his counterpart in India.

230

I didn't see violence happening here for a long time.'

'Did you find it easy or difficult to speak in the abstract?'

'I've always been bad at subjects like algebra. I'm better at expressing myself in a more tangible medium.'

'Let us talk about Seadom. What sort of impression did he make on you when you first met?'

'He's intelligent, aware, but angry. He told me that his father had been killed in the Sharpeville incident and I felt sorry for him. I didn't think anyone would lie about anything as serious as this.'

'How did Seadom dress?'

'Rather flamboyantly. If he went out to parties he would wear Zulu ear-rings and dark glasses.'

'Were his ears pierced?'

'No.'

'What sort of front was he putting on?'

'I think he was pretending to be a sort of Black Panther supporter.'

'Did he tell you how he was earning a living?'

'He said that he was going to university and that the church was providing him with money.'

'And did you believe that?'

'Yes, it seemed logical.'

'Now Seadom talked about the effect of sabotage on the economy. Did you have an interest in the economy when you were here?'

'Very much. Advertising is dependent on an expanding economy.'

'And insofar as there was any difference of opinion in your group at the studio on radicialism, liberalism, call it what you will, where did you think you stood?'

'I suppose I would call myself a progressive. I believe in competition, primarily.'

'And your university friends, did they pass any kind of judgment on you as a person?'

'Yes, they used to say in a fairly joking manner that I was middle-class.'

'And what did they think of Seadom?'

'That he was a classic angry young man out of some rather out-of-date kitchen-sink drama.'

'Did you, on your various ploys with Seadom, ever photograph bridges?'

'No. I have in other countries. I've shot London Bridge and Sydney Harbour Bridge and sold them too, but I don't think people are interested in shots of road bridges.'

'Now, when you returned to England, it was primarily to collect some money, wasn't it?'

'Yes, that's correct. I had to pick up some money in Paris and I also wanted to buy some things in London for my photographic work.'

'And before going, did you know about the ANC and the banned South African communist party?'

'No, I didn't.'

'Well, can you tell the court how you came to meet them?'

'Yes, I suppose it was an accident. Before I left South Africa I met an Indian, called Ebrahim, who said he was going to London and suggested we should go together. While we were in London, he stayed at my place and one day he said he was going to town to see some friends and I went with him.'

'Yes, and who were his friends?'

'He wanted to pay his subscription to the Anti-Apartheid Movement and I went up there with him.'

'Did he take you anywhere else?'

'Yes, on the way down he asked me if I would like to see the offices of the ANC. He said it was just round the corner, so I said, "Why not?" and we went. I met this friend of Ebrahim's called Aziz whom he'd gone to school with in Johannesburg.'

'And did you become sort of friendly with Aziz?'

'Yes, I asked if I could borrow some books on South Africa. He apparently went to LSE and he had a lot of political books.'

'And did you ask him about other books?'

'Yes, one of the books he lent me was the Che Guevara *Guerrilla Handbook* and I found it quite amusing, so I asked if he knew of others like it. He said "Yes" and showed me a newspaper cutting of a review of two other books, the *US Army Manual on Sabotage and Demolition* and the *Anarchist Cookbook*.'

'Now did Aziz tell you anything about a Dr Dadoo?'

'Yes, he did mention his name. He said that a friend of his, a Dr Dadoo, had taken an interest in civil disobedience in South Africa and he asked if I would like to meet him. I said I was quite interested to meet anyone from South Africa.'

'And when you met him, what did you speak about?'

'Mainly about films. I told him I was interested in making a film in South Africa and asked him if he knew of anyone who might be interested in financing it. He said he didn't.'

'Now did you know that Dr Dadoo was or had been a member of the communist party in South Africa?'

'No, I have since learnt that from the police.'

'You told us that you were given a book by Aziz and discussed two other books as a result of a newspaper cutting. Did he tell you where you might be able to obtain the books?'

'Yes, he said at a bookshop in Chalk Farm.'

'And did you go to the shop?'

'Yes, I went to the shop and asked if I could buy the books but they said they only had review copies and that their proper stock was arriving in three months' time. I then asked if I might photograph the books. I was given permission and went straight ahead.'

'What was your interest in the books?'

'Well, all my friends in South Africa had banned books. I just thought I would bring them back for kicks. That's all.'

I waited for the Judge to laugh.

'You say your friends had banned books. In what sort of sense did they have them?'

'Oh, as a sort of status symbol of radicalism, a bit like pornography from Scandinavia.'

I stood there thinking to myself, 'How on earth can anyone sit there and believe this drivel?'

'Did you do this photography of the book surreptitiously?'

'I did it on the staircase.'

'Was it expensive?'

'No. The film cost about two rand. It was a lot cheaper

233

than buying the book would have been. It cost six rand.'

'Now when you came back to South Africa, you brought the film with you?'

'That is correct.'

'Was there an argument on your return between you on the one hand and Cohen and Smith on the other?'

'Yes, there were several arguments. They had let the studio run down while I was away.'

'And that was the reason you felt somewhat angry?'

'Yes.'

'Now, did you try to print these negatives on your return?'

'Yes, Seadom and Buki had always been pressing me to teach them to print and I thought it would be a good opportunity to do so, mainly because they weren't in any hurry and it didn't matter if they put their fingers on the negs. They weren't all that important.'

'Did you really need the assistance of Seadom and Buki?'

'No, not really, but they wanted to learn and I quite like teaching photography, anyway.'

'Was the printing done for the purpose of giving them copies?'

'No.'

'Did you say to them they could take copies?'

'No, they never asked me, nor was it suggested.'

'Now, do you remember the evidence of Mr Cohen to the effect that he asked you what you were up to and you replied, "If I am up to anything, it isn't your concern". What do you have to say to that?'

'Well, he and Dave had become much more involved in architectural programmes which had a very long-term scale to them. I wasn't interested in their ideas; I was only interested in photography.'

'And did you ever tell him that democracy inside the studio was over?'

'Indirectly, yes. I wanted a German photographer called George Wagner to join us. He had both equipment and capital. I thought he would be good in the studio but the others didn't.'

'Now let us deal with African Explosives. Tell us about the first time you went there.'

I told them the story of going there to get the jars blown for my cigarette job.

Bizos then asked about the photographs. 'How did the transparencies get to South Africa?'

'I asked Mr Zimerman to telephone my mother and get them sent back.'

'And do you recognise your mother's handwriting on this envelope in which they came back?'

'Actually, it is my twin brother's handwriting. He must have posted it.'

Bizos turned to the Judge.

'Exhibit Number 50, My Lord. No further questions.'

When Mr Nothling rose to cross-examine me he began by telling the Judge that he had had transcripts made of the evidence of Martin and Ian and he proposed to refer to them in court.

Mr Justice Marais asked, 'And is Mr Bizos to have the advantage of a copy as well?'

'Yes, but he will have to pay for it. Unfortunately the State cannot pay for it. He went on, 'I want to read from the evidence on pages 175 and 176. Here Mr Cohen gave evidence concerning this incident about seeing the film, *Wild River*. He goes on to say that he, (that is you) described to him an "Aha" experience that you had, and that this very strong "Aha" experience told you that the place you should go to was South Africa.'

He then read Martin's evidence on the subject and ended by asking me if I agreed with it.

'No, not one hundred per cent.'

'So, it's incorrect.'

'It's inaccurate.'

'How can you say it's inaccurate? It's either correct or incorrect.'

'All right, it's incorrect.'

'But you see, Mr Jacobsen, it was not disputed when your counsel cross-examined Mr Cohen.'

'I agree it was not disputed but I am not doing the cross-examination.'

'Yes, but you are giving your instructions. I saw you often sending over notes to your attorney.'

'I was not encouraged to do this.'

'But did you do it?'

'On a few occasions, yes.'

'So you could have written such a note saying it was untrue?'

'Yes, I could, but I'm not doing the cross-examining.'

'Naturally not, but you are the man who must give your instructions to your counsel?'

'To a degree, yes, but I leave these things to my attorney. It's not for me to say. He is a professional. I am a professional, and I am a photographer. He is an attorney.'

'Yes, I know that. Very well, can you advance any reason why Martin should give a false impression?'

'We have all been under a lot of pressure in the last six months, and I think that the police have interviewed me so many times on what made me come to South Africa that I tend to exaggerate and get things out of all proportion. I can only say that Martin had been under similar pressure of this nature.'

'Now, in Ian Hill's evidence, page 18, line 2, Hill says that you wanted to make an advertising campaign to put over the idea that diamonds are not a symbol of love but of corruption, slavery and hate, because most diamonds come from this country where Africans work under shocking conditions to get them. Is this evidence correct or not?'

'It is inaccurate.'

'How can it be inaccurate? It is either correct or incorrect.'

'Yes, it is incorrect.'

'Why?'

'It was just an idea that I had. I did think there was a way through advertising to improve working conditions.'

'By placing an advertisement that diamonds are not a symbol of love?'

'I didn't say that necessarily. What I said was that one ought to have more respect for the people who mine them, and perhaps some love for them too.'

'Yes, but have you ever been to a diamond mine?'

'No, but I've read about them.'

The Judge intervened. 'What have you read?'

'I have read that they are under contract for six months and that they can't see their family for that time.'

Mr Nothling asked, 'Now, what is wrong with that contract?'

'I feel a person should have freedom of mind and choice.'

'I have difficulty in following your argument. These are the terms of employment offered to them; they can accept them or reject them. They can seek other employment.'

'There is a lot of unemployment and they can't always get other employment.'

'Well, Mr Jacobsen, I wish to refer now to another portion of Cohen's evidence, page 185, line 25. I quote: "This was our justification for being in the country, that is, investigation and discussion of the political situation."'

'Well, he was wrong there. I have no political interest in South Africa.'

'But Cohen then goes on to say that he would be prepared to join you in actions...'

'I have not said this.'

'So, is Mr Cohen lying to us in the witness box?'

'I find it very hard to remember half these discussions.'

'Now, did you ask Seadom how it feels to be black in South Africa?'

'I'm not a racialist. I don't divide people into categories. I didn't ask him, he told me.'

'When you came here did you not become aware of the sort of division there is between Europeans and Non-Europeans?'

'There is that intention and it is not easy for me to go along with it. Even buses and park benches are separate.'

'Now on page 147 Martin says, "We also discussed the possibility of mounting some sort of propaganda campaign against the country". What do you say to that?'

'I have never talked in terms of a propaganda film. I have said a documentary film to make people more aware of the situation in South Africa.'

'Well, I will continue. On page 5 of Ian Hill's evidence he says, "We then talked about how to undermine the economy" and when he was asked if he remembered who raised it he replied, "The accused first raised it". You see here Mr Hill states very clearly that you raised the possibility.'

'My Lord, when people are under detention and they are

subject to lots of interrogation—I myself had up to seventy-two hours in one go without sleep—it is very easy to agree with anything the police say, just for the sake of getting some sleep. It is ridiculous to try to get information from people who aren't in a state to give it.'

'So you think he made a false statement here against you just to save his own skin?'

'I should think it's very likely and I don't blame him.'

'He is a close friend of yours.'

'Oh, yes, very close.'

'And you see he was released from detention in December.'

'Yes.'

'And he gave evidence towards the end of March and, in fact, said in court that he was no longer suffering from the effects that detention might have had on him?'

'No, but if one gives a statement one obviously has to stick to it—the original statement, I mean.'

'Why?'

'Because, if one starts changing it, it won't look very logical to the police.'

'Well, why didn't he come to court and give a true picture of what happened?'

'You try giving him his passport back and a free life and he may well do so.'

'Do you know if he ever went to the police and asked for the return of his passport?'

'No, but if the police took it, I think it's very unlikely that they would give it back.'

'Page 6 in Hill's evidence says that you said it would be possible to obtain the plans of the telephone exchange from your father.'

'I really don't know.'

'Do you suggest that he sucked it out of his thumb?'

'No, I suggest my twin brother must have told him.'

'But how could he make a mistake about this?'

'Very, very easily. We are identical twins. You made the same mistake three times.'

'Mr Jacobsen, I was told you were identical twins. I accept that. A photograph was handed to me by the police and they told me it was of you.'

'Not one, three photographs were handed to you.'

'Can you blame me for confusing the two of you?'

'I can blame the police and yourself.'

'But Hill knew you both very well?'

'People make mistakes all the time. It's part of the fun of being a twin.'

'You see I can't recall that Hill was ever questioned on this in cross-examination.'

'Well, I can only regret not informing my attorney on this count.'

'Cohen says on page 153, line 15, "The damaging of the bus system was mentioned on two, maybe three occasions". Then we turn to Hill's evidence, page 7, line 24, "On the same occasion when the matter of the telephone exchange was discussed, the accused suggested blowing up the bus sheds". So this evidence is completely false?'

'Completely false, yes.'

'Can you advance any reasons for Hill giving this false evidence?'

'As I have said, when one is interrogated for up to seventy-two hours non-stop without sleep, of course one finds oneself agreeing to anything the interrogator tells one. It is not a situation where people find themselves trying to be truthful: it's a matter of self-survival.'

'Now, when did you talk about politics?'

'Mainly at parties.'

'I can't believe this, but apparently at every party you go to, revolution is discussed.'

'No, not every one.'

'Which is very extraordinary?'

'No, it's not extraordinary at all; this country is obsessed with politics.'

'I have been in this country slightly longer than you have been and I've never heard it being discussed.'

I couldn't help asking 'Do you mean to tell me that you have never heard politics being discussed at any party you have been to? I could pick up a paper on any day of the week and show you an article on...'

'I am just interested in all these discussions at all the

parties you attended—centred around revolution, apparently?'

'No, not at all ... They were centred round many things, girl-friends, films, work...'

Cross-examination went on for four more days and not once did Nothling refer to my evidence; it was always to the others. I've got to hand it to him, he made me look an idiot. I ran out of ideas as to why the others advanced these lies. And my script was never once questioned. Another problem was that, just before I'd gone up to give evidence, Bizos had turned to me and said, 'Now, just so you won't ever accuse me of not doing my job, I'll read you the law on Terrorism and Communism", and then added that under the Terrorism Act they can read the evidence all over again under a new indictment. So if I admitted to trying to get money for a propaganda film, it could still get me five years. The best thing, I felt, was to deny the lot.

After the first day of my giving evidence, the Judge finished by saying, 'I think the day has been long enough for you. You need a rest now.'

I felt I didn't so much need a rest as an opportunity to wallop Nothling. Some of his remarks had been obviously intended to make me angry but I had managed to hold back. When I got back to the Fort, I met Trevor in the shower. He had just come back from the court, having got four years.

'Jesus, Trevor, I'm sorry.'

'Don't feel sorry for me. From what I read in the papers, I feel sorry for you.'

'Thanks. This bastard Nothling keeps on asking each question three times. It's costing me a fortune.'

'Simple! Don't let him. Just tell him you've answered it already.'

Next day in court, Nothling resumed. 'I want now to deal with the books. Why did you bring the two books into the country?'

'I had no real purpose. If you like, it was the medium not the message.'

'But why did you not want to discuss it with Martin and Dave?'

'I'm happy to discuss it with anybody, as I am with you now.'

'The point is, why did you go to all the trouble of photographing the books?'

'It was no trouble.'

'Over two hundred pages?'

'It doesn't take any trouble. Click one, click two.'

'Over two hundred pages taken and then smuggled into South Africa, and you never told your friends the reason?'

'All my friends have banned books.'

'You see, all the time you have been referring to banned books. But did you know these books were not banned?'

'I didn't know whether they were banned or not. I would have thought they would be.'

'You went to such a lot of trouble to photograph these books . . .'

'It was no trouble.'

'Please let me continue my question. You went to such a lot of trouble to photograph these books and smuggle them in to South Africa, even at the risk of landing yourself in trouble, so that you could have a banned book and then you never show it to anyone?'

'I've answered that question already. I've said it was no trouble.'

The judge took over. 'Why did you select these two books specifically and not any other?'

'Well, I did bring in another banned book, *The Female Eunuch* by Germaine Greer.'

Nothling persisted. 'Why select two books that dealt with explosives?'

'One deals with drugs as well and other things. Anyway, I haven't read them.'

'All right. We'll leave that. Now Martin in his evidence says you went back to England to contact the Anti-Apartheid Movement and listen to any suggestions they might make and offer your assistance. Is this completely wrong?'

'Martin never said what organisation. He was asked the name and he said that it might have been planted by the police.'

'He said the Anti-Apartheid Movement.'

At this moment, a very loud and angry Bizos rose and said, 'Well. let us hear it! Let us hear it! '

Nothling answered: "Why should I, if I don't want to?'

I'd forgotten about Bizos. Good on you, I thought to myself. It was all he'd said in two days. Nothling went on as though nothing had happened.

'You see, according to Hill, page 13 lines 13-20, you told him that when you were in London you had been to see the Anti-Apartheid Movement with a view to receiving financial aid for your plans.'

'I have never said this to Hill.'

'Can you give me a reason why he should have lied in court?'

'I've answered that one already.'

'All right. Now, why did you spend 300 rand on a trip back to London for the sake of two banned books when they could have posted them to you?'

'I think it's highly unlikely that they would have got through.'

'But they were not banned.'

'It's not my fault they weren't banned.'

Nothling leant down and took up the police copy of the *Anarchist Cookbook*.

'Page 310. This is something you probably found very interesting. How to sabotage bridges, showing where to place the explosives.'

'I have not read the book. Where is the question?'

'Here on page 131 is another illustration of how a certain bridge can be blown up; 132 another bridge; and here on page 138 a pressure-trigger device under a driver's seat.'

'It may well be, I haven't read it.'

'One has to be careful when one gets into a car nowadays.'

'Is that a question?'

'You had ample opportunity in England to see what the books were about.'

'That is correct.'

'Do you agree that these books, both of them, might well be described as handbooks for the saboteur?'

'I am not a saboteur.'

'Do you agree with this bit on page 27, "Power must be taken, it is never given"?'

'Is it in the negative the police found?'

'No,' said Nothling.

'Fine. Then I don't know. No.'

'Why did you want to photograph this book?'

'I think you have yourself proved quite adequately that it is a very interesting book. I believe it's a best-seller in America.'

'You see this chapter on explosives and booby traps?'

'Yes.'

'There is this illustration called "The crazed Anarchist" showing him with a bomb in his hand. Why didn't you photograph that?'

'I may well have done. I can't remember.'

'Well, you see the police didn't find the negative of this page. It looks as if you deliberately skipped it. Isn't it really significant you started making prints of this chapter dealing with explosives?'

'Interesting, but quite accidental.'

'Oh, you say it's quite accidental. I agree it's interesting, because, on page 113, it describes how to make nitro-glycerine; on page 114, how to make mercury-fulminate, and blasting gelignite formulas for the straight dynamite series. Page 115 how to make chloride of azode; page 116 ammonium nitrate compounds; page 117, gelatine dynamite; 118 TNT. These were the prints found, the ones you actually made.'

'If you say so.'

'And you think it's merely incidental?'

'I didn't write the book.'

'Ja, you didn't write the book, but you only printed this part. I want to put this to you. It is a question your counsel put to Cohen dealing with the challenge of the younger generation to established values, and their assumed duty to challenge the philosophies all down the ages, and the part played in their discussions on the question of the right or wrong of using violence to settle disputes. What is your view?'

'Well, violence is a terrible thing. It's like hanging, it's not humane. But then, it depends whether the African can find a solution to his problem by other means. It might be that he has no alternative but to commit crimes of violence.'

'And what you have told the court during the course of your evidence, was that the truth, the whole truth and nothing but the truth?'

'It is the truth.' What else did he expect me to say?

Nothling sat down.

Now it was Bizos' turn again. 'My Lord, I too, would just like to read from the *Anarchist Cookbook*: "This is not the age of slender men in black capes, lurking in alley-ways with round bombs, just as it is not the age of political discussions in Munich beer halls. Anarchistic theory to-day places the whole weight of responsibility where it should be, on the shoulders of all the people, not just a select few. It basically relies on an unshakeable faith in human nature and the primary goodness of the human race". Now, how does that strike you?'

'Sounds great.'

No further questions.

I left the witness box with relief, though I didn't really feel I'd done much good. I felt more at home back in the dock. The next witness for the defence was called and my place was taken by a small, very harmless, prim woman.

Bizos started. 'Miss Ogilvie, you are the Assistant City Librarian?'

'Yes, that is correct.' A rather high, thin voice.

'And you have been sub-poenaed to produce these books?'

'Yes, I have.'

'What books have you been asked to get out of the Johannesburg public library?'

'I have been asked to bring about seventeen books.'

She then went on to read out, in the most delicate manner possible, a list of titles: *Modern Guerrilla Warfare, Nitro Explosives, Handbook of Intelligence and Guerrilla Warfare, Explosives Handbook for South Africa.* I felt both embarrassed and elated. To have gone to all that trouble when all I need have done was go to the local library! But the judge made a remark which somewhat damped my enthusiasm. 'Even if the accused had gone to the library with the intention of redistributing this information in order to disrupt the maintenance of law and order, he would still be guilty.'

This was distinctly discouraging.

Miss Ogilvie stood down and the court began the summing-up, which lasted for most of four days. Bizos repeated all over again in immense detail why Seadom and Hill's evidence couldn't be accepted and why I, on the contrary, was such a good witness. 'Never once did he refuse to answer questions, in fact he even asked a few.'

At one point the judge commented, 'The accused is not a Walter Mitty; he is a highly intelligent man, but the explanation of why he brought the books in is a silly and worthless lie.' I felt like clapping and wanted to add, 'You tell me of a better reason and I'll buy it.'

Then Mr Nothling gave his reasons for thinking my evidence was no good and Hill's and Martin's was. It took the inside of a week to do this and it was very boring. Finally, on Thursday afternoon the judge announced that he would give his verdict the next morning at 10.30.

I went over to speak to Zim and Bizos, who were very weary. Bizos said, 'Well, we've won a few battles, but I have my doubts about the war.'

'How was my evidence?'

'Let's put it this way, at least you didn't contradict yourself, but why the hell didn't you go along with Martin's evidence?'

'I bloody well couldn't. He tied it up with Ian's in such a way that I couldn't.'

'Anyway the judge didn't believe a word you said.'

'It's not my fault I'm guilty.'

'Well, there's nothing we can do about it now.'

They left and I waited for Ferrara. It looked like at least five years. The thing was bloody Bizos, just before I went into the box, reading me the law like that, and convincing me that practically anything was an act of communism under the Act and would get me five years. Anything, absolutely anything I could have said could be construed as an act of communism.

It started to rain heavily and I felt like crying. Five years

245

when you've already done 171 days isn't funny. Ferrara came to unlock the door. We stood there by the main exit looking at the rain.

'Hell, it's been a wet year.'

'It's not my fault,' I said.

Ferrara called over a black policeman.

'Here are my keys. The car is that yellow one over there.'

'Not me, baas.'

'Come on, it won't bloody hurt you.'

'It's not my problem.' He refused to budge.

Ferrara was furious and I could have died laughing. Somebody at last had held on to something. It was too much.

'Come on, Ferrara,' I said, 'let's all get wet. It won't hurt us, either. It will be almost worth five years to see you getting soaked.'

When we got into the car, he said, 'You can say that now, but I'll be dry tomorrow and you'll still be in the shit.'

'You never know, you never know.'

CHAPTER TWENTY

Next day, sure enough, Ferrara was dry. The only question that remained was whether I was still in the shit. We drove down to the court.

'Take a good look, Quentin, because it will be the last time you see it.'

In court, waiting for the judge, Zim came over and said, 'Don't worry. I'm going to London for my holidays and while I'm there, I'll do all I can. We might be able to appeal.'

'Appeal? We're cleaned out already. I haven't even got the fare home.'

The court was packed. No news is bad news. The press were loving it.

'When the judge comes in, you stand and remain standing till he finishes. If he acquits you, you can say, "Thank you". If he doesn't—well, keep your mouth shut.'

Zim went back to his bench. I seemed to remember having heard those words before.

The judge came in and I stood up. My whole body was rigid. I could smell my own sweat. I will not break down, I said to myself, I will not break down.

He began: 'The vital question is the main charge: did Mr Jacobsen photograph these books for the purpose of committing sabotage and other acts of violence? The State has to prove this beyond all reasonable doubt. The State, to my mind, has also to prove that the accused did this with the intention of distribution. A rational probable inference was that a person who photographs books does so for the purpose of making use of it. Mr Jacobsen has chosen to photograph the meat and skipped the philosophical introduction, apparently only being interested in the sabotage recipes.

'He smuggled in negatives and made a number of prints, and this was done when there had been talk of violence, sabotage and crippling the economy. Mr Jacobsen said he brought the books in because all his friends had banned books and it was regarded as a symbol of exceptional status. This is a silly lie unworthy of any consideration. I do not think a man of Mr Jacobsen's intelligence would do anything so puerile or be involved in such antics.

'The main charge alleges that Mr Jacobsen was guilty of terrorism in that he committed ten specific acts, conspiring with others to damage...' and he went through the list from the telephone exchange to Modderfontein. Then he dealt with the witnesses.

'Mr Seadom Tilotsane said that he had enrolled with the University of South Africa but we have since learnt that he did not even pass his matriculation examination. He also considered himself to be a martyr for the oppressed and an antagonist of government policy. He was a sponger and a parasite on Mr Jacobsen.'

I didn't like all this back-handed flattery and wished he'd get on with it.

'Mr Tilotsane has shown himself to be a completely un-reliable witness, given to parrot-like repetition of what he thought would please the authorities.

'Mr Hill, the final-year medical student, admitted he had suffered from a guilt complex over the possession of danger-ous information and he also said he was afraid of being de-tained indefinitely, or even prosecuted. These were the poss-ible features, in the circumstances, which might make his evidence unreliable. I am satisfied that the police have used suggestion and repetition as a means of obtaining informa-tion. It is a legitimate way of dealing with a witness but there is a danger of suggestion being accepted as truth. Hill was arrested after the others and told that he would be in serious trouble unless he told the truth. Mr Hill described his ex-perience in solitary confinement and the word he used was terror.

'Hill in some instances has inexplicably failed to answer questions and at times his answers were evasive.'

(But then some of the questions Bizos had asked him were pretty unanswerable.)

'But what was more serious is what he said about not being a political radical. Mr Hill's conduct was the amber light to a sinister slant. His evidence, standing alone and denied by

248

Jacobsen, was not sufficient to prove anything against Jacobsen.'

For a moment it sounded good. It meant he'd accepted my evidence.

'The first count is in furtherance of a common purpose. The State must be held to the exact indictment. Mr Bizos is right in his submission that if Mr Jacobsen had any other unlawful intent, it should be met in the indictment and not in the evidence.'

The judge was very slow. I wanted to scream, 'Yes or no? For God's sake, get on with it!' But Mr Justice Marais continued in his calm, judicial way. 'I find that Mr Cohen has not succumbed to the temptation inherent in cases of this nature. Mr Cohen is decidedly a man of integrity and the best witness for the State. His evidence shall be accepted. Cohen has said the accused was an avid reader of the English-speaking press and that he pointed out statutory injustices towards the non-whites. Mr Jacobsen denies this, but I will accept the evidence of Mr Cohen. I also accept on his evidence that Mr Jacobsen had a political motive in going back to London.'

The judge went on for two and a half hours. Eventually when the tension had everyone not just on the edge of their seat, but over it, he said, 'And it is for these reasons that, in count 1 of the indictment, I find the State has failed to prove their allegations.'

I turned my head slightly so that I could see Bizos. He was looking if anything more terrified than I was. We both knew that it was the second count that was the problem.

'So the accused is acquitted on the main charge. Now the second charge, alleging that Mr Jacobsen had obtained information that could be used in the furthering of any of the objects of Communism. I feel that Parliament must have had in mind more serious acts than those he has committed when it saw fit to deviate from the usual procedures and place a heavy onus on an accused (to prove his innocence) and to provide the penalties it did under this section of the act. (Minimum five years.) The contents of the book are not unique. The public could obtain such information from the reference section of the public library. It seems an absurdity that Parliament should not distinguish between people trained to destroy and others, and provide a difficult onus on these people. In the signed Afrikaans text to the Act, the word "information" did not have the connotation of knowledge of a general kind, but of a specific nature concerning subversion. The accused obtained essentially academic knowledge, and, therefore Mr Jacobsen should be acquitted on this charge.'

I looked at Bizos. He didn't even blink.

'Dealing with the third charge, that Mr Jacobsen had encouraged others to commit acts of sabotage, Mr Cohen was one of these but it could not be said that Mr Cohen was so involved.

'Mr Seadom Tilotsane gave evidence and his evidence is rejected, and Mr Hill's evidence falls into the same category. It would be dangerous to find that Mr Jacobsen has committed an act that involves these two men. The State has failed to prove the allegations in the third and last charge. I, therefore, find the accused innocent of all the charges.'

My whole body felt as though it was collapsing into jelly. The noise in the court was incredible. First there was uncontrollable clapping, then excited shouts of applause. I still didn't quite know what had happened, when the usher shouted, 'Silence in court! Silence in court!'

Then an ecstatic Bizos rose to say he would like all the exhibits, all my cameras and so on, to be released, 'as my client is flying back to England tonight.'

The judge agreed that that was a reasonable request and it was granted. Immediately the applause began again. I wanted very much to say thank you but Mr Justice Marais was out of the court before I could say anything.

An elderly man was the first to seize me by the hand and shake it. I just stood there and said, 'I can't believe it. I just can't believe it!'

The next think I knew, Zim was pushing his way over to me shouting at the top of his voice, 'My client does not wish to make a statement. Would you please leave him alone!'

Still stunned with the realisation that I was five years younger than I expected to be, I turned to my friends and actually touched them. My scalp was tense and I could feel my own smile. But Zim was yelling again, at me this time,

'We must go and get your cameras and lenses.' He pushed back the crowd—the old Springbok's last scrum—but Angela Lloyd, the vice-consul, stopped him.

'He's got to get his passport first.'

Zim shouted back, 'Yes, yes, of course.'

Angela dragged me along to get my passport back from the police, with Zim and supporters following. We went into the very cell I had used all the time of the trial and the door was actually left open. I was given my passport and signed for it.

'Come, let's get your equipment,' Zim said.

Everywhere we walked crowds followed and cheered, and I kept on saying, 'But I haven't done anything,' and Zim kept repeating, 'My client is not making any statements,' adding to me, 'Just you remember I've still got to live in this country.'

I was smiling so much my cheeks hurt. We arrived at the counter where all the exhibits were laid out. The court usher put them in a box for me and when we came to the surfboard and the carrier-bag of dagga, I said, 'You can have these.'

And in his excitement, he said, 'Thank you, thank you.'

Now more flashes were going off, so Angela and Zim grabbed me and said we'd go first to the Fort to pick up my suitcase. By now, all I wanted to do was stand there and hug someone, but Zim yanked me away.

'Not the main door! The side door!' But there were a couple of photographers even there. Zim shouted, 'If one of you bastards publishes a photo of me, I'll sue you. Do you understand?'

'Aw, I'm only doing my job. Don't be rotten.'

Zim pushed through. 'And I'm doing my job, too.'

Angela and I got into a cab while Zim was still outside yelling.

'Where to, Miss?'

'Anywhere, anywhere at all.'

She leant over to me. 'How does it feel to be free?'

'I don't know. I can't believe it. What do we do now?'

We both laughed.

'I must get your ticket for the plane, the very first plane.

We ordered it just in case, but we haven't actually got it. We must also get the rest of your cameras and tripods and things. I think most of the press are expecting you at the Fort so we'll go to John Vorster Square first, instead.'

She spoke to the driver.

'I didn't think we had a hope on that second charge, did you?' I said.

'I know, isn't it incredible? I mean, it's wonderful. But you heard what Zim said: you mustn't make any statements till you're out of the country.'

I nodded. 'Yes, you're right.'

It was hard, but of course Zim was right. Angela paid for the cab and we went up in the lift to the Security Department on the tenth floor and through the famous steel doors to where all my tripods and things were. Colonel Ferrara stood in the hall with his hands in his pockets, chewing a throat lozenge.

'Well, how's things?' I said, and he replied in a hoarse voice, 'Got a cold coming on.'

'Caught a wog, have you?' I don't think he liked that remark. 'Anyway, we've come to collect the rest of my stuff.'

He took us through to his office where there were piles and piles of it, pieces of paper, books, maps, everything from the studio. I noticed one thing but couldn't place it.

'What's this?'

'Oh, that's nothing.'

'Oh, yes.' And then I remembered. It was in fact an old note-book Henry had picked off the top of a dustbin. We used it for writing notes in. At the back it had hundreds of addresses and telephone numbers which had absolutely nothing to do with us.

'And I suppose you phoned all these people?'

'We had to,' Ferrara squeaked.

'You miserable sods.'

All the police gathered round with nothing to do, Ferrara with his snuffly nose and flowery shirt, and all the others too. I picked up the equipment. There was still quite a lot missing but I wasn't going to argue. Angela had told me there was the Queen's official birthday party to go to at the Consul-General's, so it didn't seem important.

I said goodbye and wondered if they would really let me get on the plane.

Angela rang for a cab and we went down to wait for it. After a few minutes, a white limousine drew up with a bloody reporter in it.

'You're Quentin Jacobsen, aren't you?'

I turned to Angela. 'Am I?'

'All right. But you've got to give us a lift to the Consulate.'

We got in and the black chauffeur drove us off.

'Well, Mr Jacobsen, how do you feel?'

'I've answered that one already.'

We all laughed.

'No, seriously, why did you bring those books in?'

'You know, I'm still trying to find a good answer to that one.'

'And what will you do now?'

'I'll give a small interview and then I'm off to the Queen's Garden Party.'

'Mr Jacobsen, how long have you been in South Africa?'

'Let me see, we arrived on April 21st last year. But that's to-day! Well, I mean, I've been here exactly a year, I didn't realise it.'

When we got to the consulate, Biggie was there smiling broadly and bigger than ever.

'Well, how did it go Quentin?'

'Fine! We bowled them out all right. My batting wasn't very good, I'm afraid, but at least I stayed in.'

'Good show! Jolly good show! Well, we're celebrating the Queen's birthday so you'd better get a glass.'

'No cider, I suppose?'

'Lord, no.'

'I don't really like champagne. What am I saying? Cheers.'

I collected a spare glass and took some over to the reporter who was on the phone, frantically trying to make the last edition.

'Here! Have some bubbly. It's my birthday.'

'Is it really?'

'No, don't worry.'

He was reading his notes over the phone and when he got to 'Asked him how he felt about his acquittal, he replied,

"I'm very shocked"', I intervened. 'Hold it.'

He put his hand over the mouthpiece. 'What did you say?'

'I said, "surprised" or "relieved" but never "shocked".'

I waited till he finished and then Angela and I went to the Fort. It was really very odd going into my old cell and collecting my case, everyone congratulating me left right and centre. I got hold of my dictionary and my letters and left the rest. On the way down I met François. He was wearing prison clothes and all his hair had gone.

'Have you got my ten bucks?'

'No, I haven't but I've got four years.'

'All right. Keep it, I don't need it.'

I connected up with Angela again and we went on to her place. She wanted to change before going on to the party. It was strange to be in a private flat.

'Where's the TV?' I asked.

'Still hasn't got here yet. But there's a gram over there.'

I went over. Freedom of choice. Not exactly my choice but it's good. I can choose between one side and the other. I put the record on. Angela shouted from the other room, 'Oh, do you like it?'

I thought to myself, 'You're back in society again,' and called back, 'Not bad. Haven't you anything newer?'

'That's only last year's.'

'I suppose it is. It feels like years ago.'

The phone rang.

'I'll get it.'

As it turned out it was for me. Another bloody reporter. I've answered that one already.

'No, I deny that,' and I put down the receiver. Angela came out and said,

'Who was on the phone?'

'No-one.'

We had a quick lunch and went down to go to the party. When I put my case in the boot of Angela's car, I noticed a whole crate of whisky.

'You couldn't spare me one, could you?'

'Sure.'

At the party, I saw Bizos, a large gin in one hand and a

sandwich in the other. I've never seen anyone look happier. I went over.

'Thank you for everything.'

He was totally relaxed and happy. 'I would have liked you to see our offices. You know we had quite a party.'

'That's good. It turned out well, didn't it? The judge was incredible.'

'It's not such a bad country, is it?'

'No, I've had some good times here.'

Biggie came over.

'Ah, there you are, Quentin. I've been trying to find you. I want you to meet the Mayor of Johannesburg.'

'You must be joking!'

Then I remembered this is what diplomacy is about. He took me over to a tall man wearing a chain of office round his neck. I shook hands and he didn't say a word.

Zim came up. 'You'd better get ready. Your plane leaves quite soon.'

I said goodbyes and got my luggage out and transferred it to Zim's beaten-up old Volvo, bits of sweetie paper on the floor, seat ripped. I wondered if this was some kind of sob story.

'Now listen, Quentin. I've still got to live in this country. I was born here.'

'Don't worry, I won't say a thing.'

At the airport, Zim did his usual shouting. I still didn't know who had paid for the ticket. Zim pushed me through the milling crowd but I managed to grab a bottle of champagne someone had brought for me. I walked across the tarmac to the plane and for a moment thought of throwing the bottle for a joke, and then decided it wasn't very funny.

I was the last one on, and mine was a seat by the window. I handed over my bottle of champagne to the air hostess and she smiled at me. The plane was full, full of good, beautiful people. I sat down, fastened my seat-belt, and the plane taxied out. I couldn't help smiling. The sound of children and just ordinary conversation.

'Would you like a sweetie?' She looked at me for a moment. 'Is there anything wrong?'

'No . . . no, there's nothing wrong.'

I looked out of the window but had to close my eyes as I felt the plane take off.